D0354337

❖ ❖ ❖

Coyote Speaks

Coyote Speaks

CREATIVE STRATEGIES FOR PSYCHOTHERAPISTS TREATING ALCOHOLICS AND ADDICTS

❖ ❖ ❖

Jacques Rutzky

JASON ARONSON INC.
Northvale, New Jersey
London

The author gratefully acknowledges permission to reprint an excerpt from Cole Porter's *I Get a Kick Out of You* in Chapter 2. Copyright © 1934 (Renewed) Warner Bros. Inc. Warner Bros. Publications U. S. Inc., Miami, FL 33014.

Special acknowledgment is given to various sources that aided in the retelling of the coyote stories:
- Page 2—Will-Mayo, G. (1993). *That Tricky Coyote!* New York: Walker & Co.
- Page 8—Caduto, M . J., and Bruchac, J. (1988). *Keepers of the Earth: Native American Stories and Environmental Activities for Children*. Golden, CO: J. Fulcrum, Inc.
- Page 18—Strauss, S. (1991). *Coyote Stories for Children*. Hillsboro, IL: Beyond Words Publishing.
- Page 72—Dove, M. (1990). *Coyote Stories*. Lincoln, NB: University of Nebraska Press.
- Page 117—Reed, E. D. (1988). *Coyote Tales*. Santa Fe, NM: Sunstone Press.
- Page 132—Caduto, M. J., and Bruchac, J. (1988). *Keepers of the Earth: Native American Stories and Environmental Activities for Children*. Golden, CO: J. Fulcrum, Inc.
- Page 150—Strauss, S. (1991). *Coyote Stories for Children*. Hillsboro, OR: Beyond Words Publishing.
- Page 179—Lalotki, E., and Lomatuwayina, M. (1984). *Hopi Coyote Tales*. Lincoln, NB: University of Nebraska Press.
- Page 197—Ortiz, S. (1977). *A Good Journey*. Berkeley, CA: Turtle Island Press.
- Page 218—Reed, E. D. (1988). *Coyote Tales*. Santa Fe, NM: Sunstone Press.

Production Editor: Robert D. Hack

This book was set in 11 pt. Berling Roman by Alpha Graphics of Pittsfield, NH.

Copyright © 1998 by Jason Aronson Inc.

10 9 8 7 6 5 4 3 2 1

Library of Congress Cataloging-in-Publication Data

Rutzky, Jacques.
Coyote speaks : creative strategies for psychotherapists treating alcoholics and addicts / by Jacques Rutzky.
p.   cm.
Includes bibliographical references and index.
ISBN 0-7657-0141-3 (alk. paper)
1. Alcoholism—Treatment.   2. Drug abuse—Treatment.
3. Psychotherapy.   4. Coyote (Legendary character).   I. Title.
RC564.R88   1998
616.86'10651—DC21   97—35408

Printed in the United States of America on acid-free paper. For information and catalog write to Jason Aronson Inc., 230 Livingston Street, Northvale, New Jersey 07647-1726. Or visit our website: http://www.aronson.com.

"No one owns Coyote."

DONALD SANDNER

❖ ❖ ❖

Contents

❖ ❖ ❖

Acknowledgments

Few endeavors are created in a vacuum, and this book is no different. As a result, there are many people to thank for their personal and professional contributions: Jill Mellick and Jean Shutes, for unlimited support and literary judgment; David Kurko, for urging me to publish more; Marcia Bradley, for her co-authorship of the Altered States chapter; Roger Lake and Debra Muse, for their contribution to the couples chapter; Tim Cermak, for his early training and guidance at Genesis; Linda Riebel, who finally challenged me to write; Stephanie Brown, for years of encouragement and inspiration; Carole Talbott at CAMFT, who generously published my early writing; Virginia and the staff at the Woodside Library, for their help finding Coyote; Sue and Marty Varady, for their encouragement and faith; Emily Gerber and Caroline Cox, for researching the academic aspects of the book.

Thanks to those who gave helpful feedback on various chapters: Junelle Barrett, Alexandra Gotsch, Beth Gorney, Tom Kirsch, Pat McCaffrey, Carol McRae, Nicholas Ney, Sterling O'Grady, Nancy Piatriowski, Mary Rimmerman, Ernie Rodriguez, Barbara Van Slyke, Lyman Van Slyke, Linda Voorhees, Penelope Zeifert.

Thanks to the many individuals who shared their pain and triumphs in the struggle toward sobriety. No one described in this book is, in and of himself, representative of any one of my patients. Rather than risk one individual's vulnerability regardless of his approval, I have combined elements of many people to create those who appear in this book.

And foremost, thanks to my wife Dyane. Her infinite patience with my obsession, possession, and determination was, and always will be, treasured.

Introduction

This book is for health care professionals who face alcoholics and addicts in any stage of addiction, abstinence, or recovery. It describes the struggle to sit unflinchingly in the midst of inordinate human sorrow, the need to balance genuine empathy with clinical objectivity, and the resilience required to endure recollections of early childhood trauma. It emphasizes the strategic mind required to challenge an alcoholic's or addict's slippery narrative, and it reveals the presence of that Native American trickster, Coyote, alive inside both therapists and alcoholics and addicts.

In the Navajo world view, sickness comes from activities that distort social relationships, like the breaking of a taboo or a self-indulgence. It comes from contact with a storm, lightning, a corpse, or a substance outside the natural order of harmony and beauty. It also comes from losing sight of the Holy Way, contact with ghosts, sorcery, or the intrusion of an evil force.

> In Coyote many aspects of evil power are embodied—he is active, with unlimited ability to interfere with people's affairs. . . . [His potential] for turning up unexpectedly is enormous. He has a life principle that may be laid aside, so that any injury done to his body affects his life only temporarily . . . he may . . . recover from apparent death . . . [and] he possesses an incredible fund of evil knowledge. . . . [Reichard 1977, p. 105]

As reported by Luckert (1979), "Coyote sickness" is known by a number of signs, including: nervous malfunctions; a shaking of the head, hands, or entire body; a twisted mouth; poor vision; loss of memory; fainting; sore throat; stomach trouble; and occasionally loss of mind. Coyote sickness is associated with gambling, prostitution, and, not unsurprisingly, alcoholism. Those under the influence of Coyote are considered neither inherently evil nor morally lacking but, like alcoholics and addicts, they suffer from a disease that infects the soul as well as the body.

When asked to intervene on behalf of those afflicted, a "medicine man" from the northern Navajo reservation leads his patient on a symbolic journey to the center of the world. The journey takes place in progressive steps. It begins with a ceremonial purification and unraveling. Repeated prayers and reparations are made to both gods and humans offended by the patient's behavior. A request is made for deliverance, a search is made for the patient's lost mind, and in the presence of the divine the patient is cleansed of shame. The same can be said of recovery from alcohol and drug dependence.

This book is about what happens in a psychotherapist's office when two people face the dark side of alcohol and drug use. It is about the struggle to learn what sometimes works in treatment, what doesn't, and the benefit of becoming aware of the Trickster in each of us. It conveys the humility we are forced to accept when we acknowledge our limitations as healers and the redemption we witness attending to a disease that is, at best, treatable. It describes those we work with as *patients*, because even though the practice of psychotherapy has an element of commerce reflected in the word *client*, the word *patient* feels more accurate with its root in the Latin *patiens* meaning "one who suffers." And psychotherapy is about suffering as much as it is about healing.

This book is about caring enough, at times too much, and knowing when to let go. It is about listening to the sound of another's voice, not just to the words but to the tone, the cadence, and to what is *not said* as much as what *is* said. And it is about listening, when Coyote speaks.

❖ ❖ ❖

Author's Note

Despite two years of work I find myself ambivalent about publishing this book. I have no cultural authority to expound on Coyote, nor do I wish to appropriate a myth from those tribes who have told Coyote tales for generations. No Native American blood runs through my veins, nor can I lay claim to knowledge by dream, vision, or apprenticeship with a shaman or medicine man.

Yet the moment my wife, Dyane Sherwood, introduced me to Coyote, my work with alcoholics and addicts was transformed. A veil lifted. For a year I collected Coyote stories, and slowly I saw a familiar face in the room with me when a patient smiled slyly and minimized his or her alcohol and drug use. The face I saw was Coyote, smiling mischievously. I read Coyote tales in both ethnographic and children's literature (a retelling of several stories is included in the text of many chapters) and heard him in the sound of my patient's voice. I heard him in the weak, falling tone at the end of a sentence telling me something important, like a weekend binge, was left out of a painful story. And the more I wrote about my work, I saw Coyote's tracks in the disease of addiction, in the alcoholic, the addict, and surprisingly, in myself as a therapist.

As an introverted, intuitive, and feeling person, I am not much of a scholar. I am more likely to describe what I see, hear, and feel in the midst of a session than weave a theoretical commentary of psychological theory and addictionology. Admittedly, this leaves a void in *Coyote Speaks*, and those academically inclined will be served by investigating the references provided.

I am also concerned about the ways in which, by revealing my own flaws and foibles, I am vulnerable to criticism by others. In my training, which continues to this day, I have learned the most from those who balance the tension of being human and a therapist. In *Coyote Speaks*, I have attempted an open and honest style of writing. I have included, where relevant, the personal distractions, the reactions that arise and complicate the work, and even my clinical blunders. It is my hope that this honesty will be helpful and reveal the presence of Coyote, not only in alcoholics and addicts, but in the therapist as well. And it is my hope that this knowledge will be used to heal.

CHAPTER 1

Coyote Speaks

The Trickster Archetype in the Alcoholic, the Addict, and the Therapist

COYOTE

In the mythology of many Native American tribes, Coyote, the archetypal trickster, is as provocative as he is potent. On the one hand, he's sly, sneaky, manipulative, and causes all sorts of trouble. He stole Water Monster's baby, brought on the great flood, and is known for being a glutton, a liar, a lecher, and a cheat. On the other hand, he recognized the value of Death as a necessary evil, hurled the stars into the night sky, and stole fire from Black God to relieve the suffering of First Man and First Woman (Henderson 1959, Sandner 1979).

> [Coyote is a] renegade . . . [an] outlaw symbolizing all that is untamable
> . . . [he] is sometimes a man, sometimes a god, sometimes an animal; a
> restless trickster, inquisitive, obscene, adventurous and diabolically chal-
> lenging—a desert Mephistopheles. [Henderson 1956, p.126]

Just for the fun of it and because it's his nature, Coyote will hide outside your house at night and wait until you're asleep. Dressed in a bearskin, he'll sneak in through the screen door, steal your TV, and turn over all your furniture, just to laugh at your expense and blame it on Bear.

Similarly, a psychotherapist treating those still using, newly sober, or years into recovery may notice characteristics of this trickster in alcoholics and addicts: slipping into your office under the cover of darkness (his denial, your lack of awareness or lack in experience), wearing the skin of another animal (the presenting problem may be depression, anxiety, or marital, work, or health problems), stealing something (your good will, your good judgment, your compassion, your patience), and, like many people in crisis, creating havoc in your professional life (by not following through with agreements, canceling appointments, or failing to maintain sobriety) and blaming it on someone else (work, stress, or a lack of understanding in others).

Coyote has another problem similar to that of many practicing alcoholics and addicts: he is virtually incapable of reflecting on the pain he causes himself and others because he has a difficult time admitting his own flaws and failings. For the alcoholic this might be due to inebriation, the discomfort and confusion from a hangover, memory loss due to blackouts, or, in chronic late-stage patients, permanent brain damage. In addicts it may be due to the perceived need to hide their drug use, as a result of the cultural stigma associated with their habit, and the risk of arrest associated with using a substance that is legally sanctioned.

In order to maintain his distorted sense of reality, Coyote tends to blame others for his problems and holds tight to his blindness. For the alcoholic and addict this defensiveness appears in the overriding need to embrace denial.

COYOTE AND HIS REFLECTION

One day, when Coyote was out wandering in search of food he came to the top of a high hill. As he looked down toward the valley below he saw a lake. He saw the sun shining in the water. He saw a cloud of bugs. And he saw fish jumping high in the air to catch the bugs.

Coyote's stomach grumbled and reminded him of how hungry he was.

"I don't want to eat just bugs," Coyote thought. "I want some fish."

And so Coyote made his way down the hill toward the lake. As he walked through the tall, tall grass it made a swishing sound as he brushed against it. As he walked across the wet sand it made a scratching sound when he stepped. Stopping at the edge of the lake Coyote looked out across the water at the swarm of bugs and the jumping fish.

His stomach grumbled again, he licked his lips, and as he looked down at the water, he saw his reflection.

"Yelp!" he shouted. "There's a monster in the lake."

Coyote was so frightened he jumped straight up in the air, then he ran back across the wet sand, through the tall grass, and he hid behind a big black rock. Even though Coyote was out of breath and panting hard, he wondered whether the monster was after him and so he peered out from behind the big black rock.

"Hmmm!" Coyote thought. "No monster?"

All of a sudden, out of the corner of his eye Coyote saw Antelope wander across the wet sand. She paused at the edge of the lake. She looked carefully, leaned her long graceful neck down, and took a drink of water.

"I wonder if the monster will frighten Antelope," Coyote thought. But nothing happened. Antelope took another drink, looked around carefully, and casually walked off.

"Maybe the monster ran away," Coyote thought, and remembering his hunger, he walked through the tall grass, across the wet sand, and down to where Antelope had been. He saw the fish jumping to catch the bugs and as he looked down, once again, he saw his reflection.

"The monster is back!" Coyote yelped and just as he was about to run away he heard a frightening sound.

"Who is making all that noise?" croaked a voice.

"It's the monster!" cried Coyote. But before he could flee the voice spoke again.

"I'm no monster," the voice croaked. "I'm just a frog." And Frog leaped from the bushes where he had been sitting and landed on the sand near Coyote's feet.

"Well," Coyote replied indignantly. "You have an ugly, ugly voice and you're ugly too."

"If you don't like what you see," croaked Frog. "Why don't you just close your eyes."

"Hmmm." Coyote thought. "What a good idea."

And so Coyote closed his eyes, bent his head down, and took a long drink. With eyes closed he saw nothing and so nothing frightened him. Nothing tried to catch him. And nothing scared him.

"Hah!" Coyote laughed out loud. "I bet I scared that monster away."

And this is how alcoholics and addicts live from day to day: eyes closed, drinking, using, and blind to the monster of a disease that can destroy their lives and the lives of those close to them. Working with alcoholics and addicts in psychotherapy is about pointing to the water, looking in together, and not drinking or using. It is about facing the pain of life stone cold sober. It is about helping alcoholics and addicts find another way to confront the monster without telling them to close their eyes.

COYOTE AND ADDICTION

In the same way that Coyote's behavior is his nature, the alcoholic and addict's predisposition is strongly linked to biology. A growing body of current research lends strong weight to the genetic theory of addiction through identical twin studies, physiological comparisons between sons of alcoholics and control groups, and genetic marker studies. Goodwin (1984, 1988), comparing twins separated at birth and raised either by their biological parents or by their nonbiological adoptive parents, found that sons of alcoholics had a fourfold increase in their risk of alcoholism. Schuckit (1985, 1986, 1994) described a variety of genetically linked effects including the different ways in which sons of alcoholics metabolize ethanol, have a decreased sensitivity to the acute effects of ethanol, and have a different level of muscle tension while intoxicated. In one of the early genetic marker studies, Blum and colleagues (1990, 1991) found a high correlation between alcoholism and the D2 dopamine receptor gene. While eventually the technology to intervene *in utero* may eventually be discovered, the problem of treating a disease that seems to have a mind of its own demands our attention.

Just like Coyote, alcoholism and drug dependence have been described as "cunning, baffling, and powerful." One patient, a woman in her early twenties, described her addiction as if it were "lying and waiting" for a moment of unconsciousness. Another, a man in his forties, told me with complete sincerity how his addiction spoke to him and tried to convince him that he had the strength to take one drink and stop there. Another looked far older than the sixtieth birthday he celebrated the night before his appointment. In complete awareness of the late stage of his illness he described with absolute certainty that he was unable to control his drinking and that he would die if he continued. Yet he wondered mischievously if maybe there wasn't some magic I might give him so he could keep drinking, just a little.

> An alcoholic said to man sitting at the bar, "How do you do it? Every couple of days you come in here and just have one drink."
>
> "I don't know." The man said. "If I feel like it, I stop in here after work. Sometimes I do and sometimes I don't. If I do, sometimes I have a beer or a glass of wine and other times I'll just have a soda. Then I go home to my wife and kids."
>
> "Amazing," replied the alcoholic. "If I could drink like that I would do it all the time."[1]

But it isn't enough to recognize Coyote inside the disease of alcohol and drug dependence. To work with and ultimately be of help to alcoholics and addicts, we must know Coyote's tricks, his ways, his tracks, and his guile. Once we learn them we must be able to master them, not only so we can spot the disease with a minimum of information and develop a second sense for the onset of a relapse, but to use his ways skillfully and with compassion when we are asked to lend a hand in the alcoholic and addict's quest for wholeness.

Our knowledge and experience can be used to help but it may also unconsciously wound a patient as well. We may think we know it all and move too quickly to confront the alcohol or drug use without establishing a safe therapeutic environment and relationship. Or we may move so slowly we collude with the patient's denial. We can forget that we are working cooperatively *with* our patients and not *on* them. We are not surgeons and our patients are never passive in the healing process. Because Coyote can at one moment be very charming and the next so infuriating, we may forget that his cleverness almost always leads to his downfall. Through his defensiveness and his rationalizing his behavior, Coyote avoids his suffering, deprives himself of knowledge, and claims to know everything. For the therapist under the influence of Coyote, omniscience may be a clever way of avoiding a discomforting silence, the unknown, or a patient's deepening confusion and pain.

---

[1] As told by Lyman Van Slyke.

COYOTE AND THE THERAPIST'S SHADOW

A therapist's delusion of omniscience has both a light and a dark side. The light side is revealed in the realm of the symbolic, the dream and the metaphor, when it arises in the mind of the patient or the therapist. The dark side or Shadow, made up of the repressed and cut-off aspects of one's personality, can manifest in a therapist's attempt to defend against a patient's pain by reducing it to a concept or a clever interpretation (see Chapter 9, Countertransference and Compassion).

In the midst of sitting with a patient I may see an image in my mind and feel inclined to describe what I see. I may want to tell the patient (in not so many words) "I understand." But there may be more to it than that. If I look closely, I may see Coyote emerging from my own unconsciousness. In the midst of my motivation to let my patient know I understand, I may also enjoy being clever. To some degree my comment may be helpful in identifying a similar experience, a shared moment, or a personal or professional reference. But I may also have strayed from my patient and enjoyed taking up the space between us as well. The comment or the interpretation may initially be appreciated and I may seem like a veritable shaman but I may also have usurped an opportunity for self-discovery that often emerges from my patient's pain.

In the midst of this cleverness I may also cater to my narcissistic need to appear wise and magical. The very act of writing this book, of describing an aspect of alcohol and drug dependence in symbolic terms, has many limitations. While evocative, Coyote is not scientific. While powerful, he does not lend himself to either statistical analysis or health care budget proposals. He cannot be measured, tested, or evaluated. He cannot be bought, bound, or dissected. No Coyote antidote will be found because Coyote cannot be killed.

Therefore, with each therapeutic encounter, I struggle with the knowledge that if I enjoy being clever, omniscient, or heroic a bit too much, my unconscious need to appear magical may take precedence over my patient's need to struggle. I may become excited by the thoughts, images, and feelings that well up inside me. I may speak too quickly in order to be seen by my patient rather than sit quietly and listen. I may want to talk and explain what I see in the hope that my knowledge alone will heal and I will be relieved of the need to hear another personal horror. And yet ironically, after years of experience, I am finally realizing that the heart of recovery and the soul of the relationship between a therapist and patient is born not from technique or magic but from conscious suffering.

> In the history of the collective, as in the history of the individual, everything depends on the development of consciousness. This gradually brings liberation from imprisonment . . . and is therefore a bringer of light as well as of healing. [Jung 1959, p. 271]
>
> Coyote is a partner in that liberation: he forces the hero to be conscious. One would not exist without the other. They are the great symbolic antagonists of world mythology, each opposing and undoing the other. Yet in their reconciliation lies the hope of mankind for vitality and wholeness. [Sandner 1979, p. 156]

This heroic urge to be an omniscient savior, common among professionals in the healing arts, is both an asset and a liability. Insight can either lead to illumination or it can create a feeling of distance and aloofness. If I open my mouth too soon in order to share a clever interpretation I may communicate that I am listening with the depth of my soul, but I may also unconsciously embarrass a patient into feeling psychologically exposed and emotionally naked. Clarity can create a sense of equanimity by giving form and feeling to a patient's narrative, or it can lead to a therapist's false sense of pride. The sense of knowing that arises when I listen for the internal feeling beneath a patient's story may lead to my relaxing or my feeling self-important. A sense of knowing can lead to an openness to listen or it can destroy one's curiosity. If I feel that I understand when a patient tells me that she feels tortured by the loss of someone she loved because I have had a similar experience, I may forget to listen carefully and ask another question that may invite a deeper understanding.

Ironically, because Coyote has such keen eyes and is so vigilant, he has an uncanny insight into other people's flaws. Unfortunately, while his clarity is admirable, his arrogance frequently impairs his ability to be empathic with those around him. Consequently, even though he may have something of value to offer, he is shunned. Coyote often has a hard time understanding that being right and being helpful are not necessarily the same thing.

COYOTE AND THE MOON

For as long as there was time, someone was the moon. But in this telling the moon was stolen. How it got stolen is another story. Anyway, because no one was the moon, it was dark at night. After a while the animals got tired of walking around in the darkness and so they all got together to discuss the situation.

"Who will be the moon?" the animals said.

"What about Yellowfox?" one of them said.

"Yes," they all agreed. "Let's ask Yellowfox."

Yellowfox agreed and became the moon. But he shone so brightly that it was just as hot as daytime. So the animals asked Yellowfox to come down.

"Who will we get to be the moon now?" the animals asked.

As soon as he heard this Coyote thought how wonderful it would be to be the moon so he could look down on the earth and see what everyone was doing.

"What about Coyote?" someone asked.

"Yes," Coyote said. "Of course I will go up and be the moon."

So Coyote went up and became the moon. He was neither too hot nor too dark. He looked down at the earth below and saw everything. And he couldn't keep it to himself.

"Who is that cheating at the moccasin game?" Coyote shouted. "And who is that stealing meat from the drying racks?" he shouted.

No one likes being found out so easily. After a while the animals got together and asked someone else to be the moon.

"The moon is supposed to be silent," they said.

But of course this hasn't stopped Coyote from snooping into other people's business ever since.

Regardless of whether I have read a library of books or seen dozens of patients with similar problems over the years, what the patient in front of me is saying is precious and deserves my attention. I caution myself against automatically answering when asked, "So what should I do?" and pause so as not to unconsciously fulfill my need to appear omniscient. I try to remember to weigh the value of my immediate response against the value of encouraging a search for a deeper personal answer to my patient's question. And, ironically, I must weigh even my tendency to overthink everything or risk stifling any human genuineness and spontaneity that remains.

Forced to cultivate an awareness of Coyote in myself as well as my patients, I have come to recognize that Coyote's greatest delusion, that he knows everything, is frequently my own delusion as well. Though I know with great certainty that I will never destroy him, because Coyote can't be killed, I struggle with the knowledge that at least I can recognize him when he comes into my office, sniffs the furniture, and plops down beside me, smiling. Besides, even in the midst of all his difficulty, ironically, Coyote can be a great deal of fun.

Psychotherapy, Addiction, and AA

BEN

From the moment Ben stepped into my office, I knew I would never forget the look in his eyes. As we shook hands, his firm grip clamping mine in a test as much as a greeting, I noticed the layers of crow's feet at the corners of two protruding sockets, waves of deep creases across his forehead, and a leathered tan that reminded me of an old Lakota warrior in an Edward Curtis photograph. He looked sad, as if he saw his world vanishing before him. I noticed the gnarled flesh on the top of his palm as I let go slightly before him, and I wondered, and feared, what I would learn about his life and his pain.

A long list of questions flooded my mind. I wanted to know about the hesitation in his voice the previous day when he asked me if I had time to see him. I wanted to know about the scar. I wanted to hear him say his name again in a deep baritone that vibrated through my chest. But as luck and my restraint would have it, I held my tongue.

As I led him into my office, Ben introduced himself, quickly scanned the furniture in the room, and identified my leather chair in the corner near the window looking out to the woods and a stream below the building. As he walked toward the couch opposite my chair, I noticed his long loping stride and was caught off guard by the economical grace of his movements.

"They said you work with alcoholics," he asked and stated simultaneously.

I nodded and smiled just a bit. With his thinning gray hair tied back in a small ponytail and taut, sinewy body, Ben looked like a man well into his sixties.

"My grandfather was a drunk," he said pausing. "My father was a drunk, and . . ." he said, stopping in midsentence.

And I realized, without his having to say it, that I understood his confession.

"My father always said, 'Never see a doc unless you have to and under no circumstances ever see a shrink.'"

With an almost imperceptible nod Ben acknowledged my smile and, while penetrating, his gaze was neither hostile nor defensive. He leaned back into the couch and took a deep breath. He crossed his legs.

I took a shallow breath and let it out slowly. I was starting to like this man. And I passed the first test.

Many alcoholics and addicts are reluctant to seek out psycho-therapy. Their hesitation may be due to a fear of being judged, given the stigma associated with alcohol or drug use. It may come from having been misunderstood, mis-diagnosed, or mistreated despite the good intentions of doctors, nurses, psychologists, and counselors. Or it may come from having heard stories from friends or other alcoholics and addicts that heightened their prejudice toward health-care professionals. In order to make sense of an historically difficult relationship between psychotherapists, alcoholics, addicts, and many members of AA, it may be helpful to summarize the conceptions and misconceptions that have evolved over the last hundred years in the slow development of alcohol and drug treatment.

MEDICAL TREATMENT

For most of the twentieth century, medical intervention with addicts and alcoholics generally fell into two distinct categories, depending on whether or not a physician considered addiction a disease and, if so, whether the disease was viewed as either biological, moral, or psychiatric in nature. Initially, the acute and chronic life-threatening medical problems common to the later stages of the disease were treated. For alcoholics, this included: a variety of wounds inflicted while under the influence, alcoholic hepatitis, cirrhosis, pancreatitis, pneumonia, liver cancer, cardiomyopathy, hypertension, cardiac arrythymias, Wernicke-Korsakoff Syndrome, polyneuropathy, alcoholic dementia, cerebral atrophy, and cerebellar degeneration (Secretary of Health and Human Services 1990, 1995). For addicts using syringes to deliver a drug of choice, initial treatment often addressed superficial cutaneous infections from dirty needles and blood-born diseases such as hepatitis.

If the physician believed that chemical dependence was due to a lack of sufficient willpower or morality, alcoholics and addicts were frequently transferred to a special ward for detoxification, referred to a charitable organization if the patient was indigent, or discharged with the oral prescription to "get a grip" or "find some shame." If the physician believed chemical dependence was a psychiatric problem, alcoholics and addicts were frequently referred to a psychiatric facility or an insane asylum. Early methods of psychiatric treatment for alcoholism and drug dependence may have included: electroshock therapy, pharmacotherapy, long periods of isolation, or, in extreme cases, the use of a straight jacket to restrain a patient during withdrawal and delirium tremens (Hestler and Miller 1995). If sufficient financial resources were available, a physician might have recommended several months in a spa or European-style sanitarium where the quiet pastoral surroundings, minimal social interaction, healthy diet, and contemplation were considered restorative in compensation for the overstimulation of a binge of drinking or drug use.

"The first time I ever got drunk I wound up in the hospital," Ben said, continuing with his story. "I was . . . maybe 13. I don't remember why I got drunk. I think it had something to do with a girlfriend dumping me." He shifted a little as he spoke, turned slightly, and adjusted the pillows behind him on the couch. "All I remember is waking up in the hospital. The nurse said I'd been in a coma and almost died. She asked me how much I had to drink. I told her I lost count after thirty."

For a brief moment I lost sight of Ben sitting on the couch and in my mind I saw a young boy in a hospital bed with a green wool blanket folded under the top of a starched white sheet.

"Because my Dad made a big stink they kept me for a couple of days and then let me go home."

I saw Ben sitting on the couch again and, as he continued, I wondered what happened when they got home from the hospital. Did his father get angry? Did he get a beating? Did he get a lecture? A hug?

"That's when he sat me down and told me about *his* drinking."

Thank you, I thought, grateful for his filling in the blanks—*a family disease*.

"He told me about the weekend after he got his driver's license. This was before the war," Ben said, and as he produced a pack of Marlboro cigarettes from a pocket inside his black workshirt, he nodded questioningly, inviting my permission to light up.

I tilted my head to the side, indicating my preference, and he pocketed the pack.

"He smashed up Grandpa's car and almost died. But he kept on drinking. Then, in his senior year in high school, he spent a week in a mental hospital and straightened up for a while. The part that scared the shit out of me," he said, looking down at the floor and then upward, his eyes rolling back, "was when he told me about being locked in a padded cell. Boy! Did that scare me. *But he still kept drinking.* Then after a year or two he saw a shrink."

Out of the blue I felt an uncontrollable urge to sneeze welling up inside me and reached for a tissue just in time. I blew hard a second time and took a moment to regain my composure. When I looked back at Ben to excuse myself I saw how his eyebrows telegraphed his surprise at my trumpeting.

PSYCHOANALYTIC TREATMENT

Popularized in Europe and the United States during the beginning of the century, the technique of psychoanalysis was applied to the few alcoholics and addicts who either could afford treatment or wandered into public institutions where psychoanalytic theory took hold. Though generally considered a problem of the lower socio-economic classes, alcoholics and addicts were thought to be unsuitable for psychoanalysis due to their perceived lack of ego strength and a preponderance of acting-out defenses (Freud 1905). Initial psychoanalytic theories of alcohol and drug dependence focused on the strength of libidinal drives and a developmental arrest at the oral stage of development, while later theories grew out of the developing paradigmatic shifts of ego psychology, object relations, and self psychology (Morgenstern and Leeds 1993). Etiologic suppositions varied dramatically but uniformly identified alcohol and drug dependence as a symptom of a variety of problems, including an underlying intrapsychic conflict, repression, a narcissistic crisis, an attempt to overthrow an overly harsh superego, a response to a flood of affect, an early trauma, an abundance of aggression, homoeroticism, and, more recently, an attempt to self-medicate a coexisting psychiatric disorder (Blane and Leonard 1987).

"He saw this shrink five times a week while he was in college and then for years after that. I don't remember how long. But I always remember him saying that if he could just figure out the real reason why he drank he knew he could lick it."

As he said "lick it," a tiny brown particle of what I assumed was chewing tobacco emerged from Ben's mouth and, with an obviously practiced dexterity, was lifted up by his tongue, transferred delicately to his forefinger, and then flicked into the wastebasket beside the couch.

Curious to know whether his father ever got sober, but hesitating to interrupt his chain of thought, I waited.

"He got sober for a year or two when I was a kid." Ben added. "But aside from that . . ." and he shook his head again.

If an alcohol or drug problem was even identified in psychoanalysis or psychoanalytic psychotherapy, the cure for the dependence, whether a focus of treatment or not, was expected only after the underlying intrapsychic conflict was resolved. Surprisingly, a cure was often expected regardless of whether the patient continued to drink or use drugs throughout the treatment (Morgenstern and Leeds 1993).

CARL JUNG AND BILL WILSON

An important relationship between psychodynamic psychotherapy and recovery from alcohol and drug dependence has been linked to one of Freud's early colleagues, Carl Gustav Jung. In 1931, Jung treated Roland H., an alcoholic from the United States. After a year of analysis Mr. H. sobered up, but later relapsed and returned to Zurich for further treatment. During the extended analysis, Jung noticed similarities between his patient's motivation to drink and the spiritual quest for relief from an existential loneliness and psychic pain that Jung was familiar with from both personal experience and his psychotherapy practice. But unfortunately, despite the additional analysis, Mr. H. continued to drink uncontrollably. Finally, in a moment of honesty and desperation after his failure to help his patient, Jung reportedly told Mr. H. that the situation was virtually hopeless. The only hope, he said, might be found in a spiritual or religious experience.

From this brief encounter we can imagine that Jung came to three important conclusions. First, formal psychoanalysis was of no help to alcoholics in their attempts to stop drinking. Secondly, the motivation to drink (and one can infer the same of other drug use) had its root in the search for an experience outside of one's ordinary human consciousness and, as such, the search had a spiritual component. Thirdly, if drinking was a misguided search for a spiritual transformation, what the alcoholic needed was a spiritual cure.

Taking Dr. Jung's advice, Mr. H. returned to the United States, joined a group of Christian Evangelicals who believed that temperance might be achieved through the surrender of one's will to God, and after a short time had the spiritual experience he was searching for. Finally, after years of pain and suffering, he was able to give up drinking.

Then in November of 1934, a traveling salesman named Bill Wilson, in the midst of yet another alcohol-induced hospitalization, was told about Jung's advice to Roland H. The advice Jung gave challenged Bill Wilson's "self-centeredness." It challenged his struggle to control his drinking through his willpower. Paradoxically, in a moment of transcendence, by giving up his belief in his ability to control his drinking, Bill Wilson had his own spiritual awakening, which eventually led to a lifetime of sobriety (Naifeh 1995).

There was a sense of victory, followed by a peace and serenity as I had never known. There was utter confidence. I felt lifted up, as though a great clean wind of a mountain top blew through and through. [Alcoholics Anonymous 1984, p. 14]

"Of course I tried just about everything," Ben said, shaking his head slightly. "You know, it sure took me a long time to get sober."

"Can you say a bit more about your getting sober?" I asked, curious about what Ben would be willing to reveal in his first session.

"Well, it wasn't enough that Dad died," he said, struggling to clear his throat.

In my mind I saw a pathology photograph of a cirrhotic liver, all dark and scarred with a bulge of fatty liver deposits.

"Cirrhosis?"

"Naw," Ben corrected. "He was drunk and fell down the steps. Broke his neck."

I winced. Ben noticed.

"Of course that didn't stop me either. I was around 17. I lied about my age and joined the Navy to get away from home. You know," he said smiling at himself, ". . . a geographic." And pulling back the sleeve of his shirt, Ben revealed an elegant tattoo of an eagle clutching a bunch of bleeding arrows in each foot.

"Nice, eh?"

My eyes widened and I leaned forward to admire the artwork.

"After a couple of years I got kicked out of the Navy," Ben said, and he swallowed. "Then in the early seventies I apprenticed as a journeyman carpenter. I was even in the brig for a month for being drunk on duty. Of course, I wasn't the only one, but they didn't give a shit. Then after my second divorce—" he said, and then paused.

He shifted again and I wondered if, given his apparent discomfort, he might have some back trouble. I was also curious about Ben's relationships but guessed that, if it was relevant, sooner or later he'd get around to telling me about them.

"I tried kicking it by myself," he said, "and you know how well that works!"

I smiled and realized how quickly I was growing fond of Ben's wry humor and his ability to laugh at himself.

"I tried Antabuse for a couple months but just stopped taking it when I wanted to drink. Even did twenty-eight days in a hospital once. The Union paid for it." And he shook his head again. "I always thought

my way of seeing things was right. I always thought I could do anything I wanted if I just thought about it and put my mind to it. I thought
I was big shit. Then about six months after my son was born four years
ago, I was up on this roof nailing plywood with a nail gun. It was after
the usual six-pack lunch. It was hot, I was smashed, and I nailed my
fucking hand to the roof. I thought I was going to die I was in so much
pain. But I didn't say a word all the way in the ambulance on the way
to the hospital. Fuck, can you believe I told the foreman I could drive
myself! The day I got out of the hospital I took in my first meeting. It
didn't take right away but about a month later something started to
click. I felt alive for the first time in a long while. I felt reborn. And then
I started to feel like shit."

COYOTE GETS HIS POWERS

Long, long ago, before the two-leggeds arrived from the lower world,
there were the animal people. The four-leggeds were the deer people,
the raccoon people, and the great big bear people. There were the snake
people, the frog people, and the insect people. In those days, because
everything of the natural world was alive, even plant people and rock
people roamed the earth. The rock people, of course, were the oldest
people in the world. And for that reason, even today, rocks deserve
great respect.

One day a great voice, the voice of the spirit that shoots up and out
in all green things, the Creator, the Great Spirit, spoke to the animal
people.

"Soon the two-leggeds will come and you will all need new names.
Come to my lodge in the morning and I will give you your new names."

Of course Coyote was so excited about getting a new name that he
started bragging about it to everyone.

"I'm going to wake up early and be the first to the Great Spirit's
lodge," he boasted in one village. Then he walked to another village
and shouted. "I'm going to stay up all night. I will be the first in line
and be . . . uh . . . I'll be Grizzly Bear. Yes, that's it. I'll be Grizzly
Bear."

And so Coyote went on boasting well into the night until he began to get tired. He got sleepy. And so he went home to his own lodge to try and stay awake.

"What will I do?" Coyote thought. "I must stay awake to be the first in line."

And he had an idea. Coyote was always having ideas.

"I know," Coyote said, and he searched around on the ground for two small sticks. "I'll take these two sticks and keep my eyes open so I don't fall asleep." And he did. Coyote placed the two sticks, one in each eye holding up his eyelid and he sat, waiting for the sunrise. But in a short time he fell deep, deep asleep.

When he woke up the sun was already high in the sky.

"Oh, no!" Coyote shouted. "I must be the first in line," and he ran toward the Great Spirit's lodge shouting, "Grizzly Bear! I want to be Grizzly Bear."

But he was too late. When he arrived at the Great Spirit's lodge all the animals had come and gone.

"Grizzly Bear is taken," the Great Spirit said.

"Then I will be . . . uh . . . how about Salmon? Yes! I will be Salmon," Coyote panted.

"Salmon swam upstream a long time ago," the Great Spirit said. "Because you are late you will have to keep your name. Besides, Coyote is a good name. It suits you. But to help you prepare the world for the two-leggeds, Coyote, I will give you two special powers. Whatever you imagine you will have the power to create and you will come back to life after you die."

Of course, Coyote felt so good about his new powers that he forgot all about the other names. They didn't seem so important anymore.

ALCOHOLICS ANONYMOUS

In May of 1935, Bill Wilson and Dr. Bob Silkworth founded Alcoholics Anonymous in Akron, Ohio. In the years that followed, the few physicians who treated alcoholics and addicts, achieved sobriety with help of the Fellowship, or knew of its tenets and effectiveness quietly referred their patients to AA. In the decades that followed, as medical researchers interested in alcohol and drug treatment took notice, the Twelve Steps became the focus of both clinical and academic attention. Although AA is rarely considered treatment, a brief description of its tenets are included in this chapter due to their educational, supportive, and beneficial results helping alcoholics and addicts throughout the world achieve and maintain sobriety at no cost.

The basic tenets of Alcoholics Anonymous and their counterparts in other substance-oriented anonymous programs focus primarily on three areas: an awareness of the individual's loss of control over the use of a substance, the development of a spiritual self, and a relationship to the fellowship of other recovering alcoholics and addicts. A more comprehensive analysis can be found elsewhere (Alcoholics Anonymous 1985, Brown 1985), but the following description of the Twelve Steps of Alcoholics Anonymous may help clear up any misunderstandings about the spiritual aspect of recovery in all substance-oriented Twelve Step programs and their psychological parallels in the relationship between a therapist and a patient.

The First Step: *We admitted we were powerless over alcohol and that our lives had become unmanageable* builds on the growing awareness, despite the presence of denial and resistance, that the alcoholic has lost control over drinking. The realization that the alcoholic has lost control over alcohol may come in a flash of instant enlightenment after "hitting bottom," or it may slowly sink in through a series of events that include: repeated hangovers; illness; or loss of job, family, friends, finances, or one's youth. It stands in stark contrast to the alcoholic's previously held belief that everything was under control. It stands in contrast to the belief that if something was out of control, it was someone else's fault.

The alcoholic's delusion that he has control over his drinking may initially appear quite innocent, especially when the alcoholic's life is only occasionally impacted by the effects of intoxication. Struggling to understand the meaning of control and loss of control over drinking, the alcoholic may ask, "How can my life be unmanageable

if my job is going so well?
if I have so much money?
if I'm still married?
if my kids are doing so well?
if my golf game (or fill in the sport) is pretty good?
if I still look good?

if I don't get as drunk as I used to?
if I don't drink as much as other people (spouse, friends, colleagues)?
if I don't have any (or many) DUI's?"

In the later stages, however, assertions that "I've got it under control" may sound increasingly bizarre in light of daily inebriation, hangovers, lost jobs, finances, disrupted relationships, and a chaotic family life. The First Step may seem like a small admission, an obvious insight, or the flimsiest of changes, but the realization that the alcoholic has lost control over alcohol is a substantial movement in the direction of sobriety. The loss of self-esteem or the shame associated with an admission of this kind may feel like too much to bear to the newly sober, but it is a beginning, because the alcoholic has, at least momentarily, stopped listening to Coyote and gazed at his reflection in the water.

The psychological parallel in the First Step of AA can be seen when the first phone call is made to schedule an appointment with a therapist. By reaching out for a consultation, implicitly or explicitly, an acknowledgment is made that something is not working, that something in life is out of balance. In effect, an admission is made that something is out of control.

The Second Step: *We came to believe that a power greater than ourselves could restore us to sanity* invites the alcoholic to follow the initial realization in Step One with a question: "If I'm not in control of everything, then who is?" The Second Step, while difficult for agnostics or atheists, invites the alcoholic to look beyond an egocentric world and gaze into the unknown. Though frequently frightening, the admission that no one is in control can shock an alcoholic out of denial and into the belief that he or she cannot do it alone. To leap from "I am in control of my drinking, my using, my life, my work, my friends, etc." to "no one is in complete control" is an opening to work with in treatment. It is the beginning in a long process in the breakdown of denial and the isolation that often accompanies an addiction.

The realization inherent in the Second Step, not the mere intellectual acknowledgment of it, challenges the alcoholic's narcissism and grandiosity. For many, a belief in a Higher Power may seem like the antithesis to a psychologically rational mind; its psychotherapeutic corollary can easily be found in the transference relationship in psychotherapy. When an initial sense of trust develops in therapy, whether consciously or not, there is an opening, a reaching out between patient and therapist. There is a belief that there is someone to turn to in the world. This blossoming trust implies that a helping force, outside of the alcoholic's almost rigid self-reliance, now exists. Unquestionably potent, this positive therapeutic alliance becomes the vehicle through which many people enter the world of dreams, come in contact with the unconscious, and face a numinosity within the darkness, the pain, and the unknown. It is the onset of the development of therapeutic trust and the foundation of a majority of the healing in depth psychotherapy.

The last phrase in the Second Step, *restore us to sanity*, is often difficult to embrace for the psychologically minded or psychiatrically phobic. For those who have difficulty with this aspect of the Second Step, substituting the word *balance* for *sanity* may ease the cultural stigma associated with mental illness pervasive in the United States today. In the early stage of the disease many "high bottom alcoholics" find the word *insane* intolerable and associate it with strong feelings of shame. Yet if explored to its final result, either through the patient's alcohol and drug history or through projecting the patient's drinking and using into the future, the notion that relying on alcohol or drugs to remove the void of one's loneliness and pain, even for the briefest moment and eventually not even that, will seem a little crazy even to an alcoholic struggling with denial.

The Third Step: *We made a decision to turn our will and our lives over to the care of God as we understood Him* invites the alcoholic to move just a bit further from the painful realization that "I'm not in control," from questioning "who's in control" to a spiritual leap that involves relinquishing control. Many alcoholics find this step difficult regardless of the alcoholic's rational or spiritual belief system. It is one thing to acknowledge a Higher Power, whether God in the Judeo-Christian sense, Christ, Allah, or Buddha; it is another entirely to give the care of oneself over. It may be frightening to trust that in a leap of faith you will be caught, cared for, and nourished. The Third Step is an active process wherein the alcoholic gives up the illusion of total control. It means not just looking, but leaping into the unknown. It is a leap to be tested over and over and not to be accepted blindly.

In psychotherapy, a similar openness develops over time, although it may feel like growth on a geologic timescale. Therapeutic trust is not based on blindly accepting whatever a therapist says. It begins with the possibility that a therapist may actually care. It develops as it becomes clear that a therapist values an inner truth more than any belief, arrogance, or delusion of the therapist's omniscience. It develops when both therapist and patient pay attention to the inner voice of the self.

The Fourth Step: *We made a searching and fearless moral inventory of ourselves* invites alcoholics to make a structured accounting of themselves and how they have treated others. The Fourth Step is, in many respects, a miracle of ingenuity. It sets in motion the healing of the confessional in the Fifth Step and an opportunity to make amends in the Ninth Step for harm caused to oneself and others. Without the possibility of redemption through self-reflection, confession, and making amends, a growing awareness in sobriety of the devastation alcohol has had on one's life and the lives of others would be intolerable.

Listing the alcoholic's character flaws and transgressions has its parallel in psychotherapy. A strong component of virtually all psychotherapy involves an active recounting of the patient's life, including both wounds received and transgressions against others. In essence, psychotherapy is part confessional, whether the accounting is done formally in a concise period of time or over years.

The Fifth Step: *We admitted to God, to ourselves, and to another human being the exact nature of our wrongs* is the embodiment of the curative in the confessional. It is interesting that the first to receive a confession is a Higher Power. This is important because it is frequently easier to admit one's flaws in a relationship where we experience or project an unlimited source of compassion. But the Fifth Step also includes a human component. The Fifth Step necessitates admitting to another human being "the nature of our wrongs." The Fifth Step evokes both the divine and the human aspects of redemption.

In psychotherapy, all three confessions may be heard simultaneously. In the sacred space of the therapist's office, as trust develops, pain is revealed, and through the numinosity of the transference, consciously or unconsciously, a shared symbolic Higher Power is evoked. In therapy, the patient's innermost thoughts are invited to be heard. They are spoken aloud. And they are received by the aspect of the therapist that is just another human being.

The Sixth Step: *We were entirely ready to have God remove all these defects of character* brings the recovering alcoholic to the brink of a transcendence. Curiously paradoxical, it is often the alcoholic's character flaws and pain that are held to so tightly. The Sixth Step challenges recovering alcoholics to remove their character defects not by willpower, which would be a futile exercise of self-control, but merely to be ready and willing to have the defects removed. It is this willingness, rather than the actual activity that precedes it, that leads to an experience of grace and relief.

Cognitively based psychotherapies, using insight as a tool for behavioral change, are the antithesis of this step. Depth-oriented approaches, however, while incorporating insight as a part of the healing process, rely both on the healing aspect of the transference and the development of a deeper relationship to oneself, to the world of dreams, and to the unconscious. This process of reaching in as well as reaching out, in AA as well as in psychotherapy, means that the ego, the belief in one's supreme ability to maintain control and exert one's willpower, must be tethered. It means looking into the unknown and not coming up with quick solutions, interpretations, reasons, and excuses for one's pain.

The Seventh Step: *We humbly asked Him to remove our shortcomings* is the active gesture of the alcoholic's request for deliverance. Taking the role of an initiate, the alcoholic psychologically, spiritually, and symbolically prostrates before the Higher Power and pleads for help. Once again, it is through divine intervention and not through willpower, like that of the Coyoteway ceremony, that the alcoholic's pain is relieved. It is by sincere request that one's wish is granted, not through intentionality or willpower.

In psychotherapy, this request is unconsciously if not explicitly expressed throughout treatment. With only a partial knowledge of one's suffering, power and wisdom are projected onto the therapist, and an active or passive request for help is made. Whether or not the therapist provides help in the form the patient unconsciously or consciously requests, the process of self-reflection, revealing pain to another, the presence of the therapist, the wish to be relieved from suffering, and the search for a cure from within the depths of the unconscious provide fertile ground for healing and transformation in psychotherapy.

The Eighth Step: *We made a list of all persons we had harmed and became willing to make amends to them all* is a continuation of the Fourth Step's "fearless moral inventory" and initiates the active aspect of the alcoholic's redemption. After literally making a list in the Fourth Step of those harmed, regardless of whether or not the individual was intoxicated at the time, the alcoholic is, in the Eighth Step, merely asked to "become willing" to lighten the burden of guilt and remorse that accompanies the actions and omissions of the past. Simultaneously and without willpower, once again, the energy required to repress memories of the past and maintain the illusion of one's perfection is cast aside in a humble gesture of supplication. Grace happens. It is not made or achieved.

A similar telling, re-telling, and holding of the emotional, moral, and psychological weight of one's actions and omissions can lead to an unburdening in psychotherapy. This unburdening and a subsequent wish to make amends occurs when a patient reveals psychological and emotional wounds inflicted on others and feels inclined to apologize or make retribution. Through this genuine accounting, a spontaneous willingness to renounce a self-righteousness may arise on its own and not through a forced spiritual ambition. In a therapeutic relationship it is modeled by a therapist confronted with an error in judgment who genuinely makes amends to his or her patient.

The Ninth Step: *"We made direct amends to such people wherever possible, except when to do so would injure them or others* is the activity that emerges from the previous step. Where the Eighth Step focused on a "willingness" to make amends, the Ninth Step clarifies the context in which the unburdening will take place. The recovering alcoholic is reminded to make amends only when he or she is ready, and not to do so when making amends would harm others. This essential aspect of the Ninth Step protects those listed in the alcoholic's fearless moral inventory from the self-centeredness and desperation of the alcoholic who tries to make amends, "whether you like it or not."

Separating the Fourth Step from the Ninth Step was either an act of pure genius or divine inspiration. If the two had been placed side by side, the impulse to get it over quickly, make the list, make the amends, and push it under the rug would be too enticing to the alcoholic unwilling to take in the weight of a painful past. Separating the steps gives recovering alcoholics time to think about their lives and their actions, and whether or not making amends might be harmful to others. It gives them time to reflect on their past, ask for guidance, and truly take in the nature of their character defects.

In psychotherapy, as unhealthy relationships to others and the self are recognized, a spontaneous urge to make amends may also arise. This is distinct, however, from the intellectually based wish to heal others or control the emergence of uncomfortable feelings such as ill will, sorrow, and guilt. This premature wish to be nice, loving, and spiritually correct may at times be genuine, but all too often it is a defense against feeling the darkness of one's anger, the desolation of having abandoned or wounded someone, and the desire to destroy or mollify the object of one's pain.

In psychotherapy, the act of making amends may also involve an intrapsychic healing, whether or not an individual harmed is unavailable or deceased. A symbolic amend, rather than an actual face-to-face confrontation, may be beneficial if taking action might harm the individual or the intended recipient. It may also be beneficial on an archetypal or spiritual level, and be revealed through a patient's dreams or in the patient's conscious feelings and actions in the transference relationship to the therapist. It may manifest when, after exploring early childhood wounds, the good in the wounding parent and the bad in the somewhat helpful parent is acknowledged and integrated.

The Tenth Step: *We continued to take personal inventory and, when we were wrong, promptly admitted it* reminds the alcoholic that making a fearless moral inventory is not a one-shot deal. It reminds the alcoholic that just because you're sober doesn't mean you're spiritually perfect. It counters the spiritual arrogance that often arises in sobriety, that redemption is a neverending process of self-reflection and awareness. It reminds the alcoholic that recovery is not an achievement one can possess. It means progress, not perfection.

From a psychotherapeutic perspective, the Tenth Step represents the stage in psychotherapy when a patient internalizes a search for consciousness in the midst of everyday life. It describes a stage at which the narcissistic wounds of early childhood have been addressed, tended, and at least partially healed, and an awareness of the ongoing nature of one's growth and development arises.

The Eleventh Step: *We sought through prayer and meditation to improve our conscious contact with God as we understood Him, praying only for knowledge of His will for us and the power to carry that out"* reminds the recovering alcoholic to seek out spiritual guidance through a relationship to a Higher Power. The Tenth Step guards against the tendency of the alcoholic, like Coyote, to own his spiritual progress. It counters the belief that the alcoholic's insight, while previously hampered by alcohol, is now new, improved, and in fact Higher-Powered. The Tenth Step guards against the development of a spiritual persona, guards against the delusion of self-knowledge through attainment, and encourages humility.

From a psychological perspective, the Eleventh Step represents the transformation in the therapeutic relationship beyond the personalities of the patient and the therapist. It is an ongoing cultivation of a relationship to the unknown, for in the known and the static the ego and the shadow take hold. It represents a shift in awareness from a reliance on the therapist to a direct relationship with the self and the unconscious.

The Twelfth Step: *Having had a spiritual awakening as the result of these steps we tried to carry the message to alcoholics and to practice these principles in all our affairs* once again clarifies the nature of the alcoholic's transformation: it is a spiritual change, not one of increased willpower, cognitive understanding, or a mere change in behavior. The Twelfth Step encourages the recovering alcoholic to reach out beyond a self-centered enlightenment and offer help to other alcoholics in pain. Alcoholics and addicts working a Twelfth Step are likely to take on tasks as simple as making coffee at a regular meeting, answering telephones, becoming a meeting secretary, or eventually sponsoring those in early sobriety. It is a step toward humility, whether the alcoholic was previously homeless or the CEO of a multinational corporation.

In psychotherapy, the parallel is similar: while therapy may end, the process of individuation and healing continues. Termination never implies an end to the development of consciousness but, rather, it points to the beginning of a life in constant contact with the self and the unconscious through awareness, through dreams, and through everyday life. It does not mean that all patients become therapists. It represents the way in which, through a transformation in therapy, an individual brings a less wounding attitude toward themselves, to others, and to the most everyday interactions.

PSYCHOLOGICAL RESEARCH AND TREATMENT

Following the Second World War, a large number of soldiers who made use of the military's "energy pills" returned from active duty dependent on amphetamines. Previously thought to be nonaddictive, amphetamines became the subject of a growing wave of addiction research that led to an attempt to identify the presence of a pathological Alcoholic or Addictive Personality Disorder. Ironically, the psychiatric stigma associated with alcohol and drug dependence persists to this day despite the fact that the American Psychiatric Association removed alcoholism and drug addiction from the subtypes of sociopathic personality disturbances in 1980 (Morgenstern and Leeds 1993).

A more positive result of this research led to the identification of *dual diagnoses*, the coexisting psychological or psychiatric disorders that exist within the population of alcoholics and addicts. Depending on the study (Blume 1989, Goodwin and Erickson 1979, Jainchill et al. 1986, Khantzian 1990, Ries 1994, Shuckit 1986), a co-morbid psychiatric disorder among alcoholics is reported as high as 80 percent of the time. Personality disorders, including Antisocial, Dependent, Schizoid, or Borderline Personality, are reported as high as 70–80 percent (Regier et al. 1990). Anxiety disorders are reported at a lifetime prevalence of 45 percent compared with 14.6 percent in the general population. Mood disorders appear only slightly higher than the general population at 9.5 percent (Regier et al. 1990, Ries 1994). Psychotic disorders, including Schizophrenia, Major Depression, or Bipolar Disorder, appear among alcoholics and addicts at 10–15 percent (Kansas 1988). In addition, of eating disordered women, 33 percent were found to have alcohol and drug problems (Zweben 1986). In the decades that followed, many hospital-based, community mental health, and private treatment centers experimented with behavioral (Blane and Leonard 1987), social learning (Blane and Leonard 1987), and control mastery (O'Connor and Weiss 1993) theories to treat alcohol and drug dependence.

As a result of a pervasive misunderstanding of the problems associated with a dual diagnosis, many alcoholics and addicts in the last century were caught in a revolving door between alcohol and drug treatment and one psychiatric facility after another. Frequently, those who entered a hospital displaying symptoms of disorientation, dissociation, or other psychotic features, once a history of alcohol and drug dependence was discovered, were transferred to the hospital's chemical dependence unit. Likewise, when a patient on an alcohol and drug unit exhibited symptoms associated with a psychiatric disorder after detoxification and withdrawal, they were transferred back over to the psychiatric unit, medicated, and then released.

SOCIAL MODELS OF TREATMENT

During the 1960s and 1970s, when drug use in the United States escalated dramatically, large numbers of young people rejected standard medical and psychiatric models of treatment. Based on the acknowledgment that a caring social environment like that in the Fellowship of AA could restore alcoholics and addicts, healing communities sprouted up across the country. Programs relying on the support of alumni to staff, provide service, and structure the healing community became known as social model programs; those utilizing mental health professionals have been called therapeutic communities. The current trend of treatment in many residential programs utilizes both mental health professionals and trained, recovering alumni, blurring previous distinctions between the two types of residential programs.

"I even joined Delancey Street for a while," Ben said, reflecting on his drinking and drug use during the seventies. "It was after my first divorce and I was broke in more ways than one. I was stoned so much most of the time I didn't even know what I was high on." He shook his head. "So I joined Delancey Street and sobered up real quick. Started working again but after a while, you know," he said, smiling. Then he shared a knowing grin. ". . . you know that old stinking-thinking grabs you and well, let's just say . . . I had to do it my way."

Social model programs and therapeutic communities, while frequently disparate in their attitude, social norms, and rules governing inclusion, exclusion, and ejection, were similar in how they organized virtually every aspect of the members' life from the moment they entered until they left the community. These community-oriented programs took virtually anyone who wanted to join and literally taught them to live again. They taught basic living skills, including the importance of personal hygiene, cooking, managing money, and how to be a valuable employee, but they also stressed the importance and value of social relatedness. They taught the value of respect, the maintenance of social boundaries, and how to remain honest to oneself and to the community. Through modeling and action they taught how to receive and give back to others in the community. They helped large numbers of individuals who lost friends, family, health, and finances to the ravages of the disease find a way back to productive, drug-free lives.

CURRENT TREATMENT APPROACHES

Identifying the successes and failures in alcohol and drug treatment over the last century, a majority of the hospital-based programs, residential treatment facilities, and therapeutic communities recognize that chemical dependence is not only a medical disease, but also a psychological, social, and spiritual disease as well. In addition, in order to meet the special needs of the dually diagnosed patient, many programs cross-train psychiatric and chemical dependence staff, defusing the controversy over whether the biological or psychiatric disorder should be treated first or whether both disorders should be treated simultaneously. Many facilities now initiate sobriety using a chemical dependence approach that includes detoxification, some degree of isolation from a familiar drug-infested environment, education, and a structured group setting. In early recovery (the first year), psychiatric consultation may be used on as "as needed" basis for the dually diagnosed addict and alcoholic. Treatment may be complimented with individual, couples, or family therapy and psychopharmacological treatment used when psychiatric, psychological, and emotional problems complicate, threaten, or sabotage sobriety.

A majority of the chemical dependence programs today are therefore eclectic, and incorporate various aspects of four treatment strategies, including:

Medical treatment for acute and chronic medical problems;
Individual, group, and occasionally family therapy;
Groups based on the Twelve Steps of Alcoholics Anonymous;
Group activities to foster a sense of community, stress management, meditation, and recreation.

LIMITATIONS IN TRAINING

Ironically, it is *least likely* that a physician will diagnose and refer an alcoholic or addict for treatment. Despite the fact that alcohol and drug dependence is acknowledged as a disease by the American Psychiatric Association, the American Public Health Association, the American Hospital Association, the American College of Physicians, and the World Health Organization, the American Medical Association and the American Nursing Association have no alcohol and drug treatment requirements for their members (Secretary of Health and Human Services 1990). Mental health care workers fare only slightly better than their medical counterparts, and then only on a statewide basis. The American Psychological Association, the National Association of Social Workers, and the American Association of Marriage and Family Therapists, like their medical counterparts, have no mandated alcohol and drug education requirements. Many state licensing agencies and professional organizations, however, are increasingly mandating continuing education requirements for alcohol and drug problems and treatment. As a result, the California Psychological Association, the California Association of Social Workers, and the California Association of Marriage, Family and Child Counselors have recently initiated minimum requirements for seven hours of alcohol and drug training.

On the front lines in most treatment facilities, though inferior in professional status among mental health professionals, alcohol and drug counselors may be licensed, unlicensed, or certified by a variety of academic institutions and professional organizations. The California Association of Alcohol and Drug Counselors (CAADC), at the forefront of the professional development for alcohol and drug counselors, requires its members to have a comprehensive academic and clinical curriculum that includes over 300 hours of training. Ironically, alcohol and drug counselors, while lacking advanced academic and clinical training, tend to have the most extensive experience in alcohol and drug problems and provide a majority of the care and treatment for alcoholics and addicts today.

WHAT PSYCHOTHERAPY CAN OFFER THE ALCOHOLIC AND ADDICT

As a result of their personal experiences or those of sponsors, sponsees, or friends, many alcoholics and addicts may be cautious when seeking help from health care professionals. Over the last decade, I have heard thousands of stories from patients, students, and friends describing a multitude of unfortunate experiences when a mental health professional has:

Discounted the centrality of a chemical dependence;
Insisted on finding the psychological root of the problem despite the patient's continued drinking or using;
Demeaned participation in Alcoholics Anonymous;
Ignored the problematic drinking entirely; or
In cases involving physicians, injudiciously prescribed other addictive medication (see Chapter 4).

"You know," Ben said, as he leaned back into the couch and took a long breath, "It took a lot to get me to call you. I thought about it for a while. Okay, it was about six months," he said. "To be honest, I'm not quite sure how to say it. I've been sober for four years now. I go to two or three meetings a week. Two are like my home meetings. I've gone through the steps twice, once when I got sober and once when I came close to a relapse. Something's still missing. There are some things I just don't wanna talk about at meetings. You know, sometimes I feel like things are way personal."

I nodded and he smiled back.

"Would you like to come back and talk some more?" I asked.
"Yeah," Ben said, "I would."

Psychotherapy, especially when a therapist is trained in the field of addiction, can provide a safe place where many alcoholics and addicts receive honest, objective, compassionate feedback about their alcohol and drug problems. It can help alcoholics and addicts reach out for treatment when reaching out appears more painful than the pain they know. It can provide a place to weigh the risks of not addressing the problem and help them pause to look ahead at a future of "more of the same" (Brown 1985, Zweben 1986). Psychotherapy can provide a sacred place to examine the multitude of feelings that arise following the admission that one's drinking and drug use is out of control. It can help explore the cultural stigma that binds shame and fear to every alcoholic and addict's admission. It can support the struggle to reach out beyond the fear. It can be a quiet place to talk when an AA meeting filled with people strikes terror in the heart of most introverts.

A psychotherapist knowledgeable about alcohol and drug dependence can help the alcoholic and addict face the painful realities associated with drinking, can help clarify the biological, psychological, social, and spiritual aspects of the disease, and maintain the continuity of care after inpatient, outpatient, or residential treatment. Once sobriety is stabilized, usually after a year or two of abstinence, psychotherapy can help the alcoholic and addict face a variety of compulsive behaviors like food, sex, work, shopping, and love that may plague the recovering alcoholic and addict. Psychotherapy can help examine the gnawing loneliness, the depression, and the fear that surfaces when the anesthetic of alcohol or drugs has been lifted.

> I get no kick from champagne, mere alcohol doesn't thrill me at all,
> So tell me why should it be true, that I get a kick out of you.
> Some get a kick from cocaine, I'm sure that if I had even one sniff
> It would bore me terrific'ly too, yet I get a kick out of you.
>
> [Porter 1959]

It is also important to identify the limitations associated with ongoing psychotherapy as an adjunct to an alcoholic or addict's recovery. In contrast to a sponsor, a member of the Fellowship, or meetings that may be available twenty-four hours a day, as a psychotherapist my time and availability are limited. Some therapists wear beepers or have answering services contact them around the clock. But unless there is a clear crisis when I check my answering machine more often, I can only be available on a limited basis. I cherish my privacy, my introverted nature, and guard my home life carefully in order to return to my office, my patients, and the work refreshed.

Another obvious limitation for many addicts and alcoholics in recovery, in contrast to the negligible cost associated with participation in a Twelve Step program, are the fees associated with psychotherapy. The cost can be substantial and varies from zero to forty dollars per hour for a supervised intern to as much as $250 or more per hour for licensed social workers, psychologists, or psychiatrists. Because I believe that depth psychotherapy should be available to those who have the inclination to seek it out, I set aside a quarter of my clinical hours for low-fee patients. Many of my colleagues do the same, but the wait for a low-fee spot in a therapist's private practice can be frustrating for the alcoholic and addict in search of immediate relief.

For many, psychotherapy is a necessity. For others, it may be one of many needs. Frequently, psychotherapy is sought out during a crisis when it seems essential. But over time, when familiar defenses and distractions gain appeal compared to the vulnerability of encountering the rawness of one's soul without the buffer of alcohol and drugs, a choice is often made. At such times many people find psychotherapy too expensive. Not unsurprisingly, when lifestyle takes precedence over the struggle toward sobriety, when my patient says he or she's had enough or wants to try some other short-term treatment, a workshop, or just take a vacation from being aware, Coyote comes alive again and makes his mischief.

For the alcoholic and addict with years of sobriety, entering psychotherapy may be a choice after having tried almost everything else. It may come from struggling with anxiety and confusion after having followed all the steps, gone to all the meetings, and still feeling like something is missing. Psychotherapy can help the alcoholic and addict explore emerging problems with the Program, with a sponsor, sponsee, the Fellowship, and one's Higher Power before the onset of a relapse. It can provide a safe place to confront the inflation that often follows the excitement and pride of speaking at meetings, sponsoring other recovering alcoholics and addicts, or sharing a personal vision of sobriety with a vast, rapt audience. Psychotherapy, especially depth psychotherapy with a therapist familiar with alcohol and drug problems, can create the sacred space to explore one's dreams, the unconscious, and the healing power of the transference, in the midst of recovery and not apart from it.

CHAPTER 3

Altered States

The Physiological and Psychological Effects of Psychoactive Drugs

co-authored with Marcia Bradley

MELISSA

Over a decade ago, when I began to realize how extensively alcohol and drug problems affected the lives of many of my patients, Melissa walked into my office, and over the course of several months gave me a postgraduate seminar in recreational psychopharmacology. Having had two years of undergraduate chemistry in a local community college and more than a little extracurricular research of her own, Melissa was a vital informant. She taught me about a majority of the subjective effects psychoactive substances have on the mind and body. She taught me a great deal about her attraction to one drug after another and another.

Arriving for her first appointment on a hot summer afternoon, Melissa wore a pair of freshly ironed, tight, tapered blue jeans, a clean white T-shirt, and white Topsider deck shoes. Tall, almost lanky, with short blonde hair tipped purple at her temples, Melissa moved with an almost physical apprehension that cautioned me to gentleness as she stepped into my office and sat down on the couch across from my chair.

❖ ❖ ❖

"I've been sober for a year," she said hesitantly. Then, removing her shoes, Melissa pulled her legs up on the couch and crossed her legs.

"I go to three meetings a week. One step study, one just for women, and I just kind of float for the third, depending on my schedule as a waitress."

In my mind I saw Melissa in a short, white skirt wrapped around a pair of shapely legs. She wore a soiled apron and stood in the middle of a crowded diner. She was carrying half a dozen plates stacked up along her arms. Suddenly, as I remembered I was in my office, I noticed Melissa's eyes searching my face for any sign of reproach or judgment. When I smiled, she went on.

As she began to tell me her long history with alcohol and drugs, I wondered why such an image occurred to me at that moment, in particular with Melissa, and at this early time in her treatment. And while it is true that I am a man and have my own personal responses to patients, I made a mental note to give it some thought later that day. I wondered about the implications of my response, both in regard to my arousal, as well as the possible ways in which Melissa might be unconsciously expressing both her vulnerability and sexuality in the subtlety of her gestures and her immediate comfort to remove her shoes and sit crosslegged on the couch.

"Thirty days after I had my last drink, I did ninety and ninety and went through the steps with my sponsor."

By *ninety and ninety* I knew Melissa referred to the way many alcoholics get sober with the help of AA by going to ninety meetings in ninety days. And while this often seems like a pain for most people who lead busy lives, at this point in my training I was just beginning to realize that while some alcoholics and addicts initially flirt with sobriety, a willingness to take *any means necessary* to recover from alcohol and drug dependence implies a very strong commitment.

"I haven't talked at meetings yet." Melissa said. "I just can't. I can't tell people about what I've done. I just feel too ashamed. It doesn't matter what everyone else did. I know I need to talk about it and I try to raise my hand. But I get cold all over and feel like fainting. Sam, that's short for Samantha, she's my sponsor, she thought it might help if I talked to you."

I nodded again. I sensed Melissa's shyness and her profound introversion. And although at that point in my life, the idea of speaking in front of a group of strangers would've given me a heart attack as well, I didn't want to minimize her discomfort or intrude by assuming I understood.

"What would you like to talk about?" I asked, and without missing a beat Melissa began by describing her childhood and her initiation into the world of alcohol and drugs.

Growing up in a relatively normal, though unhappy, middle-class family, Melissa described her father as a local evangelical preacher with a strong though silent presence. She described her mother, on the other hand, as mostly sad, frequently depressed, and prone to outbursts of irrational anger. Melissa had a normal, painful adolescence filled with the usual existential confusion. She felt isolated among her high school peers and struggled to discover her identity apart from her family's rigid, religious environment.

Although a curious teenager growing up in the late 1960s, Melissa's first experience with alcohol or drugs wasn't until she was 13 years old. She described it this way.

"The first time I had something to drink I was sleeping over at Mary's. Mary was my best friend. We went to school together and lived a block apart. I remember one weekend when I slept over. Her parents were out for the night. She'd done it before so it was pretty easy to pick the lock of her father's liquor cabinet. She'd been trying to get me to drink for months but I was too scared. You know, sinning and all that. Anyway, we took just a little from each bottle so we wouldn't get caught. After about five minutes I realized what all the fuss was about. It was like I felt okay for the first time in my life. It felt like all the pain went away. I didn't feel so alone, or bad, or separate. It was like I felt almost normal. All the edges disappeared." Melissa paused, then unselfconsciously crossing her arms, she slowly caressed her shoulders. "I felt warm all over." And in the silence of her statement and my listening, Melissa dropped her arms and, aware of the intimacy of her gesture, she blushed. A full minute passed before she spoke again.

"For the first time in my life I felt like I was all right, like I was okay, ya know?"

I nodded. I knew what it was like to be in pain and then have it go away, not only emotionally but physically as well. As someone with nerve damage in my right knee I've had a continuous, intimate relationship with pain for over a decade, and I understand the sense of relief, the sense of grace, when it passes.

"In a strange way it was almost like I felt loved for the first time," Melissa added. "And you know, of course, I got drunk."

PSYCHOACTIVE SUBSTANCES

All clinicians who work with alcoholics and addicts need to have at least a cursory knowledge of the most commonly used psychoactive substances, the four classes of drugs they fall into, and their physiological and psychological effects. All psychoactive substances that fall into one or more of the narcotic, stimulant, depressant, or hallucinogen classes find their way onto the street as either natural substances, derivatives, or synthetics.

Natural substances are the organic materials, frequently obtained from plants, in which the psychoactive agent is present. They may be ingested directly, diffused in a liquid, or inhaled as a vapor or smoke. They include marijuana, opium, peyote, coffee, and tea.

Derivatives are the isolated psychoactive agents separated from the inert compounds in the natural substance. They include heroin, alcohol, cocaine, caffeine, codeine, and morphine.

Synthetics refers to the psychoactive agents produced in the laboratory matching their derivative chemical models. They include tetrahydrocannabinol (THC), the psychoactive agent in marijuana, hydrocodone (synthetic morphine), and may also include caffeine and nicotine.

Designer drugs, a term coined by Gary Henderson at the University of California, Davis, are a special form of synthetic drugs made when slight molecular changes are produced in street illegal drugs. These new chemical variants usually have similar pharmacological properties to the original model. Not quite the same as their illicit cousins, these designer drugs have helped many drug producers and dealers avoid prosecution under the Federal Controlled Substances Act of 1970 (Seymour et al. 1989).

"I didn't start out drinking every day. By the time I was 16, though, I was getting high during the week and drunk on the weekends."

Curious about Melissa's initial experiences and how quickly she developed acquired tolerance, I asked her what it was like when she first started drinking on a regular basis.

"In the beginning I got high on half a glass of wine. But by the time I was drinking every day—that wasn't for a couple of years—I didn't feel a thing till I had three or four drinks."

My eyebrows rose up after Melissa's last statement and she noticed. I was surprised because while I knew that alcohol affected people differently; given Melissa's weight, somewhere around 105 pounds, three or four drinks without any effect indicated a significant change from her initial tolerance level to an rapid level of acquired tolerance.

TOLERANCE AND WITHDRAWAL

Changing the frequency, quantity, and route of administration of a given substance or a variety of substances will, over time, change an individual's initial or inherent tolerance to either acquired tolerance, reverse tolerance, or, when the substance is removed from regular administration, produce withdrawal.

Initial or Inherent Tolerance

The baseline effect of a given drug prior to regular administration is called *initial* or *inherent tolerance*. There is considerable variance among individuals with regard to initial tolerance due to gender differences, genetic predisposition, body weight, fat content, and metabolism.

Acquired Tolerance

The diminished effect of a drug as a result of repeated administration is called *acquired tolerance*. When metabolic and cellular adaptation to increased levels of a substance is present, a body requires a higher dose of the substance to produce the original effect. Acquired tolerance, therefore, explains an alcoholic's ability to drink large amounts of alcohol without appearing intoxicated.

Since Melissa's drinking had progressed to the point where she felt intoxicated after only six ounces of wine when she began drinking at the age of 14 to three or four glasses after several years, her acquired tolerance had increased a significant 300 to 400 percent.

Acquired tolerance will develop rapidly when a short amount of time elapses between each dose and slowly when time allows for the substance to be eliminated from the body. Acquired tolerance is evident in the binge alcoholic who drinks continually for a week except during periods of sleep and finds less effect toward the end of the binge. It is evident in the maintenance drinker who starts out with a beer or two and over the course of ten years progresses to a twelve-pack a night. It is also evident in the late-stage alcoholic or addict who drinks or uses continuously.

When alcohol or drug users want to get high after having developed acquired tolerance, they must increase the dosage or intensify the route of administration. If an amphetamine user changes from oral ingestion to intravenous injection, the immediate high will temporarily override the previous level of tolerance for a short period of time. Abstaining from alcohol or drug use for several days or weeks will also return the individual to lower and eventually initial tolerance levels. Though frequently less appealing to the addict and alcoholic, this method will produce the same result without having to alter the route of administration or increasing the dosage (Metzger 1989).

Melissa took a moment to gauge the possible meaning of my reaction and took a deep breath.

"Yeah," she said nodding. "I remember the first time I tried something other than booze. I was dating this guy my parents didn't care for. I guess that's a mild way of describing it. I believe my father's response was, 'Dan will be your companion in sin.' Of course, that just made me want to date him to piss off my father even more. You see, Dan dropped out of school as a sophomore in high school. He was 21 when we met. I was 17. He had this really boss motorcycle. He always picked me up after school and we'd go for rides up in the hills. We were living in Oklahoma at the time and there were these hills behind the school. So we'd go up there and get high. The first time we went up in the hills he brought wine. By then Mary and I were drinking several times a week so I didn't feel much from just a few glasses. After a couple of months he got into the habit of leaving me in the woods to drive down and pick up another bottle. After that he brought up some pills he got from his mother's medicine cabinet. I think it was the codeine she got from the dentist. But by that time one pill didn't do a thing so I had to take two or three to get a buzz."

Cross-tolerance

The body's accommodation to an entire class of substances, once tolerance to a single drug within that class is established, is called *cross-tolerance*. Narcotics (opium, morphine, codeine, heroin, and the synthetic opiates including methadone) produce a high level of cross-tolerance; a few depressants (alcohol, barbiturates, and benzodiazepines) slightly less so; and, to a minor extent, cross-tolerance exists with a few stimulants (cocaine and the amphetamines). Little evidence supports cross-tolerance with hallucinogens. A common example of cross-tolerance occurs when an anesthesiologist requires a larger than normal dose of drugs to produce surgical anesthesia and astutely questions the veracity of a patient's limited alcohol and drug disclosure.

A week later, Melissa showed up for her second session wearing a similar pair of tight jeans but this time she wore a black Bruce Springsteen T-shirt. Before she even sat down, Melissa laughed. I could tell there was something she wanted to tell me but that she was a bit embarrassed. I smiled and was curious to know what it might be. I was a little concerned and afraid, given the nervousness of her laughter, that she might have relapsed. In the moment before she began talking I also wondered if she wanted to stop therapy.

I waited for her to begin. She blushed.

"What?" I asked gently, raising my eyebrows.

"I guess there's more I still have to tell you." She said. "I'm just afraid you'll . . ."

"Judge you?" I said. "You know, Melissa, I've heard a lot," I said, exaggerating my experience and wisdom. I was afraid my overly youthful-looking countenance revealed more of my inexperience than I cared to admit.

"There was this time we were up in the hills and we totally forgot what time it was. I was supposed to be home for dinner at six o'clock on the dot. Not six-oh-five or even six-oh-one. Anyway, it was already six-thirty and I knew my father would be furious. He was the kind of dad who showed his anger by not showing it, which of course was worse. He'd just say how disappointed he was. I hated that. Anyway, we hopped on Danny's bike and flew down the hill. This truck turned right in front of the school, I think it was a milk truck and Danny slammed on the brakes and ducked down. I went over the top and flew about twenty feet in the air. Luckily I landed on some lady's lawn and only broke my arm.

I still remember the doctor asking me to count down from one hundred. They had to put a pin in. I got to eighty-five, then eighty, and eventually seventy-five before I passed out."

Reverse Tolerance

A rare and a somewhat controversial concept in the addiction literature, *reverse tolerance* is the effect of rapid inebriation with small amounts of alcohol despite an extensive history of dependence and acquired tolerance. Reverse tolerance is differentiated from a return to initial tolerance which requires an extended period of abstinence. Though little is known about the physiological mechanisms underlying reverse tolerance, it is generally hypothesized that it is the result of chronic destruction of liver tissue.

Withdrawal

When a drug or class of drugs is no longer administered in the frequency and quantity that led to acquired tolerance, an individual may experience one or more of the symptoms of *withdrawal*. Psychological symptoms of withdrawal are defined by a craving and a preoccupation with obtaining and using the substance. This preoccupation may be as mild as clock-watching, obsessing about the arrival of a drug source, or thinking, talking, or fantasizing to oneself or others about the next opportunity to use. In the extreme, this obsession may involve the exclusion of normal daily activities including personal hygiene, work, food, and social relationships. Though specific withdrawal symptoms may vary from drug to drug, depending on the frequency, quantity, variation of drugs used and the amount of time lapsing from the last dose, they may include a variety of the following:

TABLE 3–1

intense craving

difficulty concentrating

depression

irritability

anxiety

headaches

fatigue

insomnia

hypersomnia

muscular tension

grand mal seizures

paranoid ideation

suicidal ideation

psychosis: distorted perceptions, sensations, delirium

autonomic hyperactivity: restlessness, sweating, rapid heartbeat, hypertension, tremors [*DSM-IIIR* 1987, pp. 129–130]

"After surgery the doctor had a quiet talk with me without my parents in the room. He didn't know the half of what I was into. I quit for a couple of months anyway 'cause I could tell I was into it way too much. But it wasn't easy. For the first week I felt sick to my stomach. I got woozy all the time, especially in the morning. I felt like I was gonna crawl outa my skin. I broke down a couple of times. All I could think about was going up into the hills with Danny."

I tried to imagine what Melissa must have looked like as a teenager. Even though she was well into her early thirties, Melissa appeared youthful. At 16 she must have seemed like a child to her parents. I imagined wanting to protect her. And I was aware of the strength of how my countertransference was developing the more Melissa opened up.

"That's when I discovered the healing power of narcotics! Percodan . . . by prescription," she said, smiling, ". . . and legal. They gave it to me for the broken arm."

NARCOTICS

Known primarily for their analgesic, pain relieving effects, narcotics are primarily derived from the seedpod of the species *Papaver somniferum*, the opium poppy. The term narcotic comes from the Greek word *narco* which describes the numbing and deadening properties of the drug. The effects of opiates, whether synthetic or of natural origin, include a suffusion of relaxation, a decrease in perception of pain or stress, euphoria, and, at higher dosages, a lapse into a dreamlike state, sleep, and eventually coma and death. Opiates act on receptor sites in the brain that respond to naturally produced substances called endorphins. Although the exact mechanism underlying their effect is not fully understood, it is clear that the brain produces and then releases these naturally occurring opiates during stress, thus relieving pain.

Opium

Grown for centuries throughout the Golden Triangle of Asia (Thailand, Burma, and Laos) and the Near East (Turkey, Afghanistan, and Pakistan), opium is produced by carefully cutting the poppy's seedpod and collecting the exuding viscous liquid that coagulates on contact with air. Opium can be ingested directly, diluted in a liquid, or smoked.

Sumerian, Egyptian, Greek, Roman, Moor, and Chinese medical annals refer to opium as a potent cure for numerous ailments and diseases. The Greek physician Galen wrote that opium:

> resists poison and venomous bites, cures chronic headache, vertigo, deafness, epilepsy, apoplexy, dimness of sight, loss of voice, asthma, coughs of all kinds, spitting of blood, tightness of breath, colic, the lilac poison, jaundice, hardness of the spleen stone, urinary complaints, fever, dropsies, leprosies, the trouble to which women are subject, melancholy and all pestilences. [Seymour and Smith 1987, p. 4]

In the beginning of the twentieth century a variety of cure-alls, elixirs, and formulas containing opium were sold throughout the United States. Laudanum (opium and alcohol) and paregoric (opium and camphor) were popular treatments for pain and diarrhea respectively. The primary psychoactive agents in opium have been identified as morphine (9–20 percent) and codeine (0.5–2.5 percent).

Morphine

Named after Morpheus, the Greek god of sleep, morphine is the primary psychoactive alkaloid opium derivative. First discovered by the German pharmacist Frederich Seturner in 1805, morphine was used extensively during the American Civil War as an anesthetic. Along with the development of the hypodermic syringe, morphine use led to the development of morphine addiction, then known as "the soldier's disease."

Codeine

Opium's secondary psychoactive alkaloid, codeine, produces effects identical to morphine though it is approximately 8 percent as strong when injected intravenously. Codeine has traditionally been used as a mild analgesic and cough suppressant. When taken orally its strength is considerably lessened. Though codeine is rarely abused as a primary narcotic, it is easily found in cough medicine and may be used by heroin addicts unable to find their drug of choice. Codeine derivatives include: dihydro-codeine (Paracodin), and oxycodone (Percodan). Codeine is also combined with acetaminophen (Tylenol 3) as a more potent form of the mild analgesics.

"Oh, I loved codeine," Melissa said in her session the following week. "It made me feel warm, especially in my heart. I liked it when I made love, I mean had sex, with Danny. I know now I wasn't in love with him. But he treated me okay. We had fun. And it made my parents furious. After a while I took it without Danny when Mary and I drank together. Then I got constipated so I cut back on the codeine. I didn't get into heroin for a couple more years but I never injected."

Heroin

Diacetylmorphine, a white, bitter tasting crystalline powder was first synthesized from morphine in 1874 by Bayer Pharmaceuticals in Elberfeld, Germany (Seymour et al. 1989). Requiring minimal laboratory facilities and personnel for mass production, street heroin is generally diluted or "cut" with a variety of substances (milk powder, baby laxative, sugar, or quinine) to reduce its effects to nonfatal dosages (2–5 percent pure heroin). Potentially lethal heroin production in circulation today includes: Persian (92 percent pure), Malaysian Pink (50 percent pure), Mexican Tar (37 percent pure), and Amsterdam Marble (63 percent pure). Since the 1970s, when a major supply of drug traffic to the United States was disrupted, the majority of heroin now entering the United States comes from either the Golden Triangle or Colombia. Originally hailed as a cure for morphine addiction, heroin became a drug of choice for addicts worldwide. It is typically injected subcutaneously (skin-popping) or injected directly into the vein (mainlining). Risks correlated with intravenous injection include a variety of subcutaneous, blood-born bacterial and viral infections such as hepatitis and AIDS (Acquired Immune Deficiency Syndrome).

The immediate effect on injection of heroin is a rush of euphoria followed by a feeling of general well-being lasting several hours. Heroin addicts frequently nod out as if in a dreamlike state. Not everyone initially gets high from heroin. Many experience only nausea and discomfort the first few times they use. A few use heroin intermittently (chipping) for extended periods of time without becoming addicted, but regular use on a weekly, then daily basis produces the classic addiction symptoms of tolerance, withdrawal, and chronic physical effects.

Synthetic Narcotics

An expanding pharmacological revolution has produced a variety of synthetic narcotics including alphaprodine (Nisentil), anileridine (Leritine), diphenoxylate (with atropine, Lomotil), levorphanol (Levo-Dromoran), meperidine (Demerol), phenazocine (Prinadol), propoxyphene (Darvon), ethoheptamine (Zactane), pentazocine (Talwin), piminodine (Alvodine), hydrocodone (Vicodin), and methadone (Dolophine).

Methadone

First synthesized in Germany during World War II as an analgesic substitute for heroin, methadone has become a highly controversial heroin substitute in narcotic maintenance programs since the 1960s. Due to its low cost, ease of administration, and lack of a significant high, methadone treatment has been used for over thirty years to curb the secondary problems associated with heroin addiction. These secondary problems included the illegal activities often necessary to obtain the substance and the secondary infections associated with intravenous injection. Despite the controversy of exchanging one addiction for another, and the risk of a prolonged methadone withdrawal, medically administered methadone continues to be the treatment of choice for the majority of heroin addicts in the United States today (Seymour et al. 1989).

Designer Narcotics

China White and a variety of fentanyl analogues are a group of powerful analgesic-anesthetics, first produced by Janssen Pharmaceuticals, and distributed under the name Sublimaze and Innovar (fentanyl and droperidol). China White appeared on the streets in the 1970s and was followed by other fentanyl analogues with varying potencies. From several hundred to three thousand times as strong as heroin, these analogues dramatically increase the likelihood of overdose.

Analogues of meperidine (Demerol) were originally sold on the street as "new heroin" and had severe side effects including burning on injection, hallucinations, and paralysis.

"I remember the first time I did morphine. I really screwed up my knee playing volleyball. My doctor asked me if I wanted something for the pain. Could I turn him down? So he wrote out a prescription for thirty Vicodin. It's got synthetic morphine in it. I took two before I left his office, and when I got home I took two more just in case, because I was in so much pain. When I was fixing dinner I was drinking a beer and I started to notice how light I was feeling. My whole chest felt like it was expanding. I felt warm and my knee didn't hurt. I wasn't even hungry any more. The next day I got up and my knee was a little sore and I had to go to work so rather than ice my knee I just took a couple Vicodin with breakfast."

DEPRESSANTS

Generalized depressants, sedatives, tranquilizers, and a variety of industrial solvents are a heterogeneous collection of drugs that have common calming, relaxing, and sleep-inducing effects. They include alcohol, sedatives, tranquilizers, and various industrial substances. Despite their frequent use and abuse as pain relievers, depressants are poor analgesics. When used alone for pain relief, depressants may produce agitation and disorientation.

Due to their synergistic effects when combined with other substances, depressants should not be used in combination with alcohol. Combining them often creates unpredictable results and in many cases is known to cause overdose or death. Despite the danger however, depressants are frequently abused in conjunction with both alcohol and stimulants. Barbiturates are often combined with speed to offset the sedative effects and maintain the relaxation and subjective high associated with them. If the stimulant, however, which has a shorter half-life than the barbiturate, wears off prior to the effect of the sedative, a narcotic overdose may result. Cross-tolerance also exists between many depressants and alcohol. A patient's unresponsiveness to normal doses of medically administered narcotics may indicate tolerance and/or cross-tolerance to alcohol or other drugs.

Alcohol

The accidental fermentation of fruit is likely to have occurred pre-historically producing an intoxicating beverage and the first surprised inebriate, but it wasn't until 800 A.D. that Jabir ibn Hayan discovered distillation as a process for liquid preservation, and in his native Arabic, named its product *alkuhl*. Other alcohols, methanol (wood alcohol) and isopropyl alcohol (rubbing alcohol), though chemically related, are considerably less inebriating and significantly more poisonous when ingested (Hofmann 1983).

The degree to which alcohol effects the brain is dependent on the rising blood alcohol concentration (BAC) or blood alcohol level (BAL). Essentially, the more alcohol there is in the blood (its primary route of transportation around the body) the more alcohol reaches the brain through the circulatory system. The legal limit for drinking and driving in most states is one-tenth of one percent or .10 BAL. In California, legislation passed further reducing the definition of Driving Under the Influence to .08 for adults and .02, roughly equivalent to one drink, for minors.

Alcohol concentration is dependent upon the volume of material in which it is diluted. A standard drink contains approximately one-half ounce of the psychoactive substance ethanol, whether contained in one ounce of hard liquor at 86 proof, 12 ounces of beer at 4 percent, or 4 ounces of wine at 12 percent. A 150-pound man, after four standard drinks in one hour, will have an approximate blood alcohol level of .08. Due to the insolubility of alcohol in fat and other variable factors, a 150-pound woman after only three drinks will have approximately the same BAL. Due to a woman's greater ratio of fat to total body weight, and fewer alcohol metabolites compared to men, women are more susceptible to alcohol's effects ounce per ounce and may become intoxicated to a much greater degree if they keep up with their male counterparts (Youcha 1986).

Alcohol acts both as a stimulant and as a sedative. The immediate stimulant effects following the first drink in an individual without acquired tolerance include an increased sense of well-being, a decrease in inhibitions and frustrations, and a sense of relaxation. After several drinks, the sedative effect of alcohol causes drowsiness and slowed muscle coordination. Continued drinking results in the toxic effects of alcohol, including slurred speech, disorientation, dizziness, lack of coordination, nausea, and vomiting.

"I remember I was on a date in a fancy restaurant. This was just before Danny. Mark was 19 and I was 14. He ordered a martini for me and a few minutes after the first sip I felt a little tipsy. I heard a soft humming and felt light-headed but I ordered another drink anyway. By the time we left the restaurant I was falling off the high heels I borrowed from Mary. Daddy would never let me wear heels. Anyway, I had a hard time walking to the car. When he kissed me good night I slipped through his arms and fell. I didn't feel a thing. I'm not even sure how I got into bed that night."

The liver, the primarily site of alcohol excretion, processes no more than one ounce of pure ethanol (1–2 drinks) per hour. As a result, when alcohol builds up in the bloodstream, the blood alcohol level rises. At concentrations nearing .2 BAL, the level at which most drivers are arrested, gross muscle coordination, reaction time, and movement are impaired. The inebriated individual may stumble, knock over drinks, fall, or lose consciousness. Between .3 and .4 BAL most people will lapse into a coma. At .5 BAL respiration and heartbeat decrease. At .6 BAL most people are dead.

Alcohol affects virtually every organ in the body. Susceptibility to medical problems associated with chronic alcohol abuse vary widely based on individual physiology, genetic predisposition, and the quantity and duration of chronic use. As quickly as alcohol enters the stomach, the body tries to metabolize and excrete it. Approximately 90 percent of ingested alcohol is metabolized by the liver, 5 percent is excreted in the urine, and the remaining 5 percent is excreted through the lungs as a vapor. As a result, the blood alcohol level can be measured by a blood, urine, or breath test.

Alcohol is a local irritant in all doses. When an individual takes a drink, whether a beer, shot, or glass of wine, alcohol irritates the esophagus and passes into the stomach, where digestive juices are secreted. Within twenty minutes, 20 percent of the alcohol passes directly into the bloodstream while the remaining 80 percent enters the bloodstream through the small intestine. When aspirin is used to compensate for a hangover, chronic alcohol use increases the risk of an inflamed esophagus, esophageal cancer, chronic atrophic gastritis, and the exacerbation of peptic ulcers. Chronic alcohol use also injures the gastric lining of the stomach, and interferes with intestinal motility and the action of gastroesophageal sphincters (Secretary of Health and Human Services 1990).

Alcohol absorption irritates the pancreas, interferes with the production of digestive enzymes, and causes an increase in the death of pancreatic cells. Chronic alcohol use is attributed to 75 percent of the incidence of pancreatitis. When a person ingests over three drinks a day, levels of cholesterol, fatty acids, and triglycerides increase. If an individual has heart disease, even a small amount of alcohol may increase the risk of heart failure due to cardiac muscle inflammation, cardiac dysfunction, and other cardiovascular disorders. Heart muscle degeneration is also highly correlated with chronic alcohol use. Heavy drinkers are at an increased risk of hypertension, ischemic heart disease, and cerebrovascular disorders.

In pregnant women, alcohol crosses the placental barrier and reaches the developing fetus. Repeated administration of alcohol may cause birth defects and Fetal Alcohol Syndrome (FAS). FAS was first identified in 1973 and established alcohol as a cause of birth defects. FAS symptoms include prenatal and post-natal growth retardation, craniofacial abnormalities, central nervous system dysfunction, and major organ malformations. FAS is present in as many as three births per thousand and is considered the most easily preventable teratogen.

The liver, the primary site of alcohol metabolism, is chronically affected by the development of fatty liver deposits (present in 90–100 percent of chronic alcohol users), alcoholic hepatitis (present in 10–35 percent of chronic alcohol users), and cirrhosis. Cirrhosis, present in 10–20 percent of alcoholics, is the progressive replacement of liver cells by scar tissue and is the ninth leading cause of death in the United States (Secretary of Health and Human Services 1990).

Alcohol acts as a diuretic, causing frequent urination over and above the amount of liquid consumed. When alcohol levels drop, the production of antidiuretic hormone is increased, causing water retention, salt buildup, and the puffiness that is often noticed after a day of heavy drinking. Additional chronic effects of alcohol consumption include nutritional and metabolic disorders such as anemia, depressed hormone functioning, and immune system dysfunctions that may increase the risk of liver, esophagus, nasopharynx, and larynx cancers. In addition, in the early stages of the disease, the high caloric content of alcoholic drinks may contribute to excessive weight gain. Over time, however, in the latter stages of the disease, when the nausea caused by excessive stomach acid secretion acts as an appetite suppressant, the alcoholic may eat irregularly, lose weight, and risk malnutrition.

TABLE 3–2 Caloric Content of Alcohol

Beer, 12 oz.	173
Martini, 3 oz.	145
Olive, 1 lg.	20
Rum, 1 oz.	73
Sherry, sweet, 3 oz.	150
Fortified wines	120–160
Scotch, 1 oz.	73

(Rombauer and Beker 1964)

Alcohol is both a sedative and an irritant to the central nervous system. When used as a sleeping agent it causes sedation for approximately four hours. When the sedation wears off, anxiety, irritability, and agitation may set in. Chronic alcohol damage to the brain includes atrophy (shrinking of brain tissue), impaired cognitive functioning, impaired visiospatial problem solving, long-term memory loss or blackouts, alcohol amnestic disorder, and alcohol dementia. The symptoms of alcohol dementia include a global loss of intellectual abilities, memory loss, impairments in abstract thinking and judgment, and changes in personality.

Over one quarter of the 56,155 yearly motor vehicle fatalities reported by the National Traffic Safety Administration in 1995 were alcohol related (National Highway Traffic Safety Administration 1996). Alcohol has been strongly implicated in accidents caused by falls, fire, and fatal drowning. Of all suicide victims, 20–36 percent have a history of alcohol abuse or were drinking just prior to their suicide (Seymour 1989). It is also estimated that 75 percent of all traumatic deaths and suicides among Native Americans and Alaskan native tribes are alcohol related (Indian Health Service 1988).

Synthetic Depressants

Frequently abused synthetic depressants include glutethimide (Doriden), ethinamate (Valmid), ethchlorvynol (Placidyl), methaqualone (Quaalude), and diazepam (Valium). Developed in the 1950s and advertised as nonaddictive and safe, these synthetic depressants were equal in addictive potential to their predecessors and gave rise to an increase of iatrogenic dependencies. Methaqualone (Quaalude) quickly found its way onto the street and became a popular high. Combined with alcohol, the effects of Quaaludes are greatly potentiated. Though Quaaludes are no longer available as a prescription drug, they continue to be produced illegally or smuggled into the United States.

Sedatives

Barbituric acid, first synthesized from uric acid by Adolf von Bayer, led to the development of the first barbiturate in 1903. Under the name Vernal, it became the first of the barbiturate class to be used as an antianxiety and sleep-inducing agent. Vernal was followed by phenobarbital (Luminal) in 1912, amobarbital (Amytal) in 1923, pentobarbital (Nembutal) and secobarbital (Seconal) in 1930, and thiopental in 1935. The shorter-acting barbiturates, pentobarbital, secobarbital, and amobarbital, tend to be more commonly abused and are known generically as sleeping pills, goofballs, or downers.

The effects of barbiturates are almost identical to those of alcohol and include the development of tolerance, dependence, and withdrawal. They produce mild euphoria and a reduced sense of guilt and self-criticism. Sedative intoxication produces a decrease in motor control, slurred speech, and poor judgment. The risk of suicide and accidents increases dramatically with higher doses or when barbiturates are combined with other substances. Although usually taken orally, intravenous injection of barbiturates increases the risk of subcutaneous infection, hepatitis, and AIDS when needles are shared. Death by overdose is a danger and a commonly chosen method for suicide by the barbiturate dependent user.

During one session Melissa talked about her experience with barbiturates.

"My friends at college could never figure out why I liked downers. But I'll tell you, when I'm sober, the world has edges and I get cut on the edges a lot. People are really scary to me and a lot of time life sucks. When I'm doing barbs, life is a whole lot easier. No edges. No sweat. I feel warm and relaxed. It doesn't matter if someone is pissed at me. It doesn't matter if the rent's late. Everything's fine."

As I sat back in my chair listening to Melissa talk about the cutting edges of life, I remembered how I felt as an adolescent. I remembered wanting to curl up in a ball inside of myself and disappear. I tried to imagine how she might have felt as an adolescent girl with a critical, distant father. I found myself understanding, from the inside, her search for relief.

"Barbs let me feel normal," Melissa said.

And I remembered how she had said the same thing about alcohol.

Barbiturates differ in how rapidly they take effect and are metabolized by the body. When administered orally, the shorter-acting barbiturates (pentobarbital, secobarbital, and amobarbital) take effect within fifteen minutes and wear off in about two to three hours. Amytal, alurate, and butisol take effect in thirty minutes and wear off in about five to six hours. In the last two decades a majority of the barbiturates used as sedatives have been replaced by the benzodiazepines (Hofmann 1983).

Tranquilizers

In the midst of the search for a nonaddictive tranquilizer with fewer side effects, the benzodiazepine class of mild tranquilizers were initially hailed for their ability to decrease anxiety without producing drowsiness or addiction. Though they offer a larger safety margin between effective dose and overdose, it is now recognized that withdrawal from minor tranquilizers such as Valium, Librium, and Xanax can be severe. Side effects include increased anxiety, insomnia, tremors, weakness, light-headedness, anorexia, nausea, vomiting, seizures, and psychosis similar to delirium tremens. Benzodiazepines are currently the most widely prescribed drugs in the United States and are used by general practice physicians as antianxiety agents, sleeping pills, or anti-convulsants. Cross-tolerance and cross-dependence can exist between all depressants. At toxic overdose levels, respiration is depressed, eventually producing coma or death. Potential abusers are frequently older people who use tranquilizers for sleep or anxiety problems and young people who take them recreationally or in combination with alcohol or speed (Seymour and Smith 1987).

Melissa spent almost half an hour in the next session talking about her accidents, her feigned illnesses, and her use of multiple doctors in order to obtain prescription drugs.

"I was real good at convincing doctors that Valium helped me stay away from alcohol. I remember I was working in this hospital as a secretary. I convinced one doctor that I wanted to quit drinking and Valium helped. He agreed and wrote out a prescription. Hah!" She laughed. "A few years later I learned *he was a flaming alcoholic too*!

"Sometimes I wouldn't notice that it had any effect until I realized I wasn't reacting when my boyfriend yelled at me. Everything just seemed fine when he was screaming. Five milligrams didn't do much but when I took ten milligrams or more I felt kind of heavy. I could think and talk about things that would otherwise bother me. Unfortunately it wasn't very good for sex. I just wasn't interested."

Anesthetic Inhalants, Industrial Substances, and Aerosols

Anesthetics such as ether and nitrous oxide are most frequently abused by health care professionals (physicians, nurses, dentists, and dental personnel) who have easy access to the substances. Industrial substances such as glue (naptha, ketone, or toluene), gasoline, lighter fluid (naptha), lacquer thinner (naptha, toluol, acetone, or methanol), aerosol propellants, spray deodorants, nonstick sprays, furniture polish, spot removers (trichloroethylene), and cleaning solutions (trichloroethylene, ether, and petroleum distillates) have been historically abused by adolescents between the ages of 8 and 15 and technical professionals who use these solutions in their work (Seymour et al. 1989).

Though chemically disparate, the majority of industrial substances produce similar physiological effects, including euphoria, slurred speech, and perceptual distortions lasting 15–45 minutes. The most common method of administration is fume inhalation from an enclosed container such as a plastic bag or can. Toxic effects include amnesia (partial or total), rhinitis (runny nose), eye irritation, nausea, vomiting, diarrhea, joint pain, and anorexia (loss of appetite). Chronic use may lead to lung and brain damage. In toxic doses death is produced either by cardiac arrest, suffocation, or toxic poisoning. Little information exists regarding cross-tolerance of inhalants to other substances. Fatality reports due to inhalation of industrial substances, dating back to the early 1950s, led to a federal ban on carbon tetrachloride and strict limitations on the sale of plastic cement to minors. Though abuse of industrial substances is relatively minor compared to the problems associated with the use and abuse of other substances, a rise in the use and abuse of industrial substances has continued decade after decade.

"I remember one of my friends had some whipped cream. Whipped cream has nitrous oxide inside to blow it up. So we'd fill up balloons with the gas and inhale 'em. I remember how excited I felt, then scared, and then real horny. My heart pounded for a while and then I felt out of control. By the time I was really uncomfortable the effect wore off. So I tried it again, but it wasn't my drug. But it was fun once."

Leaning back and cupping her hands behind her head, Melissa scrunched her face up and looked as if she was getting ready to tell me something especially unpleasant.

"When I was 14 I wanted to get my hands on glue but they already made it illegal. So I started sniffing lighter fluid. I think I was with some friends. Now I remember. We went to a 7-11 and bought a can of lighter fluid and went back to the car. I was in the back seat so I squirted the stuff in a rag and inhaled it. It was awful. I felt sick to my stomach. It made my head pound. I felt groggy, dizzy, and stupid. The high definitely wasn't worth it. I think we threw it out the window. After ten minutes I felt better."

STIMULANTS

Analeptics, also called central nervous system stimulants, are known for their energizing and euphoric effects. These include derivatives of the coca plant (cocaine hydrochloride), amphetamines, methamphetamines, and the xanthines (theobromine, theophaline, caffeine, and nicotine).

Cocaine

The coca plant, *Erythroxylum coca*, is a small bush with bitter-tasting leaves. Its discovery has been ascribed to a variety of sources including observations of accidental animal encounters and the mythological revelations of local Indian tribes that live in the Peruvian Andes. The pre-Columbian Incas used it both religiously and medicinally to combat fatigue, cold, and hunger. Local references cite the coca plant as a nutritional supplement in a climate where little vegetation exists to support high altitude travelers. Approximately one gram of leaves contain 18.9 percent protein, 42.6 percent carbohydrates, and the daily recommended allowance for calcium, iron, phosphorous, vitamins A, B2, and E (Seymour et al. 1989). To this day, coca leaf tea is used medicinally in the Peruvian Andes for the nausea, headache, disorientation, and dizziness that accompany altitude sickness.

The use of cocaine in the industrialized world dates back to the late nineteenth century. Cocaine has been used as a nasal inhalant, infused with alcohol in liquid and water-based beverages including the original Coca-Cola. In 1884 Sigmund Freud discussed the effects of cocaine in his paper "On Coca":

> The psychic effect of cocaine consists of exhilaration and lasting euphoria, which does not differ in any way from the normal euphoria of a healthy person. One senses an increase of self-control and feels more vigorous and more capable of work. Long-lasting intensive mental or physical work can be performed without fatigue; it is as though the need for food and sleep . . . were completely banished. [pp. 48–73]

In the early 1900s, cocaine was listed in a variety of medical annals as a treatment for fatigue, depression, opium addiction, whooping cough, respiratory infections, fever, colds, asthma, bronchitis, and the common cold. During the 1970s and 1980s it became popular as a social and sexual adjunct. Ironically, like many drugs when used in large doses, cocaine actually impairs sexual functioning and inhibits orgasm in both men and women.

The psychoactive alkaloid, cocaine hydrochloride, is obtained when quantities of coca leaves are stomped, pounded, and doused with alcohol, sodium carbonate, benzol, and sulfuric acid. Washed in kerosene, the precipitant is mixed with sulfuric acid, potassium permanganate, sodium carbonate, toluol, dry hydrochloride gas, and methyl alcohol producing 99 percent pure cocaine base. Cocaine is administered predominantly through nasal inhalation (snorting), intravenous injection (shooting), or freebasing. Freebasing, an expensive and dangerous method of administration, involves the refinement of cocaine into base, then vaporizing and inhaling the mixture directly into the lungs where it crosses the blood–brain barrier in seconds. The elevated danger in freebasing is directly attributable to the rapid addiction potential, the extreme risk for overdose, and the highly flammable nature of the vaporizing process, which may lead to internal and external burns.

Crack Cocaine

When cocaine hydrochloride is mixed with a solution of sodium bicarbonate (baking soda) or ammonia in water, the resulting precipitant is called crack cocaine. When heated, the liquid evaporates and the remaining precipitant's melting point is reduced, eliminating the need for freebasing laboratory paraphernalia. The hard crystalline paste is then cut into small chunks or "rocks." In contrast to the expense of cocaine, crack cocaine is easily affordable ($10–20 per rock), powerful, and direct, making it the most accessible and addictive substance on the street.

The immediate effect of low doses of cocaine is an infusion of energy and an increased level of excitation, including rapid heartbeat, sweating, dilation of pupils, and a rise in body temperature. This heightened excitability contributes to the feeling of being "turned on" and may lead to acute anxiety reactions. Chronic use can lead to feelings of omnipotence, irrational behavior, delusions, and psychosis. The eventual drop from a euphoric high inevitably leads to the crash of the cocaine low, characterized by irritability, depression, apathy, and fatigue. The effects of cocaine peak 15–20 minutes after inhalation and wear off in 60–90 minutes from snorting and 30–40 minutes if smoked or injected intravenously. Until the early 1980s cocaine was considered relatively benign and nonaddictive. Unfortunately, this was far from accurate.

In one session, Melissa described her experiences with cocaine. Excited, her eyes lit up and she shifted her posture every minute or so. She gestured more frequently than she had in the past, as if in recalling her cocaine experiences she remembered the side effects of the high itself.

"Cocaine was really my drug," she said. "I thought it was a gift from God. I tell you . . . when I'm high on coke life is great. I feel strong! And no one messes with me. My head is on straight. I can work for thirty hours at a stretch, no sweat. But I have to be careful."

As Melissa spoke I became aware of how she used the present tense to describe her experience, rather than the past. I wondered if she were still using cocaine or whether she was once again remembering in the present tense.

"If I do more than a gram or two at a stretch the comedown is a bitch. I feel like shit. My head aches, and I throw up a lot. My body feels like I've been hit by a truck. But a couple of shots of Jack Daniels smoothes the rough edges, though."

Cocaine affects several major organs in the body. It is absorbed by the liver, heart, brain, kidneys, and the fatty tissues. Its vasoconstrictive properties limit the intake of oxygen, which, in turn, causes an increase of heart rate, blood pressure, and, in extreme cases, rapid breathing, angina, heart attack, and seizures. Individuals with a history of heart disease, including arteriosclerosis, are most vulnerable. Massive overdoses have been reported in smugglers or "mules" when the gastrointestinal containers used to transport the substance rupture internally. Cocaine also irritates the nasal lining, leading to an increased flow of mucus and, in chronic cases, a perforated nasal septum. If unsterile needles are used during injection, risk of subcutaneous abscesses, hepatitis, and AIDS increases dramatically.

Amphetamines

Benzedrine, called bennies, and dexedrine, called dexies on the street, were first synthesized in 1927 and medically prescribed for a variety of problems, including nasal congestion, mild depression, obesity, Parkinson's disease, sleep disorders, asthma, and hyperactive behavior. Amphetamines are currently prescribed for narcolepsy (chronic attacks of deep sleep), hyperactivity in minimally brain-damaged children, and short-term diet control. Long-term studies, however, reveal that weight lost as a result of amphetamine use is uniformly regained once the prescription is discontinued unless significant alterations are made in the patient's lifestyle and dietary habits. Non-prescription abuse of amphetamines is common among students, athletes, truck drivers, pilots, and entertainers and musicians who seek to increase performance and decrease fatigue and drowsiness.

An increase in amphetamine use in the 1950s has been attributed to the military supply of "energy tablets" given to soldiers during the Second World War. The resulting surplus supplies, later sold in civilian markets, gained a strong following among a select group of users called "speed freaks." Along with methamphetamines "speed," "crystal," "meth" (Amphedroxyn, Desoxyn, Desyphed, Dexoval, Doxyfed, Drinalfa, Efroxine, Norodin, Semoxydrine, and Syndrox), amphetamines are currently popular street drugs due to their euphoric rush, availability, and low cost. Amphetamines and methamphetamines are most commonly administered orally (dropped) and in more severe cases injected intravenously (shot).

The immediate subjective effects of amphetamine and methamphetamine use include a feeling of being energized, motivated, a heightened alertness, self-confidence, an initial increase in concentration, and a sense of well-being. Corresponding physiological responses include a rise in blood pressure, tachycardia, pupillary dilation, anorexia (loss of appetite), an increase in blood glucose, muscle tension, cardiac irregularities, and drymouth. Though it is a common belief that small doses of amphetamines act as an aphrodisiac, impairment in sexual functioning is identical to that of cocaine. Amphetamines produce increased levels of dopamine and norepinephrine that create a state of excitation mimicking the effects of adrenaline. Taken orally, the effects of amphetamines peak in two to three hours and have a half-life of approximately ten to twelve hours. Intravenous injection accelerates the development of tolerance and addiction.

Dopamine and norepinephrine are natural brain chemicals similar in molecular structure and effect to amphetamine, methamphetamine, ephedrine, and phyenylpropanolamine. Because methamphetamine crosses the blood–brain barrier more easily, it is a more powerful central nervous system stimulant. Ephedrine, unable to cross the blood–brain barrier, is more effective as an appetite suppressant, without causing the harmful central nervous system effects common to amphetamines and methamphetamines.

The crash following a binge of chronic amphetamine use can last as long as five days and is generally followed by a period of deep sleep, days or even weeks of anxiety, depression, fatigue, and a voracious appetite. These symptoms often motivate further amphetamine use in an effort to curb withdrawal, and in turn increase tolerance and dependence. Chronic amphetamine use can cause delusions of grandeur, lack of muscular coordination, impairment of problem-solving skills, panic, paranoid psychosis, hostility, and violence. Amphetamines are especially dangerous when taken by individuals who are prone to violent or destructive behavior due to their ability to increase heart rate and blood pressure, which may trigger a fight-or-flight response. Common physiological damage includes extreme weight loss (20–30 pounds is not uncommon), impaired memory, nonhealing ulcers, abscesses, and hepatitis (from dirty needles). A greater risk for contracting AIDS has also been noted in some individuals due to risky sexual behavior. Overdoses frequently result in heart attack, stroke, and death.

Xanthines

Frequently regarded as food substances rather than drugs, the xanthines caffeine and nicotine represent a group of stimulants that are used by more people worldwide than any other substance.

Caffeine

The psychoactive substance caffeine, found in coffee, cola, tea, cocoa, and chocolate, is praised throughout the world for its capacity to increase alertness and reduce fatigue. Originating in Ethiopia, coffee is thought to have been discovered by an Arabian holy man. The story describes how, after hearing the reports from local shepherds that their flocks stayed awake all night after eating the berries of a certain bush, the holy man used the berries and their stimulant effects to stay awake at night in meditation. Tea, grown for centuries in China, was attributed to a divine gift from the first Zen patriarch, Bodhidharma, also as an aid for his meditation. Chocolate, made from the seeds of the cacao tree (*theobroma cacao*), originated in Mexico and Central America and is considered nothing less than its literal translation, "food of the gods."

Coffee, tea, and chocolate, while historically included in the religious rituals of Arabia, Asia, and Central America respectively, are woven into the very fabric of daily life throughout the world. Despite being regarded primarily as foods, it is important to bear in mind the acute and chronic effects of food substances with high caffeine content. Their potent effects may include a mild sense of euphoria, elevated blood pressure, and tachycardia. Chronic use of up to eight to ten cups of coffee per day may result in a variety of harmful effects, including anxiety, irritability, nervousness, insomnia, irregular heartbeat, and gastrointestinal problems. Prolonged caffeine use eventually leads to addiction with the classic symptoms of tolerance, withdrawal, loss of control, and harmful physical effects.

Nicotine

Harvested for religious and recreational use for over two thousand years among the pre-Columbian cultures of Central America, tobacco eventually found its way to Europe aboard trading ships and was later banned in England in the seventeenth century. Currently in the United States there are over forty-nine million tobacco smokers. Tobacco has been described as the most addictive substance on the face of the earth by addicts recovering from heroin, cocaine, and alcohol.

Nicotine, the addictive substance found in tobacco, is commonly smoked in cigarettes, cigars, and pipes, or chewed. Nicotine acts as a stimulant causing both appetite suppression and an increase in respiration and heart rate. It also acts as a depressant causing mild euphoria, a subjective sense of calm, relaxation, and in some cases dizziness. Ninety percent of nicotine is absorbed directly through the lungs. Acute physiological withdrawal symptoms include jitteriness, anxiety, irritability, and hyperemotionality. Although these symptoms may disappear within one to three weeks, psychological craving may continue for months, years, or even a lifetime. The vast majority of those who smoke on a daily basis become addicted.

Toward the end of her month-long drug history, I realized that Melissa had never mentioned smoking as one of the many drugs she used over the years.

"Yeah. I know I should quit," she said when I finally got around to asking her about smoking cigarettes. "I tried a bunch of times. Once, when I stopped drinking for a couple of months, I stopped smoking too. Boy, was I a bitch. My first husband, Dave, he couldn't stand me.

He begged me to start drinking again. Anyway, I started smoking right when I started going out with Danny. He smoked Camels, so of course I smoked Camels. Those things'll kill you! But by then I was hooked. Now I smoke about half a pack a day. I'm trying to cut down, too! Honest."

Although I was keenly aware of the medical consequences of smoking cigarettes, I also knew how difficult it often was to give up cigarettes along with everything else. A year or two into recovery, smoking cigarettes often becomes an issue when an addict or alcoholic tries to abstain from more and more mind-altering substances. As newly sober as Melissa was, I was concerned that giving up smoking at this point might be too much. I hoped that in time she would come to rely on her therapy, her therapist, and a place inside herself, where in the past she depended on drugs.

Though the harmful effects of tobacco are legion and well documented despite pervasive denial by the tobacco industry, nicotine is significantly less toxic than many other stimulants. The more noxious effects of smoking are caused by the tars, gases, and other particulate irritants inhaled from the ignited tobacco. According to the statistics compiled by the American Cancer Society, the physical damage from long-term, chronic cigarette smoking is implicated in cancers of the colon, rectum, pharynx, larynx, esophagus, pancreas, uterus, cervix, and bladder. Smoking cigarettes is a major contributing cause of heart disease, and is linked to conditions ranging from colds and gastric ulcers to chronic bronchitis, emphysema, and cerebrovascular disease. Smoking by pregnant women is associated with a higher incidence of premature births, spontaneous abortion, and neonatal death. Passive secondary smoke inhalation is also cited as a contributing factor in all of the above harmful effects.

HALLUCINOGENS

From the Latin *hallucinar* (to wander mentally), this class of drugs is known for its profound illusory effects, including altered perceptions, synesthesia (cross-sensory identification, such as smelling color and tasting sound), a disengaged sense of time, and depersonalization. For thousands of years, the hallucinogenic properties of natural substances have been an essential part of religious, mystical, and shamanistic traditions throughout the world. In Greece, the onset of spring inspired pilgrims to visit the temple at Elesius near Athens, where a mixture of wine, herbs, and rye mold containing ergotomine was imbibed to help facilitate a vision of the Goddess. Ethnobotanists have since catalogued a variety of plants with hallucinogenic properties including:

> *peganum harmala* (from the seeds of the Syrian rue and the bark of several vines in the Amazon Basin), ibogaine (from the root of the West African plant *tabernanthe iboga*), DMT (N-dimethyltryptamine from South America), muscimole (from the *Amanita muscaria* mushroom), and a group called the anticholinergics that include deadly nightshade, mandrake, black henbane, and jimson weed. [Seymour et al. 1987, p. 86]

Psychedelics, a term derived from the Greek *psyche* (meaning mind) and *delein* (to manifest), comprise a vast array of substances with little chemical homogeneity, including LSD (lysergic acid diethylamide), marijuana (cannabis), psilocybin, peyote, mescaline, and MDMA (3, 4-methylenedioxymethamphetamine).

LSD

D-lysergic acid diethylamide, or "acid," is a synthetic derivative of ergot discovered by Albert Hofmann in 1938 while he worked for Sandoz Pharmaceuticals in Basel, Switzerland. Having accidentally ingested a small amount, the young researcher unexpectedly experienced its visually hallucinatory properties while riding his bicycle home from the laboratory that night. Decades later, research by Timothy Leary, Richard Alpert, and Ralph Metzner popularized the recreational use of LSD in the 1960s while they searched for new models of perception, creativity, mystical experiences, and even the social rehabilitation of convicted felons.

Relatively simple and inexpensive to produce, a standard dose of LSD is available in various forms as a powder, a solution dropped on sugar cubes, a capsule, a pill, or impregnated into paper as a "tab." Purity of the drug varies considerably between doses and may range from 0–80 percent LSD. Occasionally, what is advertised as LSD may be tainted with methamphetamine and produce unexpected effects. Odorless, colorless, and tasteless, LSD is absorbed very quickly from the gastrointestinal tract and is distributed throughout the body. Only 1 percent of the drug is actually taken up by the brain. LSD is so potent that dosages are measured in micrograms (millionths of a gram). Fifty micrograms can produce changes in perception and mood that will last approximately six to eight hours.

The physiological effects of LSD include: pupil dilation; chills; trembling; increased heart rate, body temperature, and blood pressure; nausea and dizziness; slowed deep breathing; loss of appetite; and insomnia. Documented cases of death due to overdose are nonexistent in the literature, although accidental deaths and adverse reactions, including "flashbacks" (intrusive memories of previous drug-induced experiences), panic reactions, and transient psychoses have been widely reported. An experience of LSD can be highly affected by the environment. A "good trip" or "bad trip" may be caused by both the individual's emotional state when ingesting the drug and the effects of individual suggestibility and environmental influences.

About a month later, when Melissa spoke about her experiences with LSD, she calmed down considerably and looked almost reverential.

"I can definitely say that LSD changed my life. Sure, there were lots of colors and everything seemed to change shape. It was the most alive I've ever felt in my life. It was like I could feel the colors. I remember looking at the wall in my bedroom. I'd painted it red and when I looked at it *I was the red*. I could feel it in my chest. It was like I was the wall and the wall had a beating heart and it was my heart."

For a while I thought Melissa's fascination with her drug experiences was merely an attempt to rid herself of her depression, her anxiety, and an attempt to break free from her father. But as I listened more carefully to the way in which she described feeling changed by her experiences, I realized that drugs helped Melissa discover a deeper spiritual self. To some degree, her drug experiences had both liberated a wild rebellious side of her and had tamed it as well.

"At first I was a little bit freaked," she said. "But after a while I got used to everything changing. People weren't people, they were glowing, warm things. I felt I was connected to everything."

Marijuana

Cannabis, a bushy plant that can grow to a height of twenty feet, is found throughout the major tropical zones of the world. Marijuana has been used medicinally, recreationally, and ceremonially for over four thousand years. Arabic physicians used cannabis medicinally for sedation and analgesia. *Cannabis indica* is cultivated in the Eastern hemisphere (Afghanistan, Thailand, India, Nepal, and Tibet). *Cannabis sativa*, or American sinsemilla, is grown in the Western Hemisphere (the south, central, and northern Americas, and the Caribbean) and is known by a variety of names, including marijuana, maryjane, weed, reefer, hashish, pot, dope, ganja, hemp, sinsemilla, and bhang. Grown commercially, the fibers of the plant stalk have been used in the production of hemp rope and paper, the seeds for poultry feed, the oil as a drying agent in paint, and the remaining bulk used as fertilizer and cattle feed. Generations of cross breeding have increased the psychoactive potency of marijuana dramatically. The more potent varieties are composed of the dried flower tops which contain a rich supply of the psychoactive agent THC (tetrahydrocannabinol). In the last two decades, twenty-four-hour ultraviolet lighting, climate-controlled humidity, and drip irrigation have made cannabis the largest selling industrial cash crop in the state of California.

Cannabis is typically smoked in cigarettes and pipes or baked in cookies, brownies, and other fat-containing foods. The immediate effects of cannabis, hashish, and THC are qualitatively identical and include a decrease of inhibition, perceived muscular relaxation, time distortion, mood lability, and a heightened response to sensory input. Many consider the effects enjoyable, but some experience only anxiety, paranoia, insecurity, and depression.

THC

D-tetrahydrocannabinol, the major psychoactive agent in cannabis, was first isolated by Dr. Raphael Mechoulam and his colleagues in Israel in 1964. Infrequently administered in its pure form, the direct psychoactive effects of THC are affected appreciably by the mode of administration. The effects are most immediate with injection, intermediate when inhaled as smoke, and least potent when taken orally. Hashish, an extract made by boiling the resin-covered parts of the plant, may have 5–12 percent THC. Hawaiian and Jamaican marijuana have approximately 4–8 percent THC. Mexican varieties have less than 1 percent THC. Resin contains the highest THC content, while decreasing amounts are found in the flowers and leaves, stems, roots, and seeds of the plant.

THC reaches the brain only seconds after it has been smoked. Its effects peak in ten to thirty minutes and last approximately three to four hours, depending upon the quantity and potency smoked. Although THC is eliminated from the bloodstream quickly, traces may remain in fatty tissue for several weeks until it is eventually excreted in the urine.

Physiological responses to THC include increases in heart rate, peripheral blood flow, and bronchodilation. High doses lead to increased heart rate, short-term memory disturbances, and slowed reaction time. Animal studies and sociological field evidence indicate a mild degree of tolerance. Medical uses of cannabis include the reduction of intraocular pressure among glaucoma patients, bronchodilation of asthma patients, and a nausea suppressant for chemotherapy patients. No known lethal dosage for THC has been reported. Prolonged use of cannabis and THC result in few if any physiological withdrawal symptoms, though psychological withdrawal may be profound. Chronic users report surprisingly negligible impairment in functioning, which indicates a learned ability to act while intoxicated. The most prevalent chronic effect of prolonged cannabis smoking is an amotivational syndrome characterized by loss of ambition, apathy, distractibility, and magical and short-sighted thinking.

Psilocybin

Considered sacred by tribes in the American Southwest and Mexico, the psilocybin mushrooms, *Conocybe*, *Stropharia*, and *Psilocybe*, have been an integral part of religious ceremonies and spiritual divination practices for over a thousand years. Following its suppression by the Spanish from the 1700s, *tonanacatl* (or "the flesh of the gods") was kept secret by the Oaxacan shamans of Mexico until its rising popularity in the United States during the 1960s.

The psychoactive agent psilocybin, found in *Psilocybe mexicana*, was isolated by a Swiss chemist in 1958 and is found in over seventy-five species of mushrooms. The mushrooms are eaten raw, cooked in foods, infused in tea, and in powdered form either inhaled or swallowed in capsules. With doses as low as four milligrams, the effects of psylocibin include altered perceptions and heightened sensitivity to sensation. Some experience euphoria: others may feel anxiety, depression, disorientation, or mild disassociation. Physiological effects, including pupil dilation and increased pulse rate, blood pressure, and central nervous system stimulation, are generally noticed within thirty minutes and last from four to eight hours. No withdrawal is described. Toxic doses are established at approximately two thousand times the normal dose. Rare deaths associated with psilocybin use are generally related to polydrug use or inaccurate harvesting of similar-looking but poisonous varieties.

Peyote

Preparations made from the mescal cactus *Lophophora williamsii* have been used for religious ceremonies for centuries by the Aztecs of Central and South America, as well as local indigenous tribes of the southwest United States and Mexico. The grayish-green plant supports one or more round projections called buttons. The dried buttons, usually hard and brown, are generally infused in a liquid or chewed.

Mescaline, the predominant psychoactive agent in peyote, was isolated in 1896. Roughly three hundred times less hallucinogenic than LSD, peyote was popularized in the books of the philosopher and writer Aldous Huxley, the artist Henri Micheaux, and the anthropologist Carlos Castenada (Seymour et al. 1989). The effects of peyote and mescaline last up to twelve hours and are similar to LSD, though less intense. Harmful effects include anxiety, disorientation, hallucinations, derealization, and panic.

Other Hallucinogens

A variety of synthetic hallucinogens have gained popularity over the decades and include DOM, also called STP, a synthetic related to the amphetamine group, and DMT, isolated from hallucinogenic snuffs from South American Indian tribes, and are usually inhaled as a powder or smoked in tobacco and marijuana.

PCP (phencyclidine)

Often called "angel dust" or PCP, phencyclidine was first synthesized in the 1950s and marketed as an anesthetic under the name Sernyl. PCP is generally smoked with marijuana or tobacco. It is available through nonlegal avenues in liquid, powder, tablet, or capsule form. At low doses the physiological side effects include difficulty concentrating, difficulty following a train of thought, numbness, slurring of speech, depersonalization, and a distortion of body image. At higher doses PCP increases confusion, decreases coordination, and causes an increase in muscular rigidity and psychotic symptoms. Primary effects occur after thirty to sixty minutes and last approximately five hours. PCP was removed from distribution in the 1960s due to increasing reports of its side effects, which include nightmares, muscular rigidity, delirium, physical violence, and psychosis.

During one session, when Melissa told me about her thirty or forty LSD trips, she mentioned the one time she tried PCP. She appeared exhausted that day and, having worked a full shift at the restaurant, seemed to sink lower and lower in the couch as the hour wore on.

"All I remember about being on PCP is that I felt great for about the first twenty minutes. I felt strong, I had unlimited energy, I felt like I could stop cars or buses just with the force of my will. Then I started to see things. Everybody was my enemy. I knew what people were thinking and everybody was pissed at me for being so cool. The only way to save myself was to find out who was at the root of all the fear and hatred and kill 'em. Boy! What a trip!"

Designer Hallucinogens

Over 125 analogues of PCP include PHP, TCP, PCE, PCC, PHP, and MDMA. First synthesized from methamphetamine and safrole by E. Merck and Company of Germany, MDMA is from a group of drugs called phenethylamines. Known by its street name, "Ecstasy," due to its apparent effect of reducing the neurophysiological mechanisms of fear and increasing interpersonal understanding and warmth, MDMA has a controversial research history including its use as an aid in couples therapy. Citing evidence of neurological damage in 1984, the Drug Enforcement Agency severely limited its research and availability.

After Melissa's PCP story, she paused for a long while. I wanted to ask another question but felt she was on the verge of sharing something important, something she wanted me to know but hesitated to say. In my mind I figured I'd wait a few moments. I bit my tongue, unsure whether she might interpret my silence as withdrawal.

"After a while I got tired of fighting it," Melissa said. "I got tired of going from one drug and then to another. I got tired of fighting my demons. Eventually I got turned on to spiritual stuff."

COYOTE FIGHTS SOME MONSTERS

One day Coyote was wandering far away from home across the Rocky Mountains and well into the Great Plains country where Horse lived. Back then, Horse was a dangerous monster and he was as big as a tall tree.

Walking out from a stand of tall trees, Coyote startled Horse and he ran after Coyote. With Coyote in front they ran and ran all over the bare plains. They ran up the hills and they ran down the hills. After a while Coyote was tired of running and when he looked back Horse was closer. Coyote always thought he was the fastest runner, Coyote always thought he was the best at everything, but Horse was faster. Coyote got scared. He cried out, "Help me, Guardian Spirit!"

The Guardian Spirit that watched over Coyote heard his cry and in the midst of the dry flat plains three trees grew out of the ground in front of him.

Coyote jumped into the first tree.

"Hah! You can't catch me!" he laughed.

But without breaking his stride Horse cut down the tree with his giant hoofs. Coyote flew through the air, hit the ground hard, and, dusting himself off, he leaped into the second tree. The same thing happened with the second tree and he leaped into the third tree. But the same thing happened.

"I don't want to die," Coyote whimpered. He was lying on the ground all dusty, sore, and tired. "But before you kill me, Horse, let me smoke my pipe."

"You can smoke," Horse said. After all, it was a reasonable request. "That is all. After that I will kill you." Horse was being generous, but only so generous.

Puffing on his pipe, Coyote whispered into the smoke and spoke to his Guardian Spirit and again asked for help. All of a sudden, a whip appeared in front of him. So Coyote jumped on Horse's broad back and struck him with the whip. Horse was surprised and caught off guard. He bucked, he whirled around and around, and he tried all his tricks. But he couldn't defeat Coyote. Finally, Horse begged for mercy.

"Please, don't kill me," Horse whinnied.

And when Coyote hopped off his back Horse was changed. He was not big and dangerous now. He was much smaller.

"From now," Coyote commanded, "you will let the two-legged people ride you. Only at first will you buck and be mean. Then old men will sit on you in comfort and assurance. Women will use you for carrying camp supplies, heavy packs of roots and berries and meat."

Horse bowed and Coyote wandered off.

The next day Coyote stumbled upon and defeated Dog, a big and ferocious monster. He also commanded that dog be a faithful animal for the two-leggeds. He met and defeated a monstrous human-eating tree and commanded that it let itself be used for firewood to keep the two-legged people warm. He met a human-eating canyon, defeated it, and made it become a shelter for the two-legged people. And he came across an invisible Elk, killed it, and made its flesh and hide available for the two-legged people to eat and clothe themselves.

Finally, when he was far away from his home, over by a river, Coyote saw a cradleboard propped against a tree. Inside the cradleboard was a baby. Since no one else was in sight, Coyote thought that the mother must be nearby. Hoping he would be given a reward for showing attention to the little one, Coyote walked up to the baby and rocked it back and forth and as he did, he sang it a song. He wanted the mother to hear and come by and give him a reward. Nothing happened and so he sang louder, then louder, but nobody came. Then the baby began to cry.

"This baby must be hungry," Coyote thought, and gently he poked one of his gingers into its mouth to soothe it. "Yeeoowwww!" Coyote cried, and as he jerked his hand away, his flesh was stripped clean by the baby's sharp fangs.

"This is no ordinary baby," Coyote thought. "This is a person-eating monster."

Cleverly, Coyote defeated the Baby Monster and decreed that babies would be the most helpless of all creatures.

And weary of fighting monsters, Coyote started off on his journey back home.

Ironically, Coyote brings great bounty to others through his confrontation with the monsters. Unlike the hero, who seeks out evil in order to destroy it for the good of others, Coyote merely happens upon it. Unlike the hero, motivated by altruism, fame, or glory, Coyote fights for his own life. He lacks the essential strength to defeat his demons through his own power and so he calls on another, his guardian spirit, and he is given the strength and tools to defeat his enemies. When he defeats those who try to destroy him, like the alcoholic and addict ready to reach out to others through a Twelfth Step, he turns evil into good and bends darkness to light. He transforms evil into goodness: the horse becomes a beast of burden to help those too weak to carry their loads; the dog becomes a protector; the tree becomes a resource to keep warm; the elk becomes a sustaining food; and the baby, rather than devouring those who would happen upon him, is helpless and teaches selfless giving.

Many alcoholics and addicts, understandably, experience addiction as a scourge, a burden, and a blight on their lives. Like those who find themselves recovering from a potentially fatal disease, addiction brings the addict and alcoholic to the edge of great loss and precariously close to death. Others, after years of sobriety, if they are lucky enough to find some relief from the craving and the memories of the past and make a new life, may discover an unexpected boon within the darkness and the pain. Recovery often reveals a new way of living that otherwise might have gone unnoticed in the midst of a normal life. Through recovery, the pain of addiction is transformed into a blessing, ironically dependent on the disease.

"You know," Melissa went on, " I am *so glad* I'm in recovery. I know at some point I want to stop smoking, but I have to face how much my life has changed since I stopped using and boozing. I've got a good

job. I'm gonna start back at college next semester. No more pharma-
cology. And I've just met this guy in the program."

Melissa noticed my eyebrows again.

"Oh! I didn't tell you? He's been sober for six years," she said proudly.
"This time I'm gonna take it slow, reeeeal slow."

❖ C H A P T E R 4 ❖

The Diagnostic Interview

"I've been an alcoholic and addict for twenty years.
I can spot one a mile away. What more do I need to know?"

MAKING A COMPREHENSIVE DIAGNOSIS

While an intuitive therapist or a recovering alcoholic and addict may feel as if his gut instinct can spot an alcoholic or addict with the slightest amount of information, making a diagnosis of alcohol and drug dependence is a serious responsibility and requires much more than a gut feeling. Instinct can prompt a therapist to say, "You mentioned that you don't do drugs anymore. Can you tell me about the drugs you *used to* do?" where a less attuned interviewer might hesitate to ask such a direct question. Instinct can urge you to follow up with yet another question to give a patient a second, third, or even fourth chance to reveal information about his or her alcohol and drug use. When your patient fails to show up for a Monday morning appointment and leaves a message on your answering machine that he slept through till the afternoon, instinct will arouse your suspicious nature.

But a gut instinct is far from infallible. Every now and then a feeling will remind you that something is going on, but feelings often lack a certain thoroughness. Enthusiastic to respond, a therapist may jump too quickly and assume (or intuit) that the problem is related to alcohol and drug problems. This is where the therapist's Coyote comes in. The therapist's Coyote claims to know the truth. He believes his intuition is fact and so he moves too quickly to confront and prove his insight. He judges. He offends. He forgets to ask a question so that he can appear magical and all-knowing or he asks with such a dramatic flair that he humiliates.

There are two kinds of errors in the diagnosis of psychoactive substance abuse or dependence. The first kind of error is underpathologizing. Perhaps a patient drinks as much as the therapist does or did at one time. Unconsciously, and here's Coyote smiling again, if a therapist has a positive countertransference, it may become increasingly difficult to see the patient in such a bad light. In order to maintain the positive bond and feeling, the therapist may minimize the drinking or drug use. This tendency to minimize or avoid the patient's drinking problem may take the form of not following up with another question, not probing, or not providing consequences for the patient's behavior. A therapist might feel compassionate and not charge for the missed appointment and unconsciously collude with the patient. A therapist's own drinking (or a parent's drinking) may be used as the yardstick by which pathology is measured and that measurement may contribute to minimizing the patient's problems.

The second type of diagnostic error, a risk that chemical dependence professionals are prone to, is overpathologizing. A patient casually mentions that she was exhausted all weekend, threw up on Sunday, and an over-eager therapist identifies a Friday night binge rather than the onset of the flu. Or a patient talks about years of teenage alcohol and drug experimentation, mentions getting high the previous week, and the hypersensitive therapist interrupts, even before the patient can finish telling the meaning of the story, and declares that therapy should be discontinued until the patient enters a drug treatment program. Frightened by the therapist's sense of urgency in view of such little information, and unnecessarily wounded by an empathic vacuum that appeared out of nowhere, the patient will all too often terminate therapy rather than confront the therapist and try to heal the breach and wound.

Vast differences exist among casual alcohol and drug use, abuse, and chemical dependence. While a minority of the population may believe that any chemical use compromises one's sobriety, most people recognize that the use of some substances in limited quantities has a positive place in life. For the clinician, it is essential to be aware of a whole host of life choices, beliefs, biases, and judgments about alcohol and drug use in order to discriminate between countertransference and another's alcohol and drug use, problematic use, and the various stages of dependence. This self-awareness is essential, because while many recovering alcoholics and addicts will move toward abstaining from one, then another, then eventually all mind-altering substances, the vast majority of people who use, for example, alcohol, are moderate, casual users.

EXISTING DIAGNOSTIC TOOLS

There is also a problem in the variations among competing diagnostic paradigms and definitions. What one clinician, assessment tool, treatment program, or recovering addict may mean by the term *alcoholism* or *addiction* may vary widely from the simplistic "He drinks more than I do," to the complex criteria lists used by the American Psychiatric Association (*DSM-IV* 1994), the World Health Organization (1978), and the National Council on Alcoholism and Drug Dependence (1972). All may be helpful in determining whether or not the disease is present, but few articulate an integrated diagnostic picture of an individual's relationship to alcohol and drugs. Fewer still are easily utilized in the clinical interview where they are needed most.

In the last century, medical interest in the diagnosis of alcohol and other drug dependencies has progressed from simplistic definitions toward greater conceptual clarity and complexity. As early as 1784, Benjamin Rush, a physician and signer of the Declaration of Independence, used the term *disease* to describe the problem of alcoholism. In 1849, the Swedish physician, Magnus Huss, coined the term *alcoholic*. It wasn't until 1952, following E. M. Jellinek's pioneering research, that the American Medical Association formally adopted the term *disease process* and later utilized the following general criteria to define drug related pathologies:

preoccupation
chronicity
tendency toward relapse
impaired emotional, occupational, and/or social adjustments
loss of control
progression
physical disability

[in Hester and Miller 1995, pp. 12–14]

In 1980, the American Psychiatric Association (*DSM-III* 1980) created an entire set of diagnostic categories. *DSM-IIIR* defined use,
abuse, and dependence; subclassifications of continuous use, episodic
use, and remission; and a generic psychoactive substance dependence
category that utilized the following symptoms:

tolerance
withdrawal
substance taken in larger amounts or over a longer period than
   intended
persistent desire or unsuccessful efforts to control use
a great deal of time is spent procuring, using, or recovering from
   the effects of the substance
important social, occupational, or recreational activities are
   given up
the substance is used despite the knowledge of physical or psychological problems it exacerbates or causes
                                          [*DSM-IIIR*, pp. 167–168]

In order to identify the progressive nature of chemical dependence,
the *DSM-IIIR* (1987) defined an important criterion, Severity of the
Disorder. This simplistic, progressive scale defined dependence as
either Mild, Moderate, or Severe. The *DSM-IIIR* defined the reduction of alcohol and drug use as either In Partial Remission or In Full
Remission. In 1994, the *DSM-IV* withdrew the criterion Severity of
the Disorder, simplified the progressive aspect of the disease by using
the terms "with physiological dependence" and "without physiological dependence," but then added six course specifiers including:

Early Partial Remission
Sustained Partial Remission
On Agonist Therapy
Early Full Remission
Sustained Full Remission
Controlled Environment
         [*DSM-IV*, p. 181]

Surprisingly, although the term *denial* had been used for decades
to describe the way in which alcoholics and addicts minimize, rationalize, and defend their alcohol and drug use, it wasn't until 1990

that the National Council on Alcoholism and Drug Dependence (NCADD) and the American Society of Addiction Medicine (ASAM) (Laign 1990) added the term denial, along with "distortions in thinking," to their list of diagnostic criteria.

My motivation to develop a new diagnostic framework began in the midst of my work at the Genesis with Timmen Cermak, M.D., in San Francisco. Every time I had a gut feeling about a patient's alcohol or drug problem I asked myself, "Now, what was the first criteria in the *DSM* list?" By the time I remembered the first criterion, I forgot what my patient said and then had an even harder time remembering the second criterion on the list. I found that the *DSM-IV* lacked a conceptual cohesiveness and an integrated relatedness. Of course, my tendency to think in images rather than words made using it in clinical interviews only worse.

After researching a number of the diagnostic tools including the *DSM-IV*, the Michigan Alcohol Screening Test (MAST), the CAGE Questionnaire, and the Substance Abuse Subtle Screening Inventory (SASSI) (Cooper and Robinson 1987, Ewing 1984, Selzer 1971), I examined the way in which my colleagues and I actually grouped the relevant information in a clinical interview to make a diagnosis of alcohol and drug dependence. I then took the information and unified it into a broad spectrum of symptoms, into a descriptive, mnemonic guide that clarified rather than obscured the relationship of drug-specific symptomatology on a progressive continuum from problematic use to late-stage chemical dependency. The framework below, a result of eight years of work, has been essential in my clinical practice, in training hundreds of alcohol and drug counselors at the University of California Chemical Dependence Certificate Program, John F. Kennedy University, and in particular with a patient I will call David.

DAVID

David, a 43-year-old dentist and technical consultant for a surgical supply company, and Sharon, a 38-year-old emergency room nurse, scheduled an appointment for couples therapy. As they stepped into my office, David walked over to my leather chair and sat down. Stunned at his choice, a choice taken only once in fifteen years of clinical practice, I politely offered him a seat on the couch.

"This chair is more comfortable," he said, ignoring the fact that if he sat in my chair, Sharon and I would be left sitting together on the couch.

I nodded toward the chair and waited. "Ahh, Coyote," I thought. "Do we struggle for power so quickly today?"

With a "Humff!" David stood up and took a seat next to his wife on the couch. Sharon spoke first. She described their fights, their difficulty communicating, and her resentment at David's compulsive working. David, on the other hand, was surly and silent. As I often do with couples after the initial consultation, I suggested individual sessions with both David and Sharon, with the explicit understanding that any information revealed in the individual sessions would be shared in the next conjoint session. After the individual sessions I generally have a better idea whether couples therapy was the best way to address their problems or whether some other recommendations might help them.

At the end of the initial consultation, David scheduled his appointment for the very next day, "to get things going," so Sharon scheduled hers the day after that.

Arriving for his appointment ten minutes late, David charged into my office (though the door was closed) and quickly launched into a story about his first two marriages. He described a long list of his ex-wives' flaws, placing the blame for the failure of the marriages clearly apart from himself, and then began complaining about Sharon's nagging.

For some reason, out of the blue, I found myself interrupting David and asked him if he could tell me something about his parents. Even before he responded I realized the power of my own counter-transference. I was surprised and taken aback by the forcefulness of David's inability to take any responsibility for his past and, simultaneously, I felt unnerved by his leaving virtually no space in the interview for my curiosity. I found myself feeling pushed back in my chair by the strength of his antagonism and, even though it was apparent that this might be a case of shotgun therapy, I felt as if, even before we began, we were struggling for control of the session.

"My parents? What do you want to know about my parents for? The problem is that women are just crazy. Just plain crazy," he said and, gesturing wildly, David flailed his arms about to emphasize his irritation.

Although it was my office, and I was several inches taller than David and currently training in Aikido, I found myself feeling threatened by David's excitability.

"Well," I said, trying to get a word in, "if I knew something about your parents' relationship it might help me understand yours."

"Oh!" he said condescendingly. "Well, if you need some background . . ." And he told me how both of his parents were alcoholics, how physical violence was rare but verbal and emotional tirades were a daily routine when he was growing up.

"I hid under the bed a lot but it didn't have much effect on me. I think it just made me tougher. Not much really affects me. I actually thought about being a shrink once myself but figured there wasn't enough challenge in it."

David explained that his third marriage to Sharon was "on the rocks," and how she complained about his "working too much." He admitted that when he drank he was prone to physical outbursts, though he asserted, "I've never really hit her!"

A NEW DIAGNOSTIC FRAMEWORK

As a guide and orienting schema, the Diagnostic Framework below (corresponding to the *DSM-IV* category of Axis I: Clinical Syndromes) helped organize the clinically relevant information throughout the interview process with David. The Diagnostic Framework has four sections answering five important questions about an individual's alcohol and drug use. The four sections and the corresponding clinical questions are:

Section 1. Primary Drugs of Choice
What drugs are being used?

Section 2. Stage of the Disease
What is the most *severe stage* of the disease?
What is the current stage of the disease?

Section 3. Current Status
What is the current relationship to alcohol and drugs?

Section 4. Special Features
What other important information defines the individual's use of alcohol and drugs?

Section 1. Primary Drugs of Choice

From the first moment David mentioned his drinking, I was curious to identify the substances he used. In this section, the drugs are listed in decreasing order according to the frequency of use, the quantity involved, and those drugs most strongly identified with as his drug of choice.

When I asked David about his relationship to alcohol and drugs, he replied that he didn't really drink that much. When I asked "Why not?" he confided that six months ago his doctor (also his neighbor and close friend) warned him that he was thirty pounds overweight and that he "should stop drinking" the eight to ten beers per night that had been his mainstay for the last five or six years. David said that he listened to his doctor and reported that in the last three months he drank *only* four to six beers per night with occasional "partying" on the weekends until he passed out. In addition he said he drank "a lot of coffee" (ten cups per day), used cocaine regularly for the last year (1–3 grams per week) at the office while working (36–72 hours at a stretch), and hid his cocaine use from his wife.

It might seem somewhat surprising that David revealed his alcohol and drug use so easily, and yet he appeared totally unconcerned about the implications of his disclosures. He described his experiences in a matter-of-fact tone with an air of confidence and entitlement that, while appearing superficially guileless, spoke more about his character (or possible character disorder) than he might have intended.

At this point in the interview, with only the existing information available, I might have filled out the first section as follows:

Section 1: Primary Drugs of Choice:
Alcohol (8–10 drinks/day 5–6 years, currently 4–6/day),
Cocaine (1–3 g/wk for last year),
Caffeine (10 cups/day).

It is important to remember that a single drink has approximately the same amount of alcohol whether it is contained in a 12-ounce can of beer, a 4-ounce glass of wine, or a single shot of whiskey. Because alcoholics and addicts often misrepresent the quantity and frequency that they drink or use, I often inquire how large a glass, and what proportions are used when mixing drinks or drugs. A majority of people tend to use a single drug of choice, but polydrug use may merit a diagnosis where use of a single drug does not. Potentially lethal combinations should also be noted under Section IV: Special Features.

It is also important to pay close attention to the use of illegal drugs, prescribed medications, and, in extreme cases, common household substances like mouthwash, vanilla, glue, aerosol products, wood alcohol, paint thinner, and perfume, which may induce narcotic, stimulant, depressant, or hallucinogenic effects. In order to identify problematic use of a substance, a therapist must determine whether or not it is being used for the purpose, in the quantity, or in the frequency prescribed. The use of an analgesic pain-relief drug like Demerol after receiving a bad job evaluation is not using the prescription appropriately.

Although caffeine or nicotine dependence *is* diagnosed within the Diagnostic Framework, like most clinicians I do not believe that use of these two drugs compromises sobriety or abstinence in the sense of being clean and sober. This clinical distinction, similar to that in the *DSM-IV* and the *ICD-9*, is based on the lack of significant, intoxicating effects, which places caffeine and nicotine use in a slightly separate context for evaluating sobriety as a whole. Caffeine and nicotine use are therefore considered a relapse only for a caffeine and/or nicotine dependency despite the cigarette smoker's increased risk of relapse for a primary drug of choice (Sandor 1991).

Section 2. Stage of the Disease

The second phase in David's diagnostic evaluation was to determine how far along the continuum from Non-Problematic Casual use to Problematic Use, Early, Middle, or Late-Stage Dependence the disease had progressed.

Evaluating the stage of the disease involves examining three sets of criteria:

1. Problems in Living:
   Financial, Legal, Occupational, Social
2. Physical Effects:
   Health Problems, Risk, Acquired Tolerance, and Withdrawal
3. Psychological and Behavioral Effects:
   Ability to Abstain and Control; Use to Regulate Affect
   and Denial.

Problems in Living

When alcohol and drug use becomes an integral part of an individual's life, a variety of problems tend to occur (Secretary of Health and Human Services 1990). These problems may affect both the alcohol and drug abuser and the friends, family, workmates, and the community at large. Problems in Living are defined by the impact on *financial, legal, occupational,* and *social well-being.*

Financial Problems

Financial difficulties are common when an increasing portion of an individual's or family's income, previously used for the basic survival needs of food, clothing, and shelter, is diverted for alcohol and drug use, when income is lost due to missed work or hangovers, when finances are used to cover legal expenses related to alcohol and drugs, or when finances are lost to cover the cost of accidents or penalties incurred under the influence.

Legal Problems

An individual involved with alcohol and drug use may, as the disease progresses, be convicted for: driving under the influence (DUI), drug-related offenses (possession, dealing, transporting), or offenses committed under the influence (assault, spousal abuse, child abuse). Anyone can make an error in judgment, drive in an impaired state, or be prosecuted for driving under the influence. But the casual user is generally so horrified by the legal costs, financial drain, social stigma, and fear of job loss that a second incident is generally avoided at all cost. A second DUI is therefore a clear sign of a high degree of loss of control and a strong indication of at least Early Stage Chemical Dependence (Jacobs 1989).

Occupational Problems
When an individual has been confronted, warned, or fired because of the secondary effects of alcohol and drug-related absenteeism, impaired productivity, accidents, or working while intoxicated, occupation-related alcohol and drug problems are indicated.

Social Problems
When a spouse, family members, or close friends mention concern about alcohol and drug use; when family arguments are caused by or inflamed while under the influence of alcohol or drugs; when family violence, physical abuse, or sexual abuse occur under the influence; or when alcohol and drugs are primarily associated with having a good time, alcohol and drug related social problems may be indicated.

The problems listed above may not necessarily appear simultaneously. A problematic user, in early or even middle stage chemical dependency may function without overt problems in living. The use of the term *overt* implies that problems in living may exist covertly. They may be hidden, denied, or disguised by the individual using the alcohol and drugs, or by individuals who enable the user.

While David had yet to lose a significant amount of his income due to the expense of his alcohol and drug habit, he did report that after cocaine binges, though he never used the word *binge*, he missed work for a few days. He had one DUI, found a legal loophole on the second, and had a small accident a few weeks before our session. He tried to minimize these effects by boasting that he might have lost his driver's license on the second DUI but his lawyer, a friend who he sometimes did cocaine with, found a loophole in the police report and was able to use it to have the charges dropped.

"Ahh, yes!" I thought. "Coyote at work."

When David told me about his near DUI I restrained myself from reacting visibly. He spoke in such an entitled way that I found myself irritated and angry. It felt as if he had reached down, deep inside my chest, and tugged at some deep wound that connected me to a narcissistic man. I felt vulnerable for hours after his session and found myself wanting reassurance about the smallest things that evening.

The following day, when I woke up with the same feelings lingering from a dream I couldn't quite put my finger on, I made a mental note to be more careful with David. I reminded myself that my countertransference reactions were important to pay attention to. They were important not only in regard to my own healing, but also to identify the ways in which my reactions might help me make sense of David's way of being and interacting in the world. Due to the strength of the reaction, I made a mental note to make an appointment with my consultant just in case.

Physical Effects

When alcohol or drugs become an integral part of an individual's life, physical effects may develop, including a variety of health problems, increased physical risk to the individual or others as a result of poor judgment and decision making, acquired tolerance, and withdrawal. The severity of any physical damage is directly correlated with an increase in the quantity, frequency of usage, and method of administration. A thorough alcohol and drug evaluation, especially when there is a risk of withdrawal, should also include a medical evaluation.

Health Problems

Alcohol and drug abuse can cause both acute and chronic health problems. Acute effects of heavy use or binges for many drugs may include nausea, dizziness, vomiting, headache, disorientation, fatigue, muscle tension, exhaustion, weight loss or weight gain, passing out, and blackouts. *Passing out* occurs when an individual uses a substance to the point of losing consciousness as if falling asleep. In a *blackout*, toxic quantities of a drug inhibit long-term memory formation, leaving discrete periods of time (minutes, hours, or even days) for which the person has no recall. An individual in a blackout is capable of acting intentionally despite being intoxicated. Behaviors common to individuals in a blackout include drunkenness, socially unacceptable behavior, and the tendency to repeat jokes and stories. Alcoholics and addicts are frequently unaware of the memory loss from a blackout until the following day, when witnesses inadvertently call attention to their odd or inappropriate behavior.

Risk
Alcohol and drug use can be dangerous, not only to the user but to others as well, including spouses, children, relatives, friends, and workmates. Common behaviors associated with increased risk include impaired decision-making that may result in the loss of income or health, using lethal combinations of alcohol and drugs, using alcohol or drugs during pregnancy and thus risking the health of the fetus, driving or operating machinery under the influence, exposing oneself and others to sexually transmitted diseases (STDs) or Acquired Immune Deficiency Syndrome (AIDS) by engaging in unsafe sex, or activities that risk incarceration, physical danger, or violence in order to obtain the drug.

Acquired Tolerance
As a body accommodates to the presence of alcohol or drugs and produces a subsequent need to increase the quantity, or frequency of use, or alter the route of administration of a substance to achieve the desired effect associated with initial use, acquired tolerance results. Acquired tolerance for some drugs (like alcohol) may begin on a cellular level within a twenty-four-hour binge. For the purpose of a diagnosis of chemical dependence, tolerance is indicated when an individual requires a significant (50 percent) increase in the amount of a substance to experience its initial effects. For example, if David was able to get high on two beers for several years but now needed three or four beers, or if he only drank two beers and felt nothing, he would show acquired tolerance. Reverse tolerance is a rare phenomenon of late-stage alcoholism, when as a result of chronic liver damage even small quantities of alcohol produce intoxication.

Withdrawal
The cluster of symptoms that result when alcohol and drug use falls below the level to which the body has become accustomed is called *withdrawal.* The symptoms and severity of withdrawal vary according to the substance, the degree of acquired tolerance, and may be divided into two categories. Minor and major withdrawal symptoms may include one or more of the following:

TABLE 4–1 Symptoms of Withdrawal [*DSM-IV*, p. 177]

Minor Symptoms	Major Symptoms
intense craving	grand mal seizures
difficulty concentrating	paranoid ideation
depression	suicidal ideation
irritability	psychosis:
anxiety	distorted perceptions and
headaches	sensations, delirium
fatigue	autonomic hyperactivity:
insomnia	restlessness, sweats,
hypersomnia	rapid heartbeat,
muscular tension	hypertension, tremors

Weighing the physical problems David reported, I noted his comment about passing out following binges, his doctor's warning about his weight, and his gastritis. When I asked him about blackouts David said that he'd "had a bunch of those" (4–6 per year) in the last few years.

Not wanting the extent of my inquiry about his risk to focus solely on DUIs, I asked David whether he'd ever driven when he had a bit too much to drink. He joked that'd driven "way drunk" hundreds of times, and reminded me about his "small" accident, costing $4,500. Later in the session, curious about his level of tolerance, I asked David whether he needed more to get a "buzz on" now, compared to when he started drinking.

"Well, let's see, Doc," David said sarcastically.

I tried to keep a straight face but winced at David's sophomoric dig. David knew I wasn't a physician and I wondered if he felt the need to somehow wound me or put me in my place. Coyote can be vicious when he senses vulnerability.

"I started drinking when I was 15. Mostly I drank on the weekends with my buddies. At that time I guess it only took a beer or two to lift off."

David also reported that when his doctor expressed concern about his weight he stopped drinking for a month and experienced minor withdrawal symptoms, including nausea, disorientation, and irritability. He gradually started drinking again the next month, "but only two or three beers a night most of the time."

❖ ❖ ❖

Psychological and Behavioral Effects

When alcohol and drugs become an integral part of an individual's life and a central focus of recreation, a variety of psychological effects develop. This increased focus or psychological reliance often develops at the expense of previous coping skills and strategies to deal with life stress, emotional pain, and existential pain. Psychological effects include the ability to abstain and control use, an increase in use to regulate affect, and the presence of denial.

Ability to Abstain

The capacity to resist the first use of a substance within a specific period of time is called the *ability to abstain*. For example, when I asked David if he ever promised himself not to drink or use drugs, he said,

"Sure. I've done that hundreds of times, like after a good weekend of partying."

I noticed the way David used the phrase "good weekend" and guessed that he was still identifying his drinking and drug use as a positive experience in spite of the negative consequences that were piling up around him.

"Then I'd lay off for a couple of days."

Wondering whether he fully answered my question or only answered part of it, I tried to see if there was something left unsaid.

"And on those days that you wouldn't drink, did you use cocaine or take something else?" I asked, curious about the extent of his tolerance and whether he was managing the onset of withdrawal by using other drugs.

"Sure," he replied and smiled mischievously. "I'll usually pop a valium or maybe a Tylenol 3 to get me through the day."

"Ah, yes," I said, recognizing Coyote peering over his shoulder. "That makes sense."

Control

The ability to limit use of a substance prior to intoxication is called *control*.

When I asked David if he ever tried stopping after one or two drinks, he said, "Alcohol, sure, because Sharon's been getting on my case, so I'll keep to a minimum of three or four . . ."

I remembered that David had previously reported that his lower limit was closer to six. Alcoholics and addicts often consciously or unconsciously change their stories in relation to a perceived threat.

". . . but coke. Forget it. Once I roll that hundred," referring to the way many cocaine addicts snort through a hundred-dollar bill, "I do it all. Sometimes I'll go for two or three days, and if I run out I'll call my lawyer. The least he can do is share his stash, given how much he charges me."

> "Denial ain't just a river in Egypt."
> Anonymous

Use to Regulate Affect

The pattern of alcohol and drug reliance to cope with, alter, enhance, or avoid emotions is called the *use to regulate affect*. Alcohol and drugs may be used habitually to calm down from anger, mellow out after a tense day at work, avoid hunger, loneliness, fear, or fatigue, or aid in attempts to be happy or to have sex.

Denial

A patient's defensiveness, rationalizing, and minimizing alcohol and drug use is called denial and is likely to increase proportionately as the disease progresses.

Defensiveness, in the context of denial, occurs when a patient resists or refuses to acknowledge, explore, or listen to comments, feedback, and concern about alcohol and drug use. Often accompanied by hostility, an evasive or abrasive tone, and social withdrawal, defensiveness is also often accompanied by attempts to distract the interviewer from exploring the topic of alcohol and drug use.

It was difficult to evaluate David's defensiveness because, on the one hand, he was quite open about the details of his using but, on the other, his generalized hostility simmered just below the surface of a slick businesslike persona. I was unsure at this point in the interview whether his hostility was consistent with a narcissistic character, a defensiveness about being forced into therapy, or a defensiveness related to using alcohol and drugs.

Rationalization is the attempt to explain behavior away. The reasoning may initially appear quite understandable and then, eventually, increasingly bizarre.

David rarely excused his drinking, his using, or his behavior while under the influence. When I asked him whether he would limit his drinking or drug use around people who drank or used less, he said, "Sometimes I might. Let's take Sharon, for instance. She just doesn't understand the kind of stress I'm under. And I work hard to keep up the lifestyle she wants to lead."

I was impressed. In one statement David rationalized his alcohol and drug use and simultaneously externalized the locus of his control onto his wife. In effect, he was saying that if he didn't have to work so hard to keep up Sharon's lifestyle, he wouldn't use alcohol or drugs. In other words, it was Sharon who was making him drink and take drugs.

Minimization is the underreporting of the quantity, frequency, or impact of alcohol and drug use. Minimization can be the result of consciously manipulating what others are told, or minimization may stem from an unconscious self-deception. The alcoholic, having just finished off a six-pack, may say, "I'm not drunk! I just had three beers!" Minimization may involve acts of omission. "Well, I did have five drinks, I just didn't tell you about the five I had an hour later." Minimization may involve acts of commission such as actively hiding bottles, hiding drug paraphernalia, or lying.

It is important to be aware that cultural norms vary dramatically regarding an individual's personal comfort with self-disclosure. The context of the evaluation, whether court-mandated, self-referred, in the beginning stages of ongoing psychotherapy, or whether a disclosure in the presence of family members may strongly affect a given response. Awareness of the subtle difference between caution in self-disclosure and denial should temper the tendency of a clinician to overpathologize.

As the interview went on, it was clear that David had made repeated unsuccessful attempts to abstain. He was unable to stop completely for any length of time longer than a week, although he did reduce his intake for several months at a stretch.

On several occasions when I pressed him for more information about the drugs he used, David added amphetamines and non-prescription sleeping pills to the list. This indicated his tendency to minimize his use by only partially responding to my questions. He also linked his moods with increased drinking. At this point in the evaluation I listed the three problematic areas as follows:

Section 2. Stage of the Disease
  Problems in Living:
    Social: arguments with wife about using
    Occupational: lost work due to recovering from hangovers and
      binges
    Financial: money lost due to accident under the influence
    Legal: 1 DUI conviction
  Physical Effects:
    Acute: history of passing out, blackouts (4–6/year)
    Chronic: possible complications of gastritis
    Health problems: minor symptoms of withdrawal—nausea, irrita-
      bility, disorientation
    Risk: driving drunk
    Tolerance: significant (in his 20's needed 3 beers, now 4–5)
  Psychological:
    Loss of Control/Inability to Abstain: history of going on the wagon,
      binges
    Use to Regulate Affect: his "moods"
    Denial: rationalizes use because of work and stress.

Problematic Use and Early, Middle, and Late-Stage Dependence

Psychoactive substance use varies from culture to culture, among different age groups, and over time as social norms change. Through-out the world a diversity of cultures and subcultures consider psychoactive substance use either recreationally acceptable within parameters, restricted to medical or ritual use, or incorporated within the very fabric of a society's religious, social, or economic life. Individual motivation for psychoactive substance use may vary dramatically and include relief from physical or emotional pain, peer pressure, the need to identify with a social group, or the desire for a spiritual experience outside the realm of an individual's normal consciousness.

Non-Problematic Casual User

The casual user may occasionally ingest alcohol or drugs as a part of a religious ritual, as a social lubricant, or as a mild sedative, but this limited pattern of use neither hinders social relationships nor contributes to work or legal problems. Cultivated knowledge and tastes may be a part of the casual user's hobby but it never impairs the ability to provide food, shelter, and clothing.

The nonproblematic casual user has no physical problems related to alcohol or drugs due to the relatively small quantities and infrequent intake of substances. The casual user is mindful of the effects of alcohol and drug use and therefore does not present a risk to self or others. When a social or medical situation encourages or mandates it, the casual user moderates intake or abstains without struggle, frustration, or regret. When approaching the limits of accepted norms, or sensing the onset of negative consequences associated with alcohol and drug misuse, the casual user easily adjusts the intake and frequency of substance use. The non-problematic user rarely uses alcohol or drugs as an habitual response to anger, conflict, tension, stress, or emotional or physical pain.

Since the non-problematic user is mindful of the cultural norms for alcohol and drug use and does not experience physical problems, there is nothing to deny, defend, or distort. Hiding alcohol and drug use is therefore unlikely. When questioned confidentially, the casual user generally responds frankly and openly about alcohol and drug experience. An exception occurs when a substance is not sanctioned within a wide societal framework though accepted within a given subculture. For example, marijuana in the United States is illegal though its use is accepted openly in some isolated subcommunities. David's use clearly did not fit this category.

Problematic Use

Alcohol and drug use can be considered problematic when it has progressed to the point where any one of the characteristic Problems in Living (financial, social, legal, occupational), Physical Effects (health problems, risk), or Psychological Effects (use to regulate affect, denial) occur. Whether as a result of increased frequency, greater quantity, greater effects than anticipated, having one too many, or choosing too high a dose, the problematic user is at increased risk for the transitory negative effects associated with hangovers, impaired decision making, and acting under the influence.

An isolated instance of any one of the characteristics described above qualifies as an *incident* of problematic use. A *diagnosis* of problematic user requires at least three incidents over the course of a month. Transient problematic use may be associated with external stressors such as loss of a job, grief over the death of a spouse, relative, or friend, financial loss, or other life problems. Once the individual has accommodated to the problem, however, a return to previous nonproblematic levels of substance use is likely. Due to the infrequency and/or relatively small quantities of alcohol or drug use, the problematic user has:

no chronic physical effects
no significant increase in tolerance
no withdrawal
no significant loss of control or ability to abstain.

David reported a minor chronic physical effect in his weight gain, acquired tolerance, a history of withdrawal, loss of control, and an inability to abstain. As a result of meeting these criteria, his use of substances is clearly beyond problematic use.

Early-Stage Chemical Dependence
A diagnosis of Early-Stage Chemical Dependence meets the minimum required criteria for the diagnosis of Problematic Use and is characterized by three progressive changes:

1. Initial loss of control and the ability to abstain (10%[1]);
2. The development of tolerance but no withdrawal;
3. Marked psychological reliance indicated by an increase in frequency toward daily use, an increase in quantity, and use to regulate affect.

The temporal sequence of chemical dependence tends to be progressive and degenerative, though an individual may stabilize at any stage for years (or even decades) without apparent increase in alcohol and drug use. In addition, fluctuations among stages may occur periodically. An alcoholic or addict, due to external circumstances (a spouse's ultimatum, legal mandates) or internal circumstances (cutting back after a depressive episode or near-death experience), may exercise a limited ability to reduce substance use for years at a time.

Despite the controversy over whether a reduction in alcohol and drug use following a greater period of dependence indicates a "cure" or a benign return to controlled use, untreated controlled users are at a greater risk for a return to higher levels of use and dependence when compared with abstainers and recovering alcoholics (Heather and Robertson 1981, Paredes et al. 1979, Sobell and Sobell 1978). Therefore, once an individual has met the criteria for Early, Middle, or Late-Stage Chemical Dependence the diagnosis remains for the individual's life, though the status of the person's relationship to alcohol and drugs may change over time. The statement "I was an alcoholic before but now I just have a drink every so often" is a common feature of denial. Controlled use should not be confused with nonproblematic casual drinking. This form of denial can be analogous to lighting a stick of dynamite without knowing the length of the fuse.

A high risk of relapse is associated with cross-addiction to substances within the same class, poly-drug use, and alternating a drug of choice. Fulfilling the criteria below for even one substance, therefore, warrants the diagnosis of Chemical Dependence. Once a person is diagnosed as chemically dependent, his or her use of any stimulants, depressants, hallucinogens, or narcotics is a breach of abstinence and sobriety. In cases where substances characteristically do not or

---

1. This means that when individuals have the desire and the means to use, but attempt to control or abstain, they are unable to do so 10 percent of the time.

rarely develop the classic addiction symptoms of physical damage, tolerance, and withdrawal, such as the hallucinogens, a diagnosis of chemical dependence is made without the criteria of tolerance and withdrawal.

Long-term use of prescriptive medication that produces tolerance or withdrawal does not, however, necessarily indicate a dependency. The chronic pain patient prescribed Vicodin (6–8/day) postsurgically, who develops tolerance and eventually experiences withdrawal when discontinuing use but has no other associated symptoms, would *not* be diagnosed chemically dependent. The use of narcotics, depressants, stimulants, or hallucinogens is *not* considered a relapse when the prescribing physician is:

Knowledgeable about the medical aspects of chemical dependence
Aware of the patient's addiction history
Confident regarding the need for the prescription over a medication with less relapse potential
Monitoring the patient for relapse.

David reported a significant loss of control and a decreased ability to abstain. He reported a history of attempting to quit and his inability to follow his doctor's advice. It is important to note that he never said he stopped using drugs, he only said he stopped drinking. He had acquired tolerance, needing four to five beers to "get a buzz" whereas two or three beers had been enough when he started drinking as a youth. He also had a psychological reliance on his alcohol and drug use evidenced by daily intake, an increase in quantity over time, and his use of alcohol and drugs to regulate his moods. For these reasons, David was *at least* in the Early Stage.

Middle-Stage Chemical Dependence
A diagnosis of Middle-Stage Chemical Dependence meets the minimum required criteria for the diagnosis of Early-Stage Chemical Dependence and is characterized by three progressive changes:

1. Physical effects: acute and chronic
2. An increase in tolerance with no or minor withdrawal.

3. Significant loss of control and loss of the ability to abstain (50%), evidenced by a progression toward daily use with occasional dry days or a pattern of bingeing.

During the middle stage of the disease, problems in living tend to escalate and it is more difficult for the alcoholic and addict to hide the effects of dependency on social relationships, work, and finances. Individuals at this stage frequently cultivate social relationships with other alcohol and drug users who contribute to the development of denial by validating the individual's drinking and drug use as normal.

Psychological reliance in the middle stage of the disease includes the classic addiction symptoms of tolerance, withdrawal, and minor health problems. Frequently, the transition from the early to the middle stage develops in such a gradual and subtle manner that the progression goes unnoticed by most individuals and those around them. An increased frequency of use, indicating tolerance, is more likely to be evidenced by increasing debts or the presence of numerous empty bottles or drug paraphernalia. At this stage some individuals offset withdrawal by drinking or using small quantities throughout the day, combining substances, or alternating use of alcohol with other drugs when early morning drinking might be noticed.

A significant loss in the ability to abstain and control at this stage is indicated when an individual uses in excess of his or her companions, drinks alone, or continues to drink or use when others abstain or stop. For example, an alcoholic may have an aperitif, half a bottle of wine, and a cognac after dinner where his or her dinner partners abstain or have a single drink the entire evening. The alcoholic and addict may insist on refilling other people's glasses to keep pace, covertly pressuring others by encouraging them to " Let loose! Have another line!" or overtly ridicule others' temperance as "stiff," "square," or not up to standards.

Individuals at this stage often develop a heightened, compulsive hoarding attitude toward alcohol and drugs. They may proclaim the tragedy of waste when a bottle is disposed of before it is entirely drained or secretly finish off other people's glasses prior to filling the dishwasher. In order to decrease the possibility of the dependency being noticed, an individual at this stage may "borrow" or steal medication from friends or family, obtain medication from several doctors, or purchase alcohol and drugs with cash to avoid having credit-card bills or check stubs noticed by family members. The Middle and

Late-Stage Chemical Dependent may also hide use with pronounced amounts of incense, cologne or perfume, mouthwash, breath mints, or chewing gum to camouflage the odor of a substance.

Middle and Late-Stage Chemical Dependents often have a history of "going on the wagon." Discrete periods of abstinence as short as a day or as long as several years may contribute to the individual's denial and illusion of control. The statement "I can quit. I've done it a thousand times" is a common rationalization supporting the alcoholic and addict's denial. "Going on the wagon" may be as subtle as giving up alcohol or drugs for the holidays or until a bit of weight is lost, or as obvious when the alcoholic "dries out" for longer periods of time. Keep in mind that if using alcohol and drugs were not a problem, there would be no reason to give it up.

Bingeing

Bingeing involves intermittent use of large quantities of a substance in a relatively short period of time. Bingeing may involve ingesting a fifth of vodka, a case of beer, or as much as three or four grams of cocaine in a twenty-four hour period. A binge user may remain abstinent or control use for extended periods but then use without interruption until he or she has passed out, been hospitalized, or some external action stops the alcohol and addict's continued use. *Due to the high risks associated with this type of alcohol and drug use, a binge user is always diagnosed at least in the Middle Stage of the disease* (see also section on risk).

David reported acute effects of both hangovers and blackouts. His chronic effects included his gastritis and excess weight gain. He also reported minor withdrawal symptoms, including nausea, disorientation, and irritability when he stopped drinking for a short period of time. I wondered, however, that if he had stopped using drugs for the month that his withdrawal might have been more intense. His loss of control was significant, he had a pattern of bingeing, and he was a daily drinker and user. For these reasons, David fit the criteria for Middle-Stage Dependence.

Toward the end of the session, when he appeared to feel more relaxed, I asked David directly if he thought he had an alcohol or drug problem. "Maybe," he said, "but not anything I don't have under control."

❖ ❖ ❖

Late-Stage Chemical Dependence

The final stage of the disease prior to death is characterized by dramatic increases in problems in living and life-threatening physical effects. A diagnosis of Late-Stage Chemical Dependence meets the minimum criteria for Middle-Stage Chemical Dependence and three progressive changes:

1. Physical damage: acute and chronic with extreme risk of withdrawal.
2. High tolerance or reverse tolerance accompanied by use to avoid withdrawal.
3. Extreme loss of control and ability to abstain (90%).

At this late and severe stage, the addiction to alcohol or drugs is so profound that virtually every aspect of the individual's life is affected. Problems in living are obvious, acute *and* chronic health problems are life-threatening, the threat of withdrawal or use to avoid withdrawal is continuous, and loss of control and the ability to abstain is present to an extreme degree (90 percent). This means that 90 percent of the time when individuals have the desire and means to use but attempt to control or abstain, they are unable to do so. This means that only one out of ten times, or 10 percent of the time, the late-stage alcoholic and addict is able to control or abstain for a short period. In the late stage of the disease, alcohol and drug use is continuous with only short periods of abstinence while sleeping or until the onset of withdrawal. Drinking and using proceeds unabated until the alcoholic or addict passes out, or as long as the substance is available or death ensues.

The Late-Stage Chemical Dependent's life is focused on a single goal: using. Social relationships are defined predominantly by the habit. The user associates with people to drink and use with or to obtain money to purchase alcohol or drugs, and avoids anyone who might confront or deter using such as family, friends, physician, or police. At this stage of the disease, the alcoholic and addict's occupational history is likely to be checkered, with numerous job changes, firings, or lapses of employment. Individuals at this stage may have lost friends, family, and fortunes.

A Late-Stage Alcoholic or Addict is likely to be in gravely impaired health with multiple physical problems. Malnutrition as a result of loss of appetite and poor decision-making may be present along with physical injuries, a compromised immune system, or untreated wounds. As a result of impaired judgment and the need to obtain drugs or alcohol to avoid withdrawal, the Late-Stage Addict is at an increased risk, when intoxicated, for accidents, drowning, falls, fires, and burns when intoxicated. Unfortunately, alcoholics and addicts at this late stage often hesitate to seek medical help due to the risk that seeking such help will call attention to the primary problem: the addiction. A Late-Stage Alcoholic and Addict should have a complete physical and be treated through medical intervention for drug detoxification. The primary effects of withdrawal may vary from drug to drug, but withdrawal is always a serious concern and may result in seizure, suicide, or accidental death (*DSM-IV* 1994).

Alcoholics and addicts at this late stage of the disease are often in the wrong place at the wrong time and are therefore easy targets for victimization by mugging, beating, or rape. The risk to the alcoholic and addict, as well as to others, is extremely high through self-inflicted wounds, overdose, the use of dirty needles, and high-risk lifestyles such as homelessness, drug dealing, stealing, and prostitution.

At this point in his life, David's use of alcohol and drugs did not meet the criteria for Late-Stage Dependence. His withdrawal symptoms were only minor, so far as I could determine. His tolerance, though increasing from his original level, was not extreme and he was able to exercise modest control for given periods. For these reasons I did not diagnose David at the late stage, although he might be rapidly approaching it.

If David had been in the late stage, he would have evidenced more severe chronic physical problems, which could have been confirmed by a medical examination. If he were in the late stage of the disease, his withdrawal would have been severe and his tolerance greater or reversed. I always try to remember to diagnose a patient only so far as I can provide diagnostic information. If I suspected that David was late stage due to his withholding information, however, or if I was unable to gather the relevant criteria, I would make a note under Section 4: Special Features indicating my concern.

❖ ❖ ❖

Section 3. Current Status

Once the stage of the disease has been established during an alcohol and drug evaluation, the individual's current use of alcohol and drugs can be viewed in a progressive, historical perspective from unrestricted using toward levels of health and well-being described as *controlled use, abstinence,* or *in recovery.*

Using

The repeated, problematic, or pathological administration of alcohol and other drugs is generally referred to as *using.* An individual may remain abstinent or controlled during the week or use continuously on the weekend, holidays, or special occasions such as the birth of a child, a promotion, or a death in the family. Using, however, does not refer to an individual involved in nonproblematic use of a substance.

David is clearly using alcohol and drugs in a problematic and pathological manner. Although a reduction in his drinking is notable (from 8–10 to 4–6/night), it is not controlled use. Controlled use would be the reduction to a lesser stage of the disease for at least one month or more. David's status would be listed as: Section 3: Status-Using.

Controlled Use

When alcoholics and addicts significantly reduce their levels of use to a lesser stage of the disease, it is called *controlled use.* Periods of controlled use may be as short as a month or as long as several years. They may occur by choice, or as a result of decreased resources or the inability to obtain the substance. Reducing substance use for a period of several hours or days or switching substances does not qualify as controlled use. A period of controlled use frequently supports denial, since the addict or alcoholic may convince himself or others that a problem doesn't exist or has been cured. Alcoholics or addicts may take pride in their modulated use by saying, "I can stop any time.

Now I only smoke on the weekends!" They may take pride in their acquired tolerance by exclaiming, "Hey, drinking's not a problem for me. I can go through a six-pack and not even feel it!" They may discount an inquiry and deflect exploration of their past history by saying, "I told you I stopped freebasing weeks ago. Now I just snort a little coke." Or they may boldly confront the interviewer by challenging, "I haven't gotten drunk in a month. I've been in jail. So what's the problem?"

When making the status designation of Controlled Use, the clinician should include the length of time at the reduced level of use in order to provide an accurate drug history, for example, Status: Controlled Use: Middle Stage 2 years, previously Late Stage 1 year.

Abstinence

When people refrain from using *all* mood altering drugs, they are called *abstinent*. This includes narcotics, depressants, stimulants, and hallucinogens. Abstinent does not mean refraining from alcohol, if alcohol is the primary drug of choice, but occasionally smoking marijuana or opium. Abstinent means refraining from *all* substances. Once again, medically prescribed and supervised use is not considered a relapse. Relapse is indicated only when the medication is used for a different purpose, with a different frequency, or in quantities other than prescribed. When a recovering alcoholic forgets to mention to his physician that he is an addict and accepts a prescription for codeine when a non-narcotic may be available, and then uses the prescription "when I've had a hard day," the incident should be considered a relapse.

Despite the clear position that medically prescribed substances are acceptable and do not compromise sobriety (defined by Alcoholics Anonymous in 1989), many recovering alcoholics refrain from using even prescribed medications in the belief that a reliance on any chemical is a breach of sobriety. This "pharmacophobia" can complicate the dually diagnosed alcoholic or addict's transition from abstinence to recovery. The dually diagnosed addict or alcoholic is at an increased risk of relapse when attempting to "white knuckle it" by avoiding medication that would reduce distressing symptoms.

Abstinence alone is not in and of itself an indicator of sobriety, though it is clearly a step in the right direction. Abstinent alcoholics and addicts often continue to behave self-destructively and anti-socially, and are often referred to as a "dry drunk." Dry drunks often continue to wreak havoc in their own lives and the lives of friends and family by blaming others for their problems, or engaging in compulsive work, gambling, unsafe sex, food, shopping, exercise, and other obsessions. Though a majority of those struggling to achieve sobriety do so initially without help, the notion that willpower alone is sufficient to maintain abstinence has often been referred to as "having the safest room on the Titanic."

In Recovery

Abstinence *and* participation in a rehabilitation or self-development program such as a Twelve-Step Program, regular church attendance, a group-oriented recovery program, or psychotherapy that confronts the denial, effects, and trauma associated with a chemically dependent life, is called *in recovery*. Involvement in a Twelve-Step Program unrelated to the individual's alcohol and drug use does *not* fit this criterion. For example, the abstinent alcoholic who only attends Al-Anon is not in recovery per se. In recovery distinguishes the individual who is abstinent and involved in an active program from the individual who just stops drinking or using. Individual psychotherapy alone may not qualify as being in recovery, especially if the therapist is insensitive or ignorant to the problems associated with the processes of addiction and recovery.

Section 4. Special Features

Under this section any additional information that provides a clearer, more comprehensive picture of the individual's lifestyle and relationship to alcohol and drugs is listed.

Longest Period of Abstinence or Sobriety

Knowing the longest period an alcoholic or addict has been able to totally abstain from using provides a clue to the conscious or repressed awareness of the problem, the results of any attempts to limit or control use, and the potential risk of relapse.

Dual Diagnosis

Chemical dependency is frequently implicated in the self-medication of a variety of psychological and physiological conditions including affective disorders, anxiety disorders, schizophrenia, personality disorders, disorders associated with trauma, and chronic pain (Alterman 1985, Goodwin and Erickson 1979). Alcohol and drug use often complicates an initial psychiatric diagnosis. It is easy to confuse the crash of stimulant withdrawal with depression, the high of stimulant use with a manic episode, or a psychotic episode with Korsakoff's psychosis. A clinician should keep in mind the tentative nature of Axis I and Axis II diagnoses for a period of several months until the long-term effects of withdrawal have passed and the early stages of recovery have begun. In the early recovery of a dually diagnosed alcoholic or addict, periodic reassessment is necessary. In addition, the dually diagnosed patient may require special attention during detoxification, necessitating psychiatric consultation throughout treatment, as well as psychopharmacological intervention to help contain complicating and disturbing symptomatology.

During his conjoint and individual interview David was emotionally excitable, gestured evocatively, and appeared even somewhat threatening. As I recalled feeling threatened, I reminded myself that I needed to take into account my countertransference in order to weigh his behavior accordingly. On the other hand, just because I felt threatened, in part due to my personal history with an authority figure, didn't mean he wasn't a threat to Sharon or others, or that he had difficulty with impulse control and anger.

David detailed a lifelong history of depression prior to his drinking and drug use, without any previous suicide attempts. He recalled that he would also experience periods of intense "creative energy" when he worked several days straight and then collapsed.

While my first inclination was to link his behavior with his cocaine use, I also needed to consider the possibility that David was self-medicating an underlying depression or untreated Bipolar disorder exacerbated by his alcohol and drug use. At this stage in his evaluation, I considered the diagnosis tentative.

❖ ❖ ❖

Medical Evaluations

A thorough medical evaluation will help clarify any medical complications prior to and during treatment arising from the medical disorders common to the late-stage alcoholic and addict (listed previously).

Given the volatility of David's bingeing and the initial comments attributed to his physician, I felt strongly that any recommendation should include a medical evaluation with a physician familiar with the problems of alcohol and drug dependence, not his family physician.

Medically Supervised Prescriptions

Information regarding current medication is vitally important because addicts and alcoholics often actively or passively withhold information from a treating physician. Alcoholics and addicts rarely remind their physicians, "Please keep in mind that I am currently abusing drugs." As a result, complications may arise when prescription medications are mixed or mixed with street drugs prior to or during chemical dependence treatment.

David reported that he took no prescription medication.

Initial Onset of Use

The familial and cultural environment and the circumstances under which the alcohol and drug use began provide an important framework with which to understand an individual's alcohol and drug history.

David mentioned that both parents were alcoholics. When he was 8 years old, he began drinking from their bottles when they were passed out on the couch in the living room.

A hidden and frequently underdiagnosed population includes individuals in their seventies, eighties, and older. It is estimated that between 2 and 10 percent of people over 65 have problems with alcohol, although in clinical settings this figure is considered low (Lawson 1989, Secretary of Health and Human Services 1990). Frequently socially isolated and likely to escape observation by friends and family, these older users may conceal problematic use and dependence on prescription medication or alcohol. Older substance abusers and addicts are at increased risk for the problems associated with multiple drug interactions and overdose due to the synergistic effects of substances with the same class. These problems may go undiagnosed due to the similarity between drug interactions, drug abuse, and symptoms of old age such as forgetfulness, weakness, confusion, tremor, anorexia, and anxiety.

Familial History

A careful alcohol and drug history may reveal a familial predisposition toward chemical dependence and become a powerful tool for education and confrontation while increasing the therapist's understanding of the familial milieu.

David's familial history was essential to help articulate the genetic predisposition of alcoholism and drug dependence and the risk David ran in choosing not to seek treatment.

Dealing

Selling or smuggling drugs is a dangerous activity. It increases the risk for legal, financial, and physical harm. A willingness to risk imprisonment, financial penalty, and violence is an important indicator of an individual's continued attachment to using alcohol and drugs.

DUIs and near-DUIs

Even if an individual has not been prosecuted or convicted for driving under the influence (DUI), it is important to know if there is a history of being stopped, questioned, given a sobriety test, or held in jail and having the charges dropped for driving under the influence. It is also wise to ask for all blood alcohol level (BAL) test results. A BAL of .04 might indicate an overzealous police officer or a poor driver. A BAL of .075 might indicate someone who barely missed prosecution. A BAL of .2 indicates someone who was dangerously drunk but might have gotten off on a technicality. It may also indicate an individual with tremendously high initial or acquired tolerance. A BAL of .3 indicates an individual whose alcohol use was extremely out of control. Most people at such a high level of alcohol blood toxicity are unconscious.

Unfortunately I forgot to ask for the blood alcohol level of David's DUI and his near-DUI. Because he reported he "couldn't remember a thing either time" I was unsure whether he was withholding information or had been in a blackout.

Other Arrests and/or Convictions

When alcohol and drug use becomes a major focus of an alcoholic or addict's life, the extent to which he or she is willing to risk incarceration can help determine the depth and desperation of an individual's dependence. Those desperate enough and without other financial means may resort to prostitution, shoplifting, robbery, assault, or dealing to supply their alcohol and drug habit.

History of Violence

When most drugs are used habitually, an increased risk of desperate or violent behavior may arise if the addict or alcoholic has difficulty procuring the drug to relieve withdrawal. Knowledge of the individual's history of violence is important for the clinician to keep in mind during treatment for the safety of the patient, family members, other patients, and the health care clinician alone in a dark office building on a Friday night.

David reported never having hit his current wife, Sharon. Unfortunately, I forgot to ask about his previous marriages. When I asked about his "not having hit her" he mentioned he did "push her once." When I asked him what happened, he reported that she "fell through a plate-glass window" and he minimized the results of his actions by claiming "she didn't need many stitches."

Suicide Potential

The single best prognostic indicator of suicide risk is a previous attempt. Whether or not the individual's conscious intent is to commit suicide, use of increasingly large dosages of drugs may increase the risk of overdose and death. Alcohol and drug use has long been implicated in a large percentage of suicide attempts (Secretary of Health and Human Services 1990). Impairment in functioning due to the influence of alcohol and drugs may lead to an increase in fatalities. Falling down a flight of stairs, drunk driving, misuse of medication, accidents while using dangerous equipment, or self-neglect from failing to seek medical help are possible examples of alcohol and drug-related fatalities.

Just to be sure, at one point in the interview when David was talking about his "low periods" prior to his drinking and drug experiences, I asked him if he ever considered suicide.

"Naw!" he said. "A couple of times when the business wasn't going well I might have had a passing thought about driving my car into a telephone pole but I never gave it much thought. Everyone thinks about those things once in a while. Haven't you?"

Route of Administration

The method of a drug's administration is an important indicator of the perceived need for more powerful, direct, immediate effects. A variety of drugs may be administered orally, nasally, injected intravenously, applied topically and absorbed through the skin, or inserted anally where blood vessels readily absorb chemical substances. The alcoholic and addict's need for an increased high often disregards an increased risk of infection, AIDS, heart attack, or brain damage. The transition from snorting cocaine to freebasing or injecting is significant and worthy of concern.

Other Compulsions

Alcohol and drug use is often accompanied by other problematic compulsive behaviors, including overworking, shopping, gambling, binge eating, and promiscuity. A thorough, descriptive diagnosis will take into account a variety of chronic, problematic behaviors that can influence the development of abstinence and recovery. For example, many cocaine addicts believe they are exceptionally productive when bingeing. It is only when they get sober that they realize or admit how little work they accomplished when they were high.

David indicated that he could work 60–80 hours per week when he was bingeing on cocaine.

After reviewing the information David revealed in his individual session, I was able to create a comprehensive diagnostic picture of David's relationship to alcohol and drugs.

Section 1. Drugs of Choice
Alcohol (8–10 drinks/day for 5–6 years, currently 4–6/day minimum):
Cocaine (1–3 g/wk for last year)
Caffeine (10 cups/day)
Amphetamine binges
Nonprescription sleeping pills

Section 2. Stage of the Disease: Middle Stage (6 years)
Problems in Living:
    marital problems, lost work due to recovering from hangovers
      and binges, money lost from accident
Physical Effects:
    Acute: history of passing out, blackouts (4–6/year)

Chronic: possible complications of gastritis
Risk: health problems, driving drunk
Withdrawal: minor symptoms—nausea, disorientation, irritability
Tolerance: significant
Psychological Effects:
going on the wagon, binges, rationalizes use

Section 3. Status: Using

Section 4. Special Features
Potentially lethal combinations of alcohol and cocaine
Longest period of abstinence from alcohol: one month
Dual Diagnosis: possible diagnosis of Bipolar Disorder
Familial History: both parents alcoholic (defined by patient)
History of violence under the influence (pushed third wife through a window, requiring stitches)
One DUI, one near DUI. Accident under the influence.
Driven drunk "hundreds of times"
Compulsions: work
Physician advised abstinence due to health problems
Third marriage "on the rocks"

RECOMMENDING TREATMENT

I was strongly concerned about David's alcohol and drug use. I was concerned that the couples therapy would prove fruitless if his drinking and drug use were not addressed directly. I was concerned that he was driving under the influence and using potentially lethal doses and combinations of substances. I was concerned about the risk to both David and Sharon if I took a more relaxed approach. And I was concerned that if I confronted the situation too strongly, David would reject anything I recommended and flee therapy.

As I reflected on the situation and any possible course of action I might take, I took into account seven important factors. I considered David's:

Risk of withdrawal
Physical and medical complications

Psychiatric complications
Life impairments, including social support, legal problems, job
   vulnerability, and financial resources
Extent of his loss of control and risk of relapse
Optimum recovery environment, given his situation, and
Level of treatment acceptance or resistance.

Treatment matching is currently a debatable concept in the literature. I use a general rule of thumb when making treatment recommendations: the greater the stage of the disease and risk of relapse, the greater the need for containment and structure. On the less contained end of the spectrum, a therapist can recommend that an individual in the problematic stage or an early-stage alcoholic or addict attend several AA meetings, as few as two or as many as seven meetings per week. In addition, more than one therapy session per week would help explore a lifetime of alcohol and drug use and help guide the patient into recovery. The more contained end of the spectrum includes inpatient or residential treatment from one to six months or more and may include a majority of the following:

Treatment for secondary medical problems
Detoxification under medical supervision
Psychiatric evaluation
Busy daily schedule of activities
Individual, group, and family therapy, and
Twelve-Step meetings.

Although it is often difficult to diagnose an Axis II disorder in the midst of an active chemical dependency disorder, David appeared to demonstrate depressive, narcissistic, and Bipolar symptoms. His loss of control was significant and, given his arrogance, I considered him a high risk for relapse. If he decided to give up alcohol and drugs on his own, which I thought unlikely, his chances, based on my experience, were slim. Finally, given his attitude, I figured I had one chance. I needed to be clear, compassionate, and direct.

When we met for her individual session the following day, Sharon described her childhood as "a war zone" dominated by two alcoholic parents. She described her role in the family as the *de facto* guardian to two younger siblings when her parents were drunk, which was, as she reported, most of the time. Having read several books about adult children of alcoholics and alcoholism in general, though never having had either an alcohol or drug problem herself, Sharon abstained from all substances, attended Twelve-Step ACoA meetings, and had been in individual therapy for nine months. The previous week, after another painful night of fighting, David's drunkenness, and fear of his behavior while under the influence, Sharon gave David an ultimatum. She told him that night and the following morning that if they didn't get into therapy, she was going to file for divorce.

Sharon said she was tired of his anger, his threats, his unexplained absences, and the shopping sprees that kept them in debt even though David grossed over a hundred and fifty thousand dollars a year. Since giving David her ultimatum, Sharon stayed with a girlfriend. She wanted to see if David would respond to the couples therapy before she went home.

I asked Sharon if she thought David had an alcohol and drug problem. She said she thought he had a problem with alcohol but she had no idea that David was hiding his cocaine use from her. I asked her if she thought that therapy would help.

"I want it, too," she said, "but on some level I know that nothing will improve if we don't get help. I know I'm part of the problem," she said, starting to cry, "but I just can't bring any children into this world to live like I did growing up. I just can't."

Sharon's mascara ran down her cheeks and she blew her nose quietly.

"My therapist says I don't have to take it anymore and I believe her. All the women in my ACoA group say the same thing. But I want to give him one more chance, just to be sure. Oh, I must look horrible." And noticing the black smudges on the tissue, Sharon balled the soft paper into a wad and dropped it into the wastebasket.

"Well, let's see what happens in the next session."

"I'm okay," she replied, sniffling.

I stood up, shook Sharon's hand, and we agreed to meet on Monday, three days later.

After Sharon's session, I thought it highly unlikely that David would respond positively to my opinion that couples therapy, without addressing his alcohol and drug problems, would be a waste of their time and money. I was also concerned that David might repeat a distorted view of what we talked about in the individual session at a later time when he was alone with Sharon. It also concerned me that if I gave him written recommendations he might refuse to share the information with his wife or destroy the list.

After consulting with my colleagues, I decided to be direct about the problems both Sharon and David identified. I typed a list of recommendations and named three well-respected alcohol and drug treatment programs in the Bay Area. I was prepared that if David didn't agree with my recommendations I would encourage him to call the directors of the treatment programs and schedule a second consultation. In effect, by implicitly challenging David to prove me wrong, I would actually invite Coyote into the room.

At the beginning of the next joint session, I described what I had learned in the individual sessions with David and Sharon. Initially, David's attention wandered but when I described Sharon's upbringing and how seriously Sharon was considering divorce as an alternative if things didn't change, he looked pensive.

When I summarized what I had learned from David, I mentioned my concern that he might be self-medicating other problems, though I was purposely not specific. I was extremely careful to use his exact words. I described his "low points," and his use of alcohol, cocaine, and amphetamines. I reminded him that he mentioned he thought he might have a problem and added, "even though you feel you have it under control."

I indicated that, since Sharon was attending Twelve-Step groups and was in individual therapy, if David entered treatment for his possible alcohol and drug problems, I believed their relationship had a much better chance.

I was struggling to keep my statements simple and to the point. Part of me wanted to go on and on chronicling the details I had learned from the individual sessions. I wanted to elaborate on the details of Sharon's fears. I wanted to list the details of David's history. But I kept it to a minimum of three key points. I reminded David of the effects his alcohol and drug use was having on his body, his work, and his relationship with his wife. Then I asked them if they had any comments and waited. After a long pause Sharon spoke up.

"I guess that pretty much says it," Sharon said sheepishly, "although I didn't know about the cocaine, it certainly makes sense given the way David's been acting lately."

David looked furious. His face reddened, his breathing deepened, and he stared at me intensely. He said he absolutely disagreed with my assessment. He said I blew things way out of proportion, then, emphasizing his disappointment, he added, "especially since you had come so highly recommended."

I was surprised, not at David's obvious disappointment, but at the way in which he was able to contain himself. I reminded myself of my own countertransference and took a deep breath.

Then before I could relax, shifting in his chair, clenching his hands into a fist, David repeated himself and threatened to talk with the director of the clinic "to tell him what a poor staff he has working for him."

I took another deep breath and very calmly I told David that he was welcome to talk to the director if he felt the need. I then changed the subject and asked both David and Sharon if they wanted to know what my recommendations were.

Sharon inched to the edge of her chair while David gathered his briefcase, ready to leave. I handed each of them a copy of the list I had made and described each item in detail. I invited them to call me back once David entered treatment. I suggested that afterward we might schedule another consultation to decide where to go from there. Then, casually, as if I didn't really mean it, I suggested that they could call anyone on the list for a second opinion if they weren't sure about my advice. And I wished them well.

Intentionally I reached out to shake David's hand first but he refused. He growled and stormed out of my office. I turned to Sharon.

"I'm really sorry about this," she said and she thanked me for my help.

We shook hands and I reminded her that she wasn't responsible for her husband's actions.

"Oh, I guess you're right," she said, and handed me a check for the consultation, thanked me for my help, and left.

As I sat in my chair reflecting on whether I'd chosen the right intervention, I had a strange feeling. With only a vague intention of my actions, I walked across the hall and asked Stacey, the clinic secretary, if during her lunch break she might deposit the payment for the session. She looked at me with an odd glance but said she didn't mind. She had to run some errands anyway.

An hour later Stacey knocked on my office door and told me that the check had already been stopped!

"Ah, Coyote!" I thought. "You got the better of me once again."

I took a moment to think about the four sessions I had with David and Sharon. I wondered whether I had taken the right approach. I wondered if I should have just continued to see David and Sharon without being so direct. And then I remembered so many of the couples I had seen and heard about from colleagues where the therapy seemed to go nowhere until the alcohol and drug use was addressed first. I remembered my concern for Sharon and her thoughts of having children. And I remembered that I had given David an out. If he went for a second opinion and my recommendations were seen as unnecessary, there would be little lost.

Finally, I resigned myself to the knowledge that at least one more person had confronted David and his alcohol and drug problem, that in the short time we worked together Sharon felt validated in her concerns, and, even if he rejected my recommendations, David had heard a summary of what he undoubtedly had minimized, rationalized, and compartmentalized for a long, long time.

A week later, I received a letter from David. As if to put salt in the wound, David outlined his intention to report me to the Board of Behavioral Science Examiners for failing to treat him and Sharon. He wrote that he was "disappointed in" me. After all, he was "someone important, and should've been treated like it." I "must have some kind of deficit in my training" if I couldn't recognize his "keen insight into the nature of Sharon's problems."

I thought about David's self-centeredness and how his narcissistic character defense protected him against the way in which I had wounded his fragile self-image by seeing him as less than perfect. I acknowledged that if I had treated David more carefully, more specially, I might have not aroused his rage. And yet, even in second-guessing myself, I felt I responded well. And I still wondered if I had done the right thing. More than a little anxious about his threat, I phoned the attorney for the California Association of Marriage and Family Therapists, my professional association, just in case. He encouraged me to relax. It was a clinical matter, not a legal one.

COYOTE'S FALSE COLORS

Late one afternoon, when he was out looking for food, Coyote came across Old Woodpecker, who lived in a hollow tree with his wife and children.

"How are you today, Coyote?" Old Woodpecker asked, as he ruffled his feathers

"I am fine, Old Woodpecker," Coyote said, and they talked pleasantly for a while. Because he wanted to seem generous, even though he had not caught anything fresh that day, Coyote invited Old Woodpecker and his family for dinner.

"Thank you, Coyote," Woodpecker said, and they parted.

When the sun set that night Old Woodpecker, his wife, and his children came to visit the Coyotes. As they came to rest in front of Coyote's lodge, they shook their wings this way and that and showed their beautiful red and yellow wing feathers. Badger Woman, Coyote's wife, cooked a wonderful meal for their guests and out of respect the Woodpeckers praised their hosts. When it came time to leave, they thanked the Coyotes and in return invited them to supper at their tree the following night.

Coyote is always envious of others and so he brooded for some time after the Woodpeckers were gone.

"Those Woodpeckers," he said to Badger Woman, "did you see how they show off their bright feathers?"

That night, coyote had an idea. The next day, with the wood his family gathered from the forest, Coyote built a great fire. The fire began to die just as the sun was setting. Coyote called his wife and children.

"Stand with your arms up," he commanded, "So I can tie these glowing sticks underneath your arms. There," he said admiring his handiwork. "Now we are just as handsome as the woodpeckers."

And as they walked to visit the Woodpeckers, Coyote instructed his family to lift their arms every so often to show off the bright coals underneath. But when they sat down to supper inside of Old Woodpecker's tree, one of Coyote's children was burned from the heat and whimpered.

"Sshhhh," Coyote scolded, "I don't cry."

"Wuwuuu," wept another when the fire at the end of his sticks went out.

Coyote snapped at his pup. "Be quiet."

"Coyote," asked Old Woodpecker, "why do your colors look so bright but then fade and become dark?"

"Because we are special," Coyote replied, not knowing what else to say. ". . . uh, our colors change as the night wears on."

But very quickly, the coyotes became so uncomfortable that they made an excuse and left.

When they were finally gone, Old Woodpecker laughed and told his wife and children, "Never try to appear like more than you really are. Coyote wants to be like others, but he never can. He is still Coyote."

And that is how it happened that his vanity brought them all to shame.

David and Sharon's story, at least this chapter of it, had an interesting ending. A month later I received another letter from David. This one, however, was conciliatory and gracious. David described how he went for a second opinion to bolster his complaint to the BBSE, and when the director of the program confirmed my diagnosis and recommended immediate detoxification followed by a 28-day inpatient hospital stay, David admitted himself on the spot. In the letter, David thanked me for standing up to him and enclosed a check for the previous consultation. The postscript on the letter said, "twenty-eight days sober."

With the aid of the Diagnostic Framework, a psychotherapist or counselor can determine not only the basic question of whether abuse or dependence is present but illustrate a comprehensive picture of the individual's relationship to alcohol and drugs both currently and historically. Throughout the assessment process, the Diagnostic Framework can serve both as a conceptual and mnemonic reference to help gather information. It can be used in a structured interview with a predetermined list of questions, in an unstructured interview, or as a teaching tool for graduate students, therapists, and drug and alcohol counselors.

FIGURE 4–1 Diagnostic Checklist

Section I   Drugs of Choice:
- ☐ Narcotics
- ☐ Stimulants
- ☐ Depressants
- ☐ Hallucinogens

Section II   Stage of the Disease:

Problems in Living:
- ☐ Financial
- ☐ Legal
- ☐ Occupational
- ☐ Social

Physical Effects:
- ☐ Damage
  (Acute/Chronic)
- ☐ Risk
- ☐ Tolerance
- ☐ Withdrawal

Psychological Effects:
- ☐ Loss of Control/Abstain
- ☐ Use to Regulate Affect
- ☐ Denial

Problematic Use
- ☐ Any criteria (to the left) for a
  period of at least one month

Early Stage
- ☐ Initial Loss: Control/Abstain
- ☐ Tolerance (no Withdrawal)
- ☐ Psychological Reliance:
  Progression > Daily Use

Middle Stage
- ☐ Physical Effects: Acute/Chronic
- ☐ Tolerance (no/minor Withdrawal)
- ☐ Daily Use and/or Bingeing
- ☐ Significant Loss: Control/Abstain

Late Stage
- ☐ Physical Damage: Acute/Chronic
- ☐ High Tolerance/Reverse Tolerance
- ☐ Extreme Loss: Control/Abstain

Section III   Status: ☐ Using ☐ Controlled Use ☐ Abstinent ☐ In Recovery

Section IV   Special Features:
- ☐ Longest Period of Sobriety
- ☐ Dual Diagnosis
- ☐ Prescription Medication
- ☐ Dealing
- ☐ Suicide
- ☐ DUI, DWI
- ☐ Other Compulsions

- ☐ Familial History of CD
- ☐ Medical Evaluation
- ☐ Age of Onset
- ☐ History of Violence
- ☐ Previous Overdoses
- ☐ Route of Administration

❖ C H A P T E R 5 ❖

Listening, Seeing, and Knowing When to Act

LISTENING

Listening in psychotherapy is the art of paying attention. It means paying attention to the sound of a patient's voice, the words, their timbre, and their tone. Attentive, we listen for the voice of a patient's heart and soul. We take in explicit information and we absorb, almost alchemically, the embedded poetry we hear. We compare their speech, their feeling, and their memories to our own personal experiences and eventually, if we listen closely enough, we may hear the voices emerging from the depths of our personal unconscious as well. We remember the voices from own childhood. And we remember and feel the pain from our past.

Listening, we might remember that a patient used the same tone when she described a previous event in her life that later revealed a depth of feeling and pain. Our awareness and associations alert us to the possibility that what we've just heard is the tip of the iceberg. So we wait and let the story unfold. Or is the falling tone at the end of the sentence a cue to ask another question? Is the pause or the silence an invitation to enter an internal world? Or does it imply a withdrawal from the previous, evocative statement? With each patient, the meaning behind the sound and the silence may be different. The cues may change over time. But the listening is the same, open and aware.

Listening also involves paying attention to the narrative of an unfolding story. Initially, this may involve not quite hearing the words, but the cadence and the flow of the sounds. We hear the sound roll off a patient's tongue with an even measure. We hear it shoot out like a cannon, forceful and impatient. We hear the need to expel the story, the pain, and the toxic memory. We hear the pressure behind each emphatic phrase. We hear the sound of the tongue pressing hard on the initial vowel or consonant of the first word. We hear a word begin with a bang, loft in midair for a moment, and land with the power of the patient's genuine feeling. We may also hear our patients speak in a foreign metaphoric language filled with unfamiliar phrases, oblivious to whether or not we understand, hoping we do and perhaps hoping we don't, or both. Sometimes, if we listen carefully we might remember to ask, "Excuse me, what did you mean by the phrase, 'I went into another space'?"

THE EAR OF CONSCIOUSNESS

When we listen, we also pay attention to the choice of words, to the vocabulary, and to the way a specific harshness of the moment is conveyed. We listen to the chaos of confusion, the smell of fear, and the pain of a wounded heart. We hear the attempt to minimize an affective state with words like "it hurt a bit" when you can practically see the emotional blood flowing on the floor before you. We may hear an overstated incident described as "the worst moment of my life" when the same phrase was previously used to describe a bad hair day.

Listening in this way involves less of a conscious, active mind and more of listening with the heart. Rather than listening to a symphony note by note, we pay attention to the wave of feeling that builds as instruments and emotions surge together until a great crescendo removes all restraint. Listening in this way may lead to hearing less of the narrative content of your patient's story and more of the hidden vulnerability, pain, or rage beneath the surface. Listening in this way involves attending to nothing in particular so as not to hold one's awareness too firmly and restrict the flow of images that link our unconscious with another's in the world of the symbolic. We begin to hear the texture beneath the words provoking memories not quite personal, and we may see images from a shared past, inaccessible through directed inquiry.

Listening to recovering alcoholics and addicts in psychotherapy demands the same openness as with all psychotherapy patients, but too much openness around Coyote carries a risk. Working with re- covering alcoholics and addicts with several years of sobriety may require a modest degree of vigilance because Coyote may be lurking about, but in the midst of the patient struggling to find sobriety a therapist must remain alert, because Coyote is generally running the show.

MARGIE

When Margie left a phone message on my answering machine late one Friday evening, her ambivalence about beginning therapy was more than obvious.

"Hi! This is Margie ———," she said, as if she were taping her own an- swering machine message. "I think I'd like to come in and see you sometime next week. I guess you probably won't get this message until Monday."

I looked at the clock. It was 9:00 A.M. Saturday morning. I had a patient in a crisis that week and caught Margie's message by chance. I always respond after I check my messages; I never sit on them and call at a later time. So I made the decision to call Margie.

"Someone said I should give you a call," her message went on, "but I'm pretty busy next week." Then she left her number.

"Two-thirty-two A.M." The machine toned in its mechanically feminine voice.

I picked up the phone and dialed Margie's number.

"Huh?" Margie said, clearly asleep. "Who is this?"

I guess I could have called a bit later, I thought. Hearing the irrita- tion in her voice I realized I might have been acting out my mischie- vousness. I might have reacted to her ambivalent interest in beginning therapy that she had revealed by both calling me and telling me that she probably wouldn't be available. I quickly realized I might have been challenging Margie's interest in therapy too early and hoped my mistake hadn't already blown it. So I introduced myself politely and offered to call back later.

"No," she said, shuffling what I imagined were sheets.

I heard a loud bang and imagined that she had dropped the phone.

"Are you still there?"

I answered.

"Someone said I should call you and schedule an appointment."

I told Margie that I had a ten o'clock opening on Monday but I was silently concerned that, given that she might have just woken up, she might not remember our conversation.

"That early?"

"I might be able to make a two or three o'clock appointment on Thursday," I added, but she cut me off by saying, "That won't work for me. I guess I'll see you on Monday." And she hung up without asking me where my office was.

When I checked my messages that afternoon there was a message from Margie.

"Hello, Mr. Rutzky? Could you leave a message for me at home with your address? We spoke this morning. I guess I didn't write down your address."

At ten o'clock Monday morning, as I approached the waiting room to my office, I saw a middle-aged woman who dressed more like a teenager. She wore an oversized black Rolling Stones sweatshirt and torn black jeans that revealed a pair of pale knees. Her hair, pulled into a braid on one side of her head, flowed wildly on the other. Dark rings of heavily applied mascara gave her eyes the worn look of war ravished women pictured in *Life* Magazine.

After taking a few seconds to realize I was standing in the doorway, Margie jumped up with a bright, though clearly social smile, and in a completely dissonant professional tone introduced herself.

"I'm Margie, Margie ——," she said in a professionally firm voice that contrasted with her attire. We shook hands and I gestured to my office.

Stepping into the middle of the room, Margie scanned the sitting options, recognized my chair opposite the couch, my datebook and cup on the table beside the chair, and sat down in the middle of the couch with a poise that reminded me of women who took ballet lessons as a child.

"I'm not really here on my own account," Margie said, looking down, then up at me, and then off past my eyes to the view outside the window and the woods behind my office. "You see, my husband got a DUI last week after we had dinner at Ramona's. You know, it's the Italian place south of the city? Anyway, he's the one who should probably be here since he got the ticket. He has a court date next month. I don't know why I'm the one who came."

I heard a fragile, almost hollow confidence in Margie's voice. Her attempt to deflect the responsibility of her situation piqued my awareness and I could have sworn I saw a little black nose poking out from behind Margie's overpermed, henna-colored hair. But even at this moment, I was skeptical of my tendency to find Coyote making his presence known. For all I knew at this point, Margie was coming to see me for her concern about her husband's drinking.

"Can you tell me what happened?"

"Well, we had a lot to drink that night," she admitted.

I nodded and as she spoke I studied what looked like strategically torn holes in her jeans and the worn-out look of her hastily applied makeup. Initially, I guessed Margie was in her late thirties but, when I remembered that time can pass quickly on the faces of alcoholics and addicts, I gauged downward when I saw the multiple rings on her fingers and the silver hoops along the delicate curve of her left ear.

"Don, that's my husband, he had more to drink than I did."

And I thought to myself, *Yes. I do see you, Coyote.*

In the newly sober patient, Coyote is mischievous but not necessarily the dominant voice in an alcoholic or addict's conscious or unconscious motivations. When an individual is still drinking and using, I often see Coyote on the floor near the couch. Every now and then I see his tale flitting when a fly lights, his ears alert to an opportunity to make mischief in the session.

Several weeks into therapy Margie trounced into my office, flopped down on the couch opposite my chair, and asked, "Do you mind?" and impishly removed her brightly colored sandals. The professional persona she projected briefly in the first session evaporated and it seemed as if a little girl joined us in the room.

I smiled and nodded, though it was her routine to make herself comfortable in this way after six weeks of therapy twice a week.

"Well," Margie said proudly. "It's been a whole week since I had anything to drink."

My eyebrows involuntarily rose a bit and I smiled. A tentative "Wow!" rolled off my lips and I shared her enthusiasm cautiously.

"Yep. A whole week."

"Nothing?" I asked, trying to express my genuine inquisitiveness and not a challenge or a lack of confidence in her.

"Well, on Friday I had a hard day." And she brought me up to date on the ups and downs of her life. Margie's husband, having received his second DUI, was eligible for the last chance drunk school. His unusually astute attorney, while suggesting he immediately enroll in a local outpatient program, also had the sensitivity, knowing Margie and Don for many years, to suggest she see a therapist to examine her own relationship to alcohol, though she had been exempted from any legal sanctions.

"On Friday, I got home from work at about six. Don was at his court-ordered AA meeting. Anyway, I was up for a promotion last month and got passed over. I kind of expected it, given how irregular my work had been 'cause of my boozing. But I was still bummed."

I nodded as if to say, "Sure, who wouldn't?" and was pleased at how quickly Margie embraced an awareness of how her drinking led to a variety of problems in her life.

"I don't remember driving home from work. I don't even remember parking the car in the driveway, and before I knew it I was standing in front of the liquor cabinet."

I was shocked at my lack of thoroughness and realized I must have neglected to suggest that together they empty the house of alcohol. For two people trying to get sober, keeping any amount of alcohol in the house is asking for trouble.

"I'd poured the first drink and had just taken a sip when I realized what I was about to do," she said proudly, believing that she had re-frained from drinking. From her point of view she had, though from mine I could hear Coyote scratching at the door, whimpering, asking me to believe that a sip wasn't really drinking. It was just a sip. And she didn't really do it consciously, so maybe we could still count her sobriety from a week ago and let it slide.

I decided to remember the incident for a later discussion, not want-ing to burst Margie's balloon. She was proud of her restraint. But I also didn't want to accept her naive conception of what it meant to stop drinking. The fear running through my mind was, if I didn't comment at some point, she might find herself in front of another drink and Coyote would tell her that "a sip isn't really drinking. It's just a sip."

When a recovering alcoholic and addict has been sober for several years, Coyote is often patient, waiting for a time when a complex combination of conflicting desires fogs the recovering alcoholic and addict's vision, muffles the growing inner voice of the self, and leaps forward at a vulnerable time, making life once again exciting, chaotic, and ultimately painful.

"You know, the funniest thing happened," Margie said, after three years into therapy, a year of divorce from her husband, and a week less of sobriety due to her earlier sip. "I've been going to my regular meeting for about two years now, got my sponsor, you know, Selene, I've mentioned her, and I'm working the steps for a second time since the divorce. But last week, you remember, I told you I was going to be out of town on business?"

I noticed the way Margie appeared unusually excited. Her voice was alive and buoyant compared to the first few weeks of her treatment when she practically dragged herself into my office only to burst into tears about the state of her marriage, her job, and her inability to stop drinking.

"Well, last week I was staying in the Hilton near the airport. The convention was there. So after my presentation, it went great by the way, thank you."

I smiled and imagined the contrasting ways in which Margie could present herself. There was the little girl who bounced into my office all excited and alive. There was the old woman who practically needed a walker to help her carry the burden of her depression, her sadness, and the weight of her alcoholic history, and there was the professional saleswoman who dressed in stylish business suits and a complete inventory of silk blouses that matched a large selection of exquisite shoes.

"I was having dinner with Dave, you remember I told you about him, he's in the Program."

I didn't remember the convention but found an image in my mind that I had created of her friend. Dave was a tremendous support for

Margie in the early stages of her sobriety. He was her buddy from work and a rare support in the alcohol- and drug-charged world of Silicon Valley computer sales. He was in his mid-thirties, a recovering cocaine addict, and was currently training to run ultra-marathons.

"Dave's the one with five years under his belt. Anyway . . . "

I saw an image of a man in his mid-thirties, still thin from his years of cocaine and an obsession with running.

"We were having dinner at a table next to the bar. I had scampi and a crab salad with a Perrier. He had a steak and grapefruit juice. Anyway, this really cute guy walked over, introduced himself as a rep from another company at the convention. I was hardly paying attention and then he shook my hand. It was like a lightning bolt shot through my body," Margie said. And as if recalling the moment, her face flushed a bright red that curiously matched not only the current hue of her henna-red hair but her blouse and shoes as well.

"I feel embarrassed telling you this," she said blushing again and she waited for a sign of my judgment or lack of it.

I smiled. She accepted my offer and went on.

"I came," she said. "I had an orgasm right there in the restaurant. All he did was touch me." And she shuddered. "I was speechless. I couldn't get a word out. I know I flushed because I felt a drop of sweat trickle down my side. It was like a flash. It was fantastic and at the same time it scared the shit out of me. Dave saw something was up and I guess he said something to John. I guess that's his name. Anyway, he walked off. And the scariest thought came into my mind as if it was the most natural thing in the world. *Order a double gin and tonic.*"

Years into the recovering alcoholic or addict's sobriety, I often find myself wanting to believe everything is stable so we can get on to the real work of the psyche. This desire, confusion, and delusion of mine often distracts me from a need to be vigilant to the sound of Coyote's footsteps. When I fall asleep to Coyote's mischievousness and get lost in some therapeutic reverie about an important symbol in Margie's dreams, Coyote's plaintive wail signals a phone call that tells me, as in Margie's case, that she's feeling much better and wants to reschedule her Friday appointment. She says she wants to go out of town for the weekend. Alert, I wonder if underneath her wish to reschedule, her need to go out of town on business or take a vacation, Coyote is saying, "Margie, I want to go out of town to drink." Or he might say its symbolic equivalent in regard to shopping, food, sex, gambling, or anything that involves a move toward relinquishing the burden of remaining conscious and sober.

I listened carefully when, recovering from the painful breakup of her marriage, Margie tried to reassure me that the man she met one morning was just a friend, nothing deep. She tried to comfort my expressed concern by saying, "I know I'm not ready for a relationship." Only later did I learn, not hearing Coyote clear enough, that Margie failed to mention that she had a date scheduled that night. She promised herself, and later tried to convince me, that she intended to go to a meeting the next day because "What's missing one meeting?" Only she missed more than one because she ended up at his place for the entire weekend. "Wuwuuuuuuuuuuuu!" Coyote sings, reveling in his mischieviousness.

Listening this carefully involves paying attention not so much to what the alcoholic says but to *what is not said*. It means being respectful. It means listening for the half-truth, the half-lie, or the silence in Coyote's grin. It means thinking, *Ah, yes. I see you*, then saying to the recovering alcoholic or addict, "Excuse me. Let's go over what you just said. I feel like I missed something."

THE EYE OF CONSCIOUSNESS

In the practice of psychotherapy, listening carefully can lead to an experience of almost seeing the gaps in what a patient says and can lead to an experience of almost seeing Coyote in the room. When a hole in an alcoholic or addict's logic opens up before me, I sometimes see Coyote put his spin on it. He tries to make me believe that it's only an inch deep. It was "only a platonic relationship," Margie said six months into sobriety when the passion of sex and love risked derailing her sobriety. I didn't quite catch her denial when she said it was the first time, but by the end of the session I realized I had to find a way to talk about it. I waited for an opening but when she failed to return to the subject I asked her whether this was the best time to begin a new relationship.

"Listen to what I am saying," Coyote said from behind the couch, "Don't look at the hole in her logic. I told you it's only an inch deep. Trust me."

Whenever Coyote says trust me, I shock myself into paying attention!

"But it's only one date," Margie said.

Right. But didn't she say just a moment ago it was only a platonic relationship?

Looking for the hole in Coyote's logic means not accepting his worldview when he says, "You don't need to ask me the question on the tip of your tongue," and asking the question anyway. Whenever I feel hesitant to ask a question and feel that I might somehow be disrespectful or intrusive by asking an alcoholic or addict to explain something, I know I've lost my balance. If I'm lucky, aware, and sensitive to my own countertransference, I may find my balance by saying, "Do you remember a moment ago when I asked you if you had anything to drink this week and you said, "Not really"? Could you tell me what 'not really' means?" Listening for the sound of Coyote smacking his lips, watching for his appearance, means balancing respect with an ignorant willingness to seek clarity. It means respecting Coyote, not catching him.

Listening in this way means seeing alcoholics and addicts as they are, not as they seem to be, tell you they are, or would lead you to believe they are. It means seeing the craziness in Margie's logic of entering "a platonic relationship" at such a vulnerable time in her sobriety. It means seeing the craziness in attending a party with her old drinking girlfriends the weekend of the Super Bowl and bringing a six-pack for "everyone else." It means seeing Coyote poke his nose into the room when she says, "I think I might cut back on my therapy now," just a week after she had a dream about drinking again. It means recognizing the fissure in her logic when she overschedules a business weekend and cancels therapy and her regular AA meetings in order to feel needed at work, conveniently placing her recently acquired humility on the back burner.

So the question arises: What do you do with all this listening and seeing? Where does it lead? In times other than emergent crises, the very presence of the therapist, the occasional question and comment, is often enough to help the alcoholic and addict develop a relationship to sobriety, a Higher Power, and the self. This may be true to some extent with the alcoholic or addict years into her recovery but it is rarely true for the patient struggling to achieve sobriety, newly sober or a year or two into treatment. A therapist must be constantly vigilant when Coyote is running the show because he will try to override any new-found clarity. A therapist must know when to point out the smell of his fur in the wind, the sound of his footsteps, or his very presence in the room. Pointing out Coyote's presence can be done implicitly by acknowledging the mischievousness in a patient's tone, plan, or comment. Occasionally, I may even evoke Coyote by interpreting a patient's behavior with his image. On occasion I have even been known to tell a story of his escapades to bring a conflict to light.

As therapists working with alcoholics and addicts we must constantly gauge the necessity of letting Coyote talk a bit more in order to fully explain his strange logic (or lack of it) in relation to sobriety. It means listening for the relatedness (or lack of it) when alcoholics and addicts talk about their sponsors, the Program, therapy, their friends, and their families. Whether consciously or unconsciously, through intuition or volition, as therapists we must choose either to remain silent or to act. In acting we must present another view of reality different from Coyote's. As therapists we must be the eyes, ears, and voice of the struggle toward consciousness when a patient listens to or is under the influence of Coyote. When Coyote says, "Nothing bad will come of this. In fact, I see it as a good thing that I don't need to go to so many meetings. I feel like I'd like to start reaching out to people who aren't in the Program," we must ask, "What does that mean? Just what is it that you find missing?" Because what Coyote is often saying is, "I'd like some excitement. These AA people are boring. I'm tired of always being conscious. It's so rigid, so dull. Let's shake things up again." We can call Coyote out and ask, "What thoughts or feelings might be underneath your plan to cut down on meetings?"

Knowing when to keep silent and when to say something has always been a difficult problem of mine. In the infancy of my training, during the first ten years of private practice, I found myself talking a great deal in order to justify my presence, my fee, and my need to be needed. Unconsciously, I feared that if I didn't prove myself with fancy interpretations, good advice, or comments, I would be seen as a charlatan. Like the man behind the curtain in *The Wizard of Oz*, I failed to realize that I had something of real value to offer my patient and that I did not need magic. The balloon, the fire, and the flash may have inspired awe and fear in the land of Oz, but the magic created distance and was ultimately a sham. In the midst of the struggle to find one's therapeutic voice, the question remains, when do we intervene? When do we say, "Wait a minute," and confront the alcoholic and addict in therapy?

Listening to an addict or alcoholic, I often find myself trying guess what Coyote's game is. Is the game, "I don't want to work. It's hard to feel pain," when a patient says that everything is going fine? Empathizing with the difficulty of the struggle to remain aware of one's pain and consciousness, I may simply nod and acknowledge how hard it is. I may ask if Margie would like to have another session, given how difficult things are this week. I may suggest that she take in another meeting and talk about how difficult it is to stay honest and aware.

Or is Coyote's game, "I'm going to tell you that things are all right but what's really going on is that I'm going to have a drink"? In situations like this we must look beneath the surface, encourage self-honesty, and call Coyote out of hiding. We must remind a patient respectfully, "Wasn't this the same sort of thing you were talking about when you almost drank last week?" and not let it go when the response is, "No, this is different. I'm not thinking about drinking." Right. Of course, if it happens anyway, if the drink begins with lust and ends with a hangover, at least we have a reference point, not to say, "I told you so," but to remember what preceded the slippery fall into a relapse.

POINTING TO REALITY

Knowing when to act means questioning Coyote's way of thinking, his way of acting, and then saying, "Something doesn't sound right about this," without being condescending, angry, or punitive. It means asking Margie, "If you were someone's sponsor who just told you what you've told me, what would you think?" It means asking, "If there was something going on underneath what you've told me, what do you think it might be?" Or it might involve stating outright, "I'm really concerned about what I hear. I wonder if underneath what we're talking about there might be another agenda." It means looking inside and asking, "Are you sure this is such a good idea?"

COYOTE AND GRANDFATHER ROCK

One day Coyote was out wandering in search of food. It had been a long time since he had something to eat and his ribs poked out from his hide. Tired and weak, Coyote crawled to the top of a big hill and saw a huge rock. Coyote knew that rocks are the oldest living things worthy of respect and, with his hunger defeating him, he took out his fine flint knife and said, "Grandfather Rock, I give you this fine flint knife. Please help me find some food. I am so hungry."

Coyote waited but nothing happened. He waited a bit more. Nothing happened even more. He got bored. He watched the flies buzzing around the grass and he saw the clouds floating overhead but still he was hungry. He forgot about Grandfather Rock and went over the top of the next hill. Looking down into the next valley, at the bottom of the hill, he saw a freshly killed buffalo.

"I have such fine eyes," Coyote said boasting to himself, "I am the one who spotted this buffalo and I will tell everyone how bravely I fought and killed it . . . but how can I butcher this buffalo without a knife?"

Coyote remembered how he offered Grandfather Rock his knife and without a second thought he ran up the hill, took the knife, and ran down the hill, licking his lips in anticipation. But when he got to where he had seen the buffalo only the dusty bones of a buffalo killed ages ago remained.

"Where is *my buffalo!*" Coyote shouted, and throwing down his knife, he stamped his feet and ran in a circle looking for his meal. Then he heard something that made his stomach forget how hungry he was. A rumbling sound rose up from the ground, through the pads of his feet and into the hollow of his stomach. He turned toward the sound and saw Grandfather Rock rolling down the hill after him.

"GA-DA-RUM, GA-DA-RUM, GA-DA-RUM," Grandfather Rock said as he rolled down the hillside.

Terrified, Coyote ran across the valley until he came to a bear den hollowed out underneath a hillock..

"Help me, Brother Bear," he called.

The bears poked out from their den and saw Grandfather Rock chasing Coyote.

"Grandfather Rock deserves respect," the bears said. "You must have done something to make him angry."

"No, I didn't," Coyote lied, and he cursed the bears.

Coyote ran across the valley until he came to a cave where the mountain lions lived and he called out again.

"Help me," Coyote panted. He was almost out of breath.

The mountain lions peered out from their cave, saw who was after Coyote, and said, "We can't help you against Grandfather Rock. You must have done something to anger the Old One."

Coyote kept running, though he was slowing down, and he called out to an enormous bull buffalo grazing just ahead of him.

"Help me," Coyote cried, "I don't know why but Grandfather Rock is angry at me." Buffalos are often sympathetic animals and, turning around, it stepped in front of the great boulder. But Grandfather Rock was so big and moving so fast that he smacked the buffalo hard, pushing his head into his shoulders and bouncing him over to the next hill. And that's why, to this day, buffalos have no neck.

By now Coyote was limping. Spying a nighthawk overhead, breathless, he called out. "Brother Nighthawk, I was talking to Grandfather Rock and he said you have a small beak, your eyes are too big, and you are ugly. But I said that you are handsome. When I spoke up for you he started to chase me."

Hearing Coyote's tale, Nighthawk became angry and called out to his brothers. Suddenly the sky was filled with nighthawks. One by one they swooped down from the sky and pecked a pebble from Grandfather Rock until, slowly, all that was left was a pile of pebbles on the ground.

Coyote turned and seeing that he was out of danger he could not restrain himself. "Ha, ha, ha!" Coyote mocked, trying to catch his breath. "Grandfather Rock didn't say that you were ugly. I, Coyote, am saying it now. You nighthawks are ugly birds. You have small beaks and your eyes are too big." And laughing he started off toward the next hillside.

The nighthawks were furious at being tricked, let alone having attacked someone as old as Grandfather Rock, and together they swooped down to where all the pebbles lay and fanned their magic wings. They kicked up a cloud of dust and when they flew away there he was in all his power . . . Grandfather Rock.

But by the time Coyote heard the sound, it was too late.

Frequently, a Coyote story begins with an understandable or almost spiritual aim. In this case, Coyote wants to relieve himself of his hunger and suffering. But as he moves along, his mischievous nature surfaces and ultimately brings about his destruction. A therapist listening to the alcoholic or addict can hear the gesture of supplication, the request for help from a Higher Power, from a friend, from a therapist, or anyone to relieve the pain, even if it means avoiding it entirely or passing it onto someone else. But when help arrives, Coyote has difficulty accepting it with humility. He must own it, possess it, and ultimately believes that his windfall is a result of his own skill and cleverness. At this point, a therapist listening to the alcoholic or addict in psychotherapy will begin to see a familiar pattern in the form of the alcoholic's arrogance and self-centeredness.

Just as I was about to greet her in the waiting room, Margie burst into my office. Until that moment she had always waited for me to greet her in the waiting room.

"I'm running late today and have to work all night for this project at work," she said, presenting me with a check for the session already made out. Her briefcase was filled to the point of overflowing. She wore a stylish gray business suit jacket and skirt. Her rings were absent and her makeup was impeccable. Rather than pulling her feet up onto the couch like she usually did, Margie launched into her agenda for the session.

"First of all, I have to leave about fifteen minutes early today. I've got this report due next week and I want to get a head start on it."

I felt my toes curl inside my shoes as Margie announced how the session would proceed. While it was true that she made a difficult choice scheduling a meeting right after her therapy, it felt as if she was trying to control the session in order not to be ruffled emotionally. It felt like she was saying, "Let's get to work but let's not go into anything I can't handle 'cause I'm busy."

"I've got an appointment with a Program friend who wants me to sponsor her. Then at seven I'm supposed to meet Don to talk about our post-divorce relationship. Then by nine I've got to get back to the office."

STEPPING IN AND ACTING

At such a moment, we have an opportunity to ask Coyote one or more of the following questions. We can ask, "What is going on here? What is going on underneath your rush, your sense of self-importance, and your 'let's get on with it' attitude? Tell me, where did last week's humility go? What happened to the woman who admitted she was powerless over people, places, and things? Where did this pride come from all of a sudden?"

A second opportunity presented itself when Coyote tried to take back his beautiful flint knife. The alcoholic and addict may talk about having made a gesture of good will toward another, made amends to a friend or loved one, made a commitment to sobriety and the Program, or made an offering in the form of giving up a sense of pride and self-importance. In Margie's case, she acknowledged the value of her therapy and, although rarely, her therapist. Then in the next sentence, Coyote whispered, "Take it back."

"So I told Don I made a commitment to go with Sue to another meeting and it was too bad that it was his birthday, his real birthday not his sobriety birthday. I told him what my plan was. He agreed to meet on the weekend. Besides, Sue is only two days sober. I'm the only Program friend she has. He tried to make me feel guilty. So I told him I was the one with three years of sobriety and not him. I said if he was feeling so bad he should go to a meeting. I told him that if he wanted to feel better he should buckle down and work his program. I figured that since things were looking good for me, I shouldn't let him drag me down."

Coyote has the ironic ability to boast about his generosity and simultaneously describe the depth of his humility and selflessness. At one moment Margie could boldly declare that someone else could take over her responsibilities because she had more important things to do. After all, she was overextended and taking care of herself was important. She confronted me by questioning whether I disagreed that taking care of oneself was, in part, the cornerstone of sobriety. Once she even commented about how good therapy had been for her. Then half an hour before the next session she called and cancelled. The following week, after I reminded her of our agreement that without twenty-four hours notice I needed to charge for cancelled appointments, she was outraged.

We must watch for Coyote's constantly reemerging self-importance and his wasteland of narcissism. We can empathize with Coyote's energy and then question the way he tends to go back on his word.

We can question how slippery he is when he decides that other people can handle his problems without considering what impact his actions might have on others. We can use the opportunity to ask Coyote to consider, just for a moment, what possible outcomes taking back his offering to Grandfather Rock may have on himself and others. We can seize the opportunity to be the voice of reflection, of consciousness, of nonself-centeredness.

If we miss the initial tale or even the first incident, there are always other chances. Few moments such as these are single events unto themselves. Because Coyote takes his time getting into a fix, he will take his time in trying to extricate himself from it as well. Fleeing from Grandfather Rock, Coyote comes across the bears and asks for help. But he doesn't ask in order to face his problem. He wants someone else to get him out of a sticky situation.

A year before entering therapy, Margie hoped her lawyer would solve her DUI related legal problems, that her accountant would juggle the books, that she would find a way to fudge her job-mandated urine test by eating half a dozen poppyseed rolls and claim that the positive test for opioids was due to her ingesting pastries and not the Vicodin she "borrowed" from a friend.

Listening to Coyote's tale of woe we can begin to see a crack open up in the floor in front of us. We hear, "Let someone else get me out of this," and the fissure becomes a hole. When we act to explore or confront the situation, we can encourage the alcoholic and addict to own the difficulty and face the music. We can intervene and question the alcoholic and addict's version of the story by asking,

"Excuse me, Margie. A moment ago you told me that you made an amend to Don. Then you said that he yelled at you out of nowhere. Is it possible that you might have forgotten to tell me about something in between?"

Or a therapist can question the alcoholic's tactic directly by commenting,

"I understand you want me to call Don to tell him how hard you're working in therapy. Isn't that a bit slippery? Where is the honesty

you spoke about before? Where is the integrity that you wanted to develop—vowing to face the music of your past?"

If Coyote waits to tell you about his mishap until after the fact and then gloats about how clever he was, manipulating others to take care of his problem, listening to his pride, even his relief at having gotten off easily, we can point to the seeds of his self-importance. We can question the wisdom of the alcoholic and addict's short-term view of the situation. We can encourage them to think about the possible outcomes that may arise from manipulating, lying, and bending the truth to their own benefit. We can even ask how they feel about their integrity.

But the opportunity doesn't stop there. Even when alcoholics and addicts pick themselves up, limp into the office, wounded, black and blue, ego flattened, humiliated, and dejected, there is still an opportunity to invite a return to sobriety, clarity, and humility.

"I'm trying to be as honest with you as possible," Margie said between sobs, unabated tears, and running mascara.

"I thought I could handle the relationship," she said, sobbing again, then reached for another tissue to blow her nose.

I knew that in spite of our talking last week, in spite of her admission that calling up the man she met at the convention was a mistake, the memory of his touch had haunted her for months. She had easily succumbed, as many do, to the magic of sex and love in the absence of alcohol and drugs.

"I just couldn't get him out of my mind," she tried to explain. "It was like he was a drug," she said almost frantically.

"It's every bit as powerful," I said, trying not to say, "I told you so."

"It was. Every time I thought about him, I thought of drinking. But I called him up anyway. I was in town for another convention and he wasn't there. I don't remember a thing that happened that whole week. I didn't have dinner with Dave. I just waited in my room for him to call back. I paged him practically every hour. I ordered room service. I didn't even think to call my sponsor, someone in the program, or even you . . ."

"It would've been okay."

"I know. But I didn't want to bother you." She countered, immediately realizing the falsity of her statement. "Actually, I didn't want to call you. I didn't want to talk to anyone. I didn't want to be talked out of it."

"What happened?" I asked, inviting her to recount the misadventure and in the telling of her story bring light to her darkness, bring understanding to her insanity, and, ultimately, bring a fresh start to her sobriety.

"Well," she said, sniveling, "it started almost a year ago. Do you remember when I told you about . . ."

❖ C H A P T E R   6 ❖

Confronting the Alcoholic and Addict

WHY CONFRONT?

For most people, the word *confrontation* carries with it an uneasy feeling of both apprehension and danger. For the psychotherapist or drug counselor the word may evoke painful memories from a familiar and familial past. It may evoke the confusion of a life prior to sobriety, or it may arouse insecurities and anxieties buried deep inside a life of unresolved feelings and relationships. Yet, to be effective as a therapist, especially with alcoholics and addicts, it is necessary, at times, to step out of the role of the listener. It is necessary to hold a mirror up and challenge the insanity of a life mired in alcohol and drugs. It is necessary to say something if any progress is to be made in treatment. The passive therapist, waiting for the alcoholic to "get" it will grow old with patience. The tolerant therapist will have wasted time, energy, and money on someone who almost got it and become frustrated. The nurturing therapist, hoping the addict will heal through love, will end up drained, bitter, and resentful.

There are many reasons to avoid saying something when your patient mentions a need to cancel a Monday morning appointment because the weekend was "a bit much." You may want to keep silent when the latest alcohol or drug related job firing is recalled after a year of treatment. Perhaps you're apprehensive that asking a probing question might offend, provoke hostility, or invite denial. Or maybe you fear discussing a subject associated with a taboo, something that might provoke an emtional withdrawal and prematurely cut short any benefit received from therapy thus far. Or does the fear seep into your mind, the fear all therapists in private practice have, that a patient will terminate therapy and remove a substantial portion of your income?

If you've thought or felt any of the above, then you're like all the rest of us who are short of sainthood. The question is, once you feel the twinge in your stomach, the hairs on the back of your neck rise up, the muscles in your forearm stiffen as your hand tightens around the arm of your chair when your patient lets it slip that for some reason he can't remember how he got home last night, what do you do? Do you let it go? Do you wince at the confusion that numbs your clarity, at the memories that flood your mind and the sadness that rises up inside your chest? Do you remind yourself to schedule a session with a consultant to discuss the case in order to get feedback on how to proceed more effectively? Do you call your own therapist and schedule an appointment to work on your own countertransference reactions? Or do you do nothing and hope it will go away and correct itself?

The bottom line, whether you resist it or not, is that at some point you just have to say something. You can't wait and hope it will fix itself. You can't pretend you didn't hear it. When you get to the point of acting (because alcohol and drug problems don't just go away on their own) the question is, what do you say? How do you say it? And when do you say it?

The question of *when* is easy: sooner rather than later. Experience will help a therapist wait patiently for the moment to ask a question rather than leap too quickly. Calling out the specter of alcohol and drug problems like a fire-and-brimstone preacher rarely leads to a greater willingness to discuss things. The question of *how* may be as simple as questioning the logic of the patient describing an intention to cut down gradually but allow himself the opportunity to drink as much as he wants on the weekends or at parties. You can reframe how the patient's expressed "need" to drink stands oddly in contrast to his desire to be in control of his life. Or you might express concern, amazement, or comment directly on how crazy it sounds when the alcoholic and addict says in one moment how important his children and his wife are, but continues to drink and get drunk despite his wife's threat to divorce him and take the children. By questioning, reframing, expressing concern or amazement, or commenting as directly as possible, a therapist can step out from the sphere of an enabling silence and move to confront a patient's alcohol and drug use.

MICHAEL

A robust and tanned young man in his late twenties, Michael had been in therapy for over a year with only modest improvements in his mild depression, his feeling lost in his life, and his diffuse anxiety about his future. He kept his appointments on a weekly basis and appeared to benefit from talking about the many things that troubled him. On a particularly hot summer day, after opening my office window in a pathetic attempt to relieve the heat, I invited Michael into my office.

Falling limply into the large burgundy-colored couch in my office, Michael took a deep breath and lamented, "I don't know what to do, Jacques. Sheila's at it again."

I didn't know what Michael meant by "at it again," so I waited to hear the rest.

"She's really pissed this time!"

"What happened?" I asked, both curious and concerned. I really liked Michael. He was sensitive, bright, introverted like me, and he talked about the odd dream that bothered him every so often. Every couple of months he brought in a wood carving he made in the workshop behind his garage, and he was articulate and charming in a way that made being his therapist almost a bit too easy.

"Well," he said, looking down, "I came home from the new job site as usual and she was out," he said, pausing, "and as usual I lit up, laid back, and watched some TV. I think it was tennis on ESPN."

Though Michael had never described his den, in my mind I saw a large green corduroy couch. I saw a golden retriever by his feet, and I saw a pair of muddy workboots by the door. Aware that Michael had paused to catch his breath, I realized I didn't know what ESPN was but, not wanting to seem ignorant, I didn't ask. Then, when I remembered he said he "lit up," three images flashed in my mind in ascending order according to the degree to which they alarmed me. One of course was a cigarette, the second was a joint, and the third a crack pipe. Initially, as I thought about this last option, Michael didn't seem like a person to get hooked on crack, but I had long since learned that addiction didn't have "a look."

"About two hours must have gone by. When she finally got home from work I guess it was around six. I heard her car drive up and was excited to see her, but when she walked in the house all of a sudden she got furious. For nothing at all."

"Nothing?" I said, wondering what she'd seen and he hadn't. I saw a young woman's face framed by a long mane of straight blond hair, though I had never seen a picture of Michael's wife.

"Well," Michael admitted sheepishly, "I guess I forgot to do the laundry."

"Oh?" I said, wondering what else he had been avoiding telling me to make himself appear less Neanderthal.

"Last night it was my turn to do the dishes and they were still in the sink."

I nodded and waited, imagining a scene I myself had difficulty tolerating, especially given the summer's heat.

"And Max must've gotten into the garbage because it was all over the kitchen floor. I guess I didn't notice it when I went to the fridge for a beer."

"What else did she say?" I asked, probing for more information than the Cliff Notes Michael doled out so parsimoniously.

"She got on my case again about my pot smoking."

And I thought, "Oh shit! First the beer. Well that was only one. Or was it? Then the pot. What else did I miss?" And suddenly the pieces came together. His low-grade depression, lack of motivation, and loss of interest in his work were all symptoms of marijuana dependence combined with the depressant effect of alcohol. I had missed it all along. Then I wondered how I was going to handle the situation. I was concerned that if I confronted the issue of his pot smoking too strongly, Michael might get irritated, as he obviously was with his wife. Would he perceive that I was siding with her or would the fragile bond I thought we shared carry him through this?

DEFINING CONFRONTATION

A *confrontation* in the context of psychotherapy with alcoholics and addicts is defined as any interaction that helps an individual identify the direct or indirect effects of their behavior related to their alcohol and drug use and, in the process, clarifies their options. Experience and training can improve your chances of knowing when to keep silent and gather more information, when the timing is right to respond, and which of six types of confrontations to use.

In order for a therapist to maintain a sense of perspective when the moment arrives to say something and face alcohol and drug problems head on, several guidelines may be helpful. First, confrontation without compassion is almost always experienced as criticism. A patient who feels criticized will usually lump a therapist in with all the rest of the people who just don't understand the need to drink, smoke, or shoot up. As a result, the alcoholic and addict may defend, deny, attack, or distance himself from the comment, the therapist, and any further exploration of the subject.

Second, an effective confrontation always aligns with the alcoholic and addict's own concerns, and as a result the alcoholic and addict is more likely to relax rather than defend, retreat, or attack. Aligning with the alcoholic and addict's concerns means engaging in a reflective process on the nature of alcohol or drug use, its benefits, and the problems connected to even looking into the subject. It means acknowledging that while exploring the question of alcohol and drug use may cause discomfort, the benefits often outweigh the initial discomfort. The trick, and this is where the therapist's Coyote comes in, is to find a way of engaging in the exploration of the dark side of an addictive relationship to alcohol and drugs that is neutral though inquisitive, where the emphasis is not on the evil of drugs but on the cultivation of curiosity, awareness, and consciousness.

Third, the goal of a confrontation is to assist in the breakdown of denial, and increase an awareness of the patient's alcohol and drug use, their thoughts, their behavior, and the results of continuing on a path that revolves around alcohol and drugs. The goal is not to nail the alcoholic, or force the addict to see something. Coyote just runs away when forced, anyway. The goal is not to fulfill some unconscious countertransference need to punish the alcoholic or addict. The goal is to explore the way in which alcohol and drugs may buffer against pain, the vulnerability of intimacy, anxiety, stress, memories, fear, inhibition, or self-criticism.

Fourth, an effective confrontation leads to an exploration of the patient's options for recovery and treatment if they embrace a new perspective on their drinking and using.

Though I clearly misjudged Michael's previous lack of interest in his marriage, conveniently interpreting it as a form of spiritual non-attachment similar to my own undeveloped, youthful view of life, it was clear by the strength of his anger and the look of extreme vulnerability that spread across his face that his relationship to Sheila was more important than he had previously let on.

"It's not like she hasn't brought this up before," Michael said. And in a single comment, Michael let me know that his marijuana use was more than likely not a minor issue. His statement opened a door to an important part of his life. Unknowingly, I had either ignored, remained ignorant of, or blindly collaborated with his use of marijuana or other drugs.

After the session with Michael, I found myself searching for the signs that I had missed. And I missed a great deal. It was as if a light bulb had gone off and I saw how I misinterpreted his lack of interest in his job, his career, and his relationship. I failed to recognize the amotivational syndrome common to marijuana dependence. I totally missed the fact that at least once a month he came to his sessions slightly stoned. I let him down when he repeatedly mentioned his slight depression at the end of the day and his ritual beer or two along with a joint to make him feel a bit better. But I never followed it up.

But I didn't want to jump the gun. I didn't want to rush headlong and accuse Michael of marijuana abuse and then, with a searing omniscience compensated for my previous lapse, bring up the past to bolster my newfound insight. I also wasn't sure to what extent his marijuana use was indeed problematic and whether other drugs were involved. With considerable effort, I literally bit my tongue and restrained myself from leaping too fast.

"Would you like to tell me something about your relationship to marijuana?" I asked, struggling to keep the session from turning into an inquisition or, worse, a lecture.

SIX TYPES OF CONFRONTATIONS

The following six forms of confrontation, when used in the context of a consultation, intervention, or psychotherapy with the alcoholic or addict, have the potential to contribute to the breakdown of denial. While no single confrontation is likely to produce magical results and an enlightening experience for a patient, the timing of any given confrontation, along with the strength of the therapeutic alliance, can have a profound therapeutic effect. Each form of confrontation may be used, based on the discretion of the therapist, the strengths style of the therapist, and the needs of the individual.

Asking Questions

By simply asking a question in an open, nonjudgmental way, a therapist can convey, by tone and timing, the value of exploring a patient's alcohol and drug use. If a therapist is too eager, however, the patient is likely to feel pressured or criticized, and rightly warned of the therapist's countertransference and personal agenda. Timing is everything.

"Sure," Michael said. "Where should I start?"

And I shrugged, surprised at his willingness to talk about it.

"I guess I've been doing drugs for about ten years or so," Michael said.

And once again, in one sentence, having asked a fairly general question (rather than a pointed one like, "How much do you smoke a day?"), Michael gave me a great deal of information. He told me he had been "doing drugs" and not just marijuana. He told me that I'd need to ask an entire series of questions to explore his drugs of choice. And he told me with some quick calculation that he'd been using, to one extent or another, since he was in his late teens.

"I started out smoking cigarettes like most of my friends. When a cousin turned me on to pot in my senior year of high school, it felt like I found my best friend."

I blinked and slowly took in what Michael was telling me. He conveyed the strength of his relationship to his drug of choice ("it felt like

I found my best friend") and implicitly hinted at a depth of loneliness he had been medicating.

"Can you tell me a little bit more about the way pot has been like a best friend?" I asked, continuing to inquire about his relationship to marijuana.

Positive Reframing

A therapist can increase the depth of a confrontation by calling attention to the ways in which alcohol or drug use may serve a positive function rather than a negative one. When a therapist acknowledges the positive aspect of drug use, a patient may relax rather than become defensive, join in the exploration, and tell more stories rather than withdraw, and as a result learn something about his relationship to alcohol and drugs.

"It's like my best friend," Michael said again. "Usually I get home before Sheila. Max is around. But it's not the same." Then he looked down, and in an almost sad whisper said, "To be honest, I don't really have any close friends. Sheila has loads and we do stuff with 'em every other week. But I'm not really close with any of the guys. They're all shirts. You know . . . they're office types."

"So smoking," I said, meaning his pot use and searching for a verb he might accept, "helps ease the loneliness?"

"I guess so," Michael said sheepishly.

I bit my tongue again trying not to interfere with his reflection.

Questioning the Wisdom

Intuition and experience can help a therapist choose one form of confrontation over another, but a general rule of thumb involves a gradual increase in the directness of the confrontation if previous methods fail to engage the patient or emphasize the seriousness of the therapist's concern. This increasing directness may take place in a single session, over the course of several weeks, or even over a period of years as circumstances dictate. It may require the use of more direct means, given the severity of the situation, the risk to self and others, and the likelihood (or not) that a patient will return for another session.

Having gathered information and engaged the patient about his alcohol and drug use through what may be either a single question or a series of questions spread out over many sessions, a therapist may increase the weight of a confrontation simply by questioning the wisdom of the patient's thinking, intention, or action. This type of confrontation may take form either as a question, a comment, or a declaration. By questioning the wisdom of the patient's thinking, intention, or action in a nonjudgmental manner, alcoholics and addicts are invited to stand back from their usual, habitual way of thinking and develop a reflective attitude. This step, concrete in the therapeutic interview and eventually internalized by the patient, may seem like a small gain, but it actually represents a significant leap toward the realization in the First Step of Alcoholics Anonymous, *"We admitted we were powerless over alcohol and that our lives had become unmanageable."*

After pausing to take in the depth of Michael's comment about his need to numb himself against the loneliness he carried inside, as gently as I possibly could, fully aware of how vulnerable Michael felt in his silence, I asked, "How's it working?"

"Not all that well," he said. "Even if I get plastered, I still know it's there. So I have to do something else."

I cocked my head.

"Then I'll turn on the TV."

"And if that doesn't do it?"

"I get a beer from the fridge."

"And . . ."

"Another joint," Michael interrupted. "Then another beer."

I nodded and placed a series of questions about alcohol on my list for another time when the situation was right. But for the moment, given that the end of the session had arrived, I thought I might plant a seed for further discussion. As we shook hands and moved toward the door I said, "Michael, where does it end?" And to my surprise, the look on his face actually seemed to say something like, "Gosh. I never thought of that."

Therapeutic Concern

Authority and compassion are powerful assets when a therapist conveys a generalized or urgent need to pay attention to alcohol and drug problems. Whether by nature of the therapist's knowledge or the strength and power of the transference, when a therapist makes a comment a certain weight of authority is carried along with it. Likewise, when a therapist steps out of a reflective listening mode and shares a genuine concern or a personal feeling rather than an observation, interpretation, or question, patients always take notice. The personal comment stands in relief to the majority of the therapist's silence in the session. The genuineness of the expression, rather than a tactically staged comment, will have enormous impact even on the alcoholic or addict in denial and resistant to examining the thorny issue of alcohol and drugs.

As psychotherapists, we often have concerns about revealing personal information to patients in therapy. We might be concerned about stepping out from behind our precious therapeutic objectivity. We might be afraid of being consumed by our own feelings if they rise to the surface. We might be concerned about the impact a personal story or comment may have on the patient or the transference. Or we may wonder whether or not the disclosure is of benefit to the patient. These fears are important and deserve careful reflection with each circumstance and each patient.

A personal revelation in the context of therapy always involves a slight risk. It may risk the therapist's sense of objective balance. It may ignite and invite additional questions or reactions by the patient. The patient may experience a concerned comment as intrusive or place the therapist in the company of the people who don't understand the "need" to drink or use drugs. But the risk of passivity, in light of a disease that rarely goes into remission by itself, is so great that, with some thought and reflection, a gesture of concern is a small risk. Sometimes, even the most modest of comments will have a profound effect when it can (or can't) be fully digested.

COYOTE AND THE GRASS PEOPLE

One day Coyote was wandering in the Great Plains. He was feeling all puffed up because he had killed great monsters and avoided a great deal of trouble. He felt powerful. Just when he started to brag to no one in particular, he heard the faint singing off in the distance.

"Weeee are the strongest people in the world."

I wonder who is singing? Coyote thought, and with his keen ears he walked into the great expanse of the grasslands.

"Weeee are the strongest people in the world," sang not one voice but many voices. And then it stopped.

Coyote listened but all he could hear was the grass whistling in the wind. Then he heard it again. These were the Grass People.

The further into the grasslands Coyote walked, the louder the song became.

"Weeeee are the strongest people in the world," the Grass People sang.

"Hah!" Coyote boasted. "You are not strong. I, Coyote, am the strongest." Coyote grabbed bunch after bunch of grass and stuffed them into his mouth. "You see," Coyote said chewing. "I can eat you. I am the strongest."

Then the Grass People started to sing.

"Weeee are the strongest people in the world."

"Hah!" Coyote shouted.

"Because we will make you fart."

And with that Coyote heard his stomach rumble. It rumbled again. And then a small one came out . . . pooof!

"That was nothing!" Coyote challenged.

Then came another one only this one was stronger . . . POOF!

"Hah!" Coyote said. "Is that all you can do?"

And then Coyote heard a great rumbling and the biggest one came out . . . POOOOOOOOOOOOOOOOFFFF! And Coyote rocketed across the Great Plains.

During the following session, Michael spoke in detail about his history of alcohol and drug use. Without much prompting, he talked about how he and his friends got drunk on the weekends and how he moved on to pot in his senior year of high school.

"I forgot about drinking for a couple of years," he said almost proudly. "Once I started smoking pot I felt like I just didn't need to drink."

"Did you feel a need to drink before?"

"Well, not really," he said unconvincingly. "But I did count the days until we'd meet to divvy up the booze we stole from our parents. You know . . . that's how I feel now about pot. I start thinking about it around two-thirty in the afternoon. Even if I'm feeling okay and not so moody, I start fantasizing how a joint is gonna feel when I'm riding home. And then how cool a beer will feel going down after the joint."

Suddenly, Michael became silent, as if he were reliving the moment of reflection right there in my office. He took a deep breath and let it out slowly as if he were exhaling a toke from a joint.

"Hmmm. So you fantasize about smoking and drinking," I said. Then I paused, took a breath, and said, "You know, Michael, the way you describe your smoking and drinking concerns me."

Michael's eyes lit up alarmingly, as if my concern was somehow threatening.

"Why?"

"Well, I wonder whether people who don't have a problem with smoking or drinking actually fantasize about it like you?"

Michael's face went blank. His jaw relaxed. And I could've sworn I heard him think, *Oh, shit.*

Therapeutic Amazement

When that sinking feeling in your stomach tells you it's time to take out the big guns, listen. After asking questions, commenting, and expressing concern fail to make an impression, you may notice yourself feeling a need to bring out the big artillery. Therapeutic amazement, however, doesn't mean blasting your patient, although you may feel the adrenaline rush up through your temples and your voice rise in preparation for the bomb you'd like to drop. It also doesn't mean judging, criticizing, or telling your patient that they're acting insane (although you may be thinking it). The first of two direct forms of confrontation unite the reality of the patient's alcohol and drug problems with your natural bewilderment.

"Well, Jacques," Michael said the following week, "I don't know. I just don't know," and he dropped his head into his hands and sat motionless.

As I waited for him to continue, my stomach tightened once again, my breathing shallowed noticeably, and I prepared for the worst.

"I didn't mean to get plastered," Michael went on.

His head was still in his hands and as he vibrated ever so slightly, I wondered if Michael was crying.

"What happened?" I asked, gently inviting him to continue.

"Well, I told myself I wasn't going to drink for a month like we talked about . . ." although I suggested three, "and I was all set to *just* have a joint . . ." although I had suggested giving up everything to really tell if he could control his smoking and drinking. "Then before I knew it, Sheila was walking through the door and there were six empty beer cans on the coffee table."

A long silence filled the room. The space between us seemed enormous.

"She left," Michael mumbled. Sitting silently, a single tear welled up in his left eye for the longest time and then, humiliatingly, rolled down his cheek. He didn't reach for a tissue.

"She didn't say a word. She just packed a suitcase and left. I know she's at Debbie's. I told her I would start over. I even told her I'd stop everything for a few months. But it didn't even slow her down."

Then he looked away. Michael's gaze froze on a scene I imagined took place several nights before. I waited. I took a deep breath. I knew he'd held on to his pain for days, not having any friends to confide in, not feeling comfortable to call me in the middle of the week and appear needy. I was afraid that if I jumped in I'd cut off his story and his release. I wanted to comfort him. I wanted to reassure him that it would be okay. I wanted to tell him that he would survive. I wanted to tell him what to do, "to get sober," "get into recovery," "do the steps," or "go to a meeting." But I knew I had to wait. I had to wait for *his* timing, not mine.

"She didn't say a goddamn word."

Finally, whatever restraint I had evaporated and I burst.

"Michael," I said emphatically, drawing his attention. "Listen to yourself. Last week you were so positive. You were going to turn things around. You were really going to get a handle on this. And now you're telling me that you want to try to control your drinking and smoking again?" My voice rose in both tone and fervor. "How can you say this?" By this time I was almost shouting.

Michael stared at me and suddenly I realized I'd never spoken to him so strongly. And I wasn't finished.

"I can't believe that even when Sheila walks out on you, you still believe you can control it. Michael, you've got a chance here, but it's a slim one. You can face your problems directly or you can lose everything you care about."

He looked stunned and dazed. At first I thought he'd walk out, but I knew he had no one else to talk to. I wanted to say more and I wanted to take it back. I feared that I had blown it by reacting too strongly. And I knew I had to wait. I knew I needed to see how he took it and at the same time I didn't want to take away what possible benefit my outburst may have initiated.

Finally, when he shifted his right leg to a more comfortable position and a small cloud of sawdust buried in the creases of his jeans floated lightly down to the floor, he broke the tense silence that stood between us.

"Damn," he said.

And I knew something had changed. How much I wasn't sure. But something shifted, as if all the wind had been knocked out of his chest. And he began sobbing, silently.

Direct and to the Point

A direct confrontation is a special resource and should not be used indiscriminately. To do so dissipates its power and its effectiveness, and will be perceived as the act of a therapist too quick to cut to the chase or make judgments. There are times when, either as a result of a crisis or the growing unlikelihood that a patient will return for another session, the risk to the health and safety of the patient and his or her family is too great and we need to pull out all the stops.

Being direct and to the point doesn't mean badgering, criticizing, or blasting the patient. A direct confrontation involves an almost methodical precision of presenting the information given you, point after point, leading to the obvious conclusion that the patient's alcohol and drug problem is out of control. Then, with the permission given you either implicitly by a patient having sought out your consultation, or explicitly after your asking if they'd like to know what you think, the confronting therapist goes one step further and predicts the future. At this point it is important to speak carefully and simply. This form of direct confrontation often has a stunning effect and the long-winded therapist's eloquence will be lost in the fog of the patient's shock and bewilderment.

Predicting the future in an alcohol- or drug-related confrontation involves postulating what the patient already knows but is afraid to admit. It involves expressing once again the concern or fear that, unabated, your patient will lose what is most valued in life. It may involve articulating that if your patient continues to drink or use in the manner they themselves have described, given your experience (and theirs) the following . . . (fill in the blank with what you have learned through a consultation or treatment) . . . will occur. Finally, a direct confrontation always provides hope, options, and an opportunity to choose another direction through abstinence, treatment, and recovery.

Regardless of whether your patient accepts the confrontation and embraces the harsh reality of their situation, or says, "Well, maybe," and walks out the door, a seed has been planted. The therapist left standing alone when an alcoholic or addict terminates treatment prematurely can hold fast to the knowledge that an attempt was made to convey the seriousness of the situation. We may not be able to help someone hit bottom faster, but maybe we can raise the floor a bit. It is a risk—to act clearly and decisively, or hope your patient will, alone, get it and take a first step before passing out, going into a coma, or ending up in an accident while under the influence.

"What do you think I should do?" Michael asked after a week of solitude, nightly smoking and drinking to the point of passing out.

"Well, Michael, trying to control your smoking and drinking doesn't seem to be working," I said, starting out with the obvious.

Although my voice sounded casual and reassuring, inside I felt overwhelmed with concern and fear that if he continued on a binge Michael might hurt himself or, worse, someone else if he drove under the influence. I was also frustrated and angry. I was frustrated because last week he seemed to have embraced the futility of his drinking and his smoking, and then dove back in full force. And I was angry because I felt like I was doing my best and, on the surface, not only was the situation not getting better, it was getting worse. Of course, sometimes things getting worse is a good thing.

In my inflation of trying to work magic with Michael I had lost my own sense of balance. Unconsciously, I had become the moon when

Michael appeared to turn a corner. I felt good, a bit puffed up. And I felt powerful until he arrived eager to deflate my grandiosity. In effect, Michael had disappointed me and I was pissed.

"I don't know, Michael," I said, feeling defeated. But since he asked me what I thought, I figured I had one last chance. I felt our alliance wavering and anticipated the possibility of his terminating therapy.

"Trying to control it hasn't worked," I said. "There's only one other option. Michael," and I looked him straight in the eyes, "you've got to give it up." And I waited for the weight of our mutual defeat to sink in. I figured that Michael's history made him a low risk for withdrawal but reminded myself, if he agreed to try going sober, that I needed to be vigilant for any signs of withdrawal in case he needed a medically supervised detoxification.

"I'd kinda like to try controlling it again," he said, holding on to a thread of hope that he could get his life and wife back and still keep drinking and smoking.

"You could do that," I responded in an obviously controlled and sarcastic manner. I was amazed how he held on to the hope of continued use. Then I remembered that marijuana was his best friend.

"But Michael," I said, realizing I was up against the full force of his denial and resistance, "let me put it this way. You have a remarkable chance here. You can face your dependence on pot and alcohol," I said, using the clinical terminology for the first time, "deal with the pain you've been medicating for years, and turn your life around. Or you can keep doing more of the same and watch your life go down the tubes."

Then I stopped short, hoping the bluntness of my comment would say more than a plethora of words and admonitions. I was going for broke, partly out of desperation and partly out of fear that if Michael continued on this path, his drinking and pot smoking would push him into a hole he might never climb out of. I was hoping that whatever relationship we had would help him face the difficult decision of facing his pain without his anesthetic. I figured that once he made the decision to get sober, getting him to increase the number of therapy sessions per week, encouraging him to check into an outpatient treatment program, or getting him to go to AA or MA meetings would be a breeze.

"What's holding you back?" I asked, not really expecting an answer and fearing he'd just pack it in and walk out.

There was a long pause and I held my breath.

"I'm afraid of being alone," he said, with the most exquisite vulnerability I'd ever witnessed. "I'm just afraid," he repeated again, tearful.

I waited, not wanting to jump in too quickly. "Michael," I finally said,
leaning forward and looking him eye to eye, "you've got a lot to deal
with ahead of you but I guarantee you won't have to go it alone."

And a long silence held us both. The clock seemed to tick by unusually loudly. I realized I had no idea how he'd respond.

"Where do we start?" he finally said.

And we smiled, together.

CHAPTER 7

Relapse Risk Assessment

Monitoring the risk of relapse is essential at all stages of therapy with alcoholics and addicts, regardless of whether a clinician is treating those struggling to control their use, those recently abstinent, or those clean and sober for years. Assessing relapse risk may be as simple as reflecting on the status of the individual's sobriety, his attitude toward recovery, and the magnitude of life stressors. In situations that necessitate a formal case presentation or a court-mandated report, relapse risk evaluation may include a summary of the individual's alcohol and drug history, a *DSM-IV* diagnosis, treatment recommendations, and a comprehensive assessment of the following criteria associated with relapse:

Relationships
Recovery/Treatment
Patterns of Use
Dual Diagnosis
Lifestyle
Family History/Treatment
Drug(s) of Choice
Work History
Relapse Plan
Attitude Toward Sobriety

A formal assessment may also be a beneficial framework with which to view relapse risk assessment in general and to examine each of the criteria and their relationship to an individual's continued sobriety.

FORMAL EVALUATIONS

In contrast to the anonymity and intimacy we share with our patients in the quiet, sheltered atmosphere of our offices, court-ordered evaluations require a professionally neutral, informative stance. Formal evaluations are not therapy, and as such rarely permit the development of a therapeutic alliance based on time, trust, and a shared history. They require, aside from common courtesy, tact and an ability to conduct a thorough interview in adherence to the clarity of one's perceptions and an understanding of the subject in question. They require an ability to make the distinction between a fact, such as *Mr. K. reports that he has remained clean and sober for six months though he has six positive tests for alcohol and opioids in the last twelve weeks* and an opinion, such as *Mr. K.'s inability to comprehend the difference between sobriety and casual drug use are characteristic of his denial that he has relapsed and may contribute to his returning to previous levels of dependence.*

Formal evaluations expose a clinician to cross-examination by attorneys. They open up a clinician's work to review by peers. They commit a clinician's opinions to the kind of intense scrutiny that will humble even the most confident psychiatrist, psychologist, or counselor. Forensic reports and evaluations of any kind are not for the fainthearted. The responsibility of producing a report that may determine whether an individual is incarcerated, given parole from a previous conviction, or restrained from the visitation and custody of young children is sobering to say the least. On the other hand, formal evaluations provide an important community service. They educate the courts, and they aid children who, by default, rely on the courts for protection from abuse and neglect despite an innate desire to maintain contact with their alcoholic or addicted parents. The courts and court-appointed personnel, though frequently aware of an individual's drug problem, often lack the education and clinical skill to explain the implicit risks associated with a variety of chemical substances.

An attorney may not understand that an addiction to crack cocaine requires relatively constant readministration in order to avoid a rapid withdrawal. A crack cocaine addiction, therefore, will rapidly lead to neglect, poor decision making, and one of the highest relapse rates compared to an addiction to a longer-acting narcotic like heroin. A judge may not be aware how vulnerable a child is when parents appear normal and functional despite being middle-stage alcoholics, or that as a result of regular blackouts a parent can't recall whether a child received medication an hour ago or needs it immediately. In cases like this, blackouts increase the child's risk of a medication overdose.

The substance abuse professional is therefore in a position to advise the court that, given the high relapse rate for stimulant addicts, an amphetamine-addicted mother is *not likely* to benefit from the simple recommendation or requirement to seek help from a counselor and attend Twelve Step meetings. At a minimum she may need more support from an agency or treatment center that can provide a respite from childcare, can provide job and life skills training, and can provide years of aftercare. A requirement to fill out a Nar-Anon attendance card will be as helpful as saying, "Just don't do it."

JOHN AND SARA

In two completely unrelated case illustrations, a financially well-off, divorced father living in San Francisco and a homeless, single mother living in San Jose were referred by different county courts through their respective attorneys for alcohol and drug evaluations. Written reports were requested to include: a list of interview dates, a list of documents and sources examined, a *DSM-IV* psychoactive substance diagnosis if present, a relapse risk assessment, a summary, and a list of recommendations. For the purpose of this chapter, however, only the last three items are described in detail.

John H. shared custody of his son with his ex-wife from a marriage that ended in a difficult and protracted divorce. John was 41, two years sober, and had a long work history. Sara M. broke off her relationship with the father of her daughter only months after conception. She received no economic support other than a minimum amount from the state. Sara was in her mid-thirties. Sara's longest recorded period of sobriety, according to written and verbal reports never exceeded two months. John's son, Nathan, was 5 years old. Sara's daughter, Marietta, was 6.

On a cold, rainy winter morning, after stopping off at a local bakery for a poppyseed roll and a cup of hot tea, I settled into my office, hit the speaker button on my phone and dialed in my answering machine for messages that may have arrived during the night. The machine beeped three times.

"I was referred by Dr. Richardson," a deep voice said in a somewhat stiff and uncomfortable tone. I imagined a tall, thin man with bushy black hair. I saw him dressed in a dark suit. He sounded as if he was trying hard to act properly in what was obviously an awkward moment. I put down my tea, swallowed a bite of the poppyseed roll, and picked up my notepad.

"I have a custody trial coming up next month. I've been referred for an evaluation by Dr. Richardson. I would appreciate a call to see if we could schedule an appointment as soon as possible." Then he gave me his home, office, and pager numbers. The machine beeped twice, indicating two messages were left. I hit the pause button, took a sip of tea, and pressed the button again.

"I don't know why I'm supposed to call you," a gravelly-voiced woman blurted out accusingly. "My lawyer said it's something about needing some kind of evaluation to get the kid back. You can call me at . . ." and then she gave me her phone number.

What struck me initially, aside from the deep tone of her voice, was the way in which she used the phrase, "the kid." I found it disconcertingly generic, a bit cold and aloof.

The machine beeped again.

"Oh," she said, having called back, "my name is Sara."

Since I start work at seven in the morning three days a week, I waited a few hours before I tried to reach John. After several attempts, I found him at his office. After an obviously awkward introduction, he reminded me again that he was referred by the psychologist assigned to the custody case regarding his 5-year-old son, Nathan. He also mentioned that both his and his ex-wife's attorney had agreed that I was acceptable to do the alcohol and drug evaluation. He said right off the bat that he didn't do drugs. He said that he'd been sober for two years since his last DUI.

Surprisingly, in contrast to his initially stiff phone message, John spoke openly about his alcoholism. In his brief description of the uncomfortable situation he found himself in, he sounded more concerned with the possible effect his drinking history might have on his son if the visitation schedule was altered or terminated. Given his interest in completing the evaluation as quickly as possible, John scheduled the first of three hour-long interviews that afternoon.

"I don't know why I'm supposed to talk with you," Sara said again when I finally reached her around noon. "I don't have a drug problem any more and things are just fine."

"Well," I replied, "you could come in and tell me how good things are. That way we could get this out of the way as quickly as possible."

"Couldn't you come to my place? I'm kind of busy."

"No," I said bristling at Sara's somewhat understandable and yet entitled request. "I'm not able to do that. But if you'd like to come here I have an opening at one today," I offered.

"Today wouldn't work," she said. "I'm busy."

"Wednesday at two?"

"No," she said. "Do you have any weekend appointments?"

And though I was giving her the benefit of the doubt that she might have a work conflict, I was also getting slightly irritated at Sara's unwillingness to adjust to my schedule. Actually, I thought I was being generous. But then, like all people, I like it when others adjust to my needs.

"Is there a problem with work?"

"No, I'm just busy."

I wondered what Sara felt was so important that she would erect an obstacle to regaining custody of her daughter.

"Well," I said. "I have the one o'clock today and the two o'clock appointment tomorrow. That's it." I did have one other opening, but a regular patient hadn't gotten back to me about whether she needed a second appointment that week. I didn't want to give the time away to someone who I didn't know from Adam and who might not even show up.

"Okay," she said, "I'll see you tomorrow at two."

Then I gave her careful, detailed directions, confirmed the time once again, and said goodbye.

That afternoon, when I met him in the waiting room, I was surprised. In contrast to the image in my head, John was only slightly over five feet tall and balding. John was polite, understandably a bit nervous, and clearly ashamed that his drinking contributed to his current circumstances. After a brief discussion of his situation and the intended reason for the evaluation, I informed John about the limited confidentiality involved in this type of assessment in contrast to the depth of confidentiality inherent in psychotherapy. This meant that the information he gave me would be kept confidential between the two of us, his attorney and his wife's attorney, and the court. I told him that I would not reveal the information to anyone else unless required to do so by the judge presiding over the case and, as a courtesy, I would inform both his and his wife's attorney in the event that a request was made for additional information.

I described the time and fees involved in the interview. I mentioned that I needed an hour of report preparation time for every interview hour and that three interview hours was normal for these types of evaluations. I described, in brief, the basic content of the report I was asked to produce, the possibility that I might need to interview his ex-wife or other family members, and what role I might have if asked to testify in court.

As expected, when I mentioned the possibility of interviewing his ex-wife, John stiffened, and I could have sworn I heard the bones in his hands crack as he rubbed them together. When I commented on the often combative nature of many custody disputes, he nodded. I conveyed how strongly I felt about the objectivity of my professional opinions. I said that I would do my best to accurately represent both his strengths and any problems he might have. I also told him that I was not a hired gun. "If anything is unclear," I promised, "I will state that it is unclear. And I will do my best to describe what I see and not make guesses or assumptions."

John relaxed a bit, shifted from his stiff, upright posture, and leaned back into the softness of the couch. He took a deep breath and said, "Okay, let's do it."

Over the course of three hour-long interviews scheduled over the next two weeks, John talked openly about his marriage and required little prompting for me to gather information. Though an obviously stressful experience, the interview also seemed to be surprisingly cathartic for John, and I sensed that he might benefit from some individual therapy to help him deal with the current stress in his life. John spoke at length of how rapidly his marriage deteriorated after the birth of his son, Nathan. He described how his drinking increased when his wife filed for divorce a year later. He admitted how the three DUIs he received in the eighteen months following the divorce led to his episodic attendance at Alcoholics Anonymous. Because he appeared so eager to unburden himself and confess the length and breadth of his inebriety, I rarely found it necessary to ask questions aside from the occasional need to determine discrete clinical distinctions.

At two o'clock the following day, remembering that I forgot to tell Sara to press the button in the hallway to announce her presence, I ventured out and checked the waiting room to see if she had arrived. The room was empty and so I left my office door ajar to listen for any sound of her arrival. I waited five minutes, ten, then fifteen minutes. When I checked my answering machine to see if she called to say she was running late, the door swung open and closed rather loudly.

Stepping out into the hallway I introduced myself to a woman slightly over five feet tall, dressed in a worn flowing skirt and a multicolored tie-dyed T-shirt. She had long, tangled brown hair, a tattoo on her right forearm in the shape of a cross, and a look that expressed both fear and rage. The hand I offered as a matter of politeness appeared to startle her out of some lingering disorientation and I felt cautioned to her fragility. So as not to force myself on her, I pointed in the direction of the door and invited Sara into my office.

"I don't know what this is all about," Sara said, adjusting the contents of a very large bag she carried with her. "I'm not an addict anymore. And besides, I only use now for medicinal purposes."

I took a moment to catch my breath because, while most people let me begin a therapy session, interview, or evaluation, Sara asserted herself quickly, and defensively at that. I hadn't asked a single question and yet I had learned a great deal. She let me know that from her point of view she thought she had been an addict. She let me know she was having a difficult time understanding the reason for the evaluation, the impact previous alcohol or drug use may have had on her daughter, and the nature of the concern the referring psychologist had with regard to the potential impact and risks associated with her drug use. She also let me know that she believed she needed to medicate some condition.

Later that afternoon I received a message from Sara's referring psychologist. She described the context of her request for the evaluation and mentioned that my fees would be paid by the court. She requested that a copy of my report be sent to her office, Sara's court-appointed attorney, and the attorney provided by the court to represent the interests of Sara's daughter, Marietta.

Over the course of the three interviews we scheduled, the second interrupted by two no-shows, Sara alternated between normal vigilance and the hostility one might expect from someone who is subjected to the inconvenience and humiliation of a court-ordered evaluation. Occasionally her mood changed into an almost childlike compliance and she referred to me as "her kind doctor." I gave Sara the same description of the interview process I had given John and asked if she had any questions.

"Nope," she replied blankly. Then she stared out the window and off into the trees behind my chair.

None of Sara's friends or close relatives were available for collateral interviews. The attorney appointed for her daughter by the court faxed me the social worker's report summary detailing a history of various diagnoses including Depression, Bipolar Disorder, Explosive Disorder, and ten years of alcohol, crack cocaine, and amphetamine use and dependence. Sara had a long history of involuntary hospitalizations following at least two clearly defined suicide attempts, repeated episodes of violence against others, and a history of episodic withdrawal from social contact lasting as much as eighteen months.

SUMMARIES

The summaries below describe two individuals with a variety of strengths and vulnerabilities on a continuum from a low risk of chemical dependence relapse, in John's case, to a very high risk of relapse in Sara's. The recommendations included in their reports weigh not only the number of positive and negative criteria but the content of criteria themselves. And while no one can accurately predict the future, I have found that a general measure of three or less negative criteria totals in the combined list of criteria will indicate a low risk of relapse, three to five negative totals a moderate risk of relapse, and five or greater a high risk of relapse.

Both positive and negative criteria valences are added together to provide a given criteria total. Each criterion is evaluated both in the context of its influence on the individual's sobriety and its possible effect on a minor child. When resources were limited, treatment programs requiring little or no fee were included. Recommendations, therefore, gave strong consideration to the vulnerability of the children versus any inconvenience to the parents.[1]

John H. reports being clean and sober from alcohol for the last two years. Prior to his sobriety, which began in December of 1995, he had a five-year history of moderate to heavy drinking that fulfilled the minimum criteria for Alcohol Dependence. His symptoms included: (1) *substance taken in larger amounts than intended*—evidenced by his unsuccessful attempts to limit his drinking; (2) *persistent desire or unsuccessful attempts to control use*—evidenced by his inability to abstain for any length of time greater than his current period of three months; and (3) *the substance was used despite knowledge of a recurrent problem that is likely to have been caused or exacerbated by the problem*—indicated by his increasing use of a depressant while depressed.

His drinking was characterized primarily by a psychological reliance, characteristic of the early stages of the disease. He also drank to excess when under situational stress, anxiety, and depression. Mr.H. reported occasional marijuana use in college and a single incident as a senior when he drank to the point of passing out. He reported that his heavy drinking began when he met his ex-wife in 1989, and escalated to the point where they would share a bottle or more of champagne nightly. He reported a history of daily drinking (4+ drinks) with significant increases (6–10 drinks) for periods of 1–2 weeks from 1993 to 1995. He believes his excessive drinking was triggered by the onset of both anxiety and depression concurrent with his ongoing custody disputes. He reported never drinking during his son's visitations.

Mr. H. has two DUIs (4/94: BAL=.17; 9/94: BAL= .12) and one wet reckless driving (3/95: BAL= .11). He reported complying with

---

1. This format evaluating relapse risk has yet to be subjected to statistical scrutiny.

all fines, classes, and community service (confirmed by the probation report).

Mr. H. has been prescribed Xanax for anxiety and Zoloft for depression by Dr. Marion B. in the last month. He reports taking Xanax on only three occasions due to his concern for its addictive potential, and has yet to take the Zoloft.

In each of three interviews, Mr. H. was candid and did not appear to minimize his responses. He appeared concerned that the effects of his drinking might affect visitations with his son. He presents a strong motivation to comply with all recommendations in order to maintain visitation with his son.

Sara M. has a history that indicates a pattern of reliance on alcohol and other drugs that easily fulfills the criteria for Poly-Substance Dependence including: (1) *tolerance*—evidenced by her need for increasing amounts of methamphetamine over a six-month period of heavy use; (2) *a persistent desire or unsuccessful attempts to cut down or control use*—indicated by her inability to test consistently negative when required to do so by the court; (3) *a great deal of time spent using the substance or recovering from its effects*—indicated by her reports of numerous binges followed by periods of extended sleep; (4) *important social, occupational, or recreational activities given up or reduced because of substance use*—evidenced by her loss of interest in recreational activities, friends, and the care of her daughter; and (5) *the substance was used despite knowledge of a recurrent problem that is likely to have been caused or exacerbated by the problem*—indicated by her use despite the knowledge that it contributes to her depression, suicide attempts, legal problems, and loss of custody of her daughter.

It is impossible to overstate the difficulties caused by Ms. M.'s lack of sobriety and its contribution to the loss of custody of her daughter. Given the reports and references to Ms. M.'s history of depression, suicide attempts, violence toward others including her daughter, and an attempt to abort the pregnancy of her daughter with excessive alcohol and drug use, any use of alcohol or drugs would dramatically increase a risk to her daughter.

Any recommendations should include treatment that provides a maximum structure, education, and support, including inpatient or long-term residential care, a full psychiatric evaluation and treatment, vocational training, and parenting classes.

TEN CRITERIA ASSOCIATED WITH RELAPSE

A thorough evaluation of relapse risk from sobriety, abstinence, or controlled use to previous levels of substance abuse or dependence is likely to include an assessment of some or all of the following ten criteria. A formal evaluation should be conducted with the same clinical integrity as described in the diagnosis chapter. The clinician should rely on either direct information supplied by the individual or information noted in reports by doctors, mental health care professionals, or various government agencies. It is also important to remember that alcohol and drug dependence is a medical condition. Terms such as *addict, alcoholic, suicidal,* and other psychiatric terminology are used by professionals lacking the clinical training to make a diagnosis and, as a result, such information deserves careful scrutiny.

Due to the tendency for many alcoholics and addicts to underreport or misrepresent their alcohol or drug use or the effects of their use, it is often helpful to obtain additional information from family or friends. This indirect or collateral information requires a high degree of circumspection. The alcoholic and addict's friends, family, or spouses are likely to have their personal reactions, investments in the outcome of the evaluation, and judgments about alcohol and drug use in general. Statements from friends and relatives, therefore, must be weighed carefully, with caution, and their source stated in any report to clarify the possibility of any bias.

1) Relationships

Is There a Long-Term Relationship?

A stable, long-term, primary relationship is a powerful asset for individuals struggling with the task of piecing a life back together from the effects of alcohol and drug dependence compared with people who have lost family and friends as a result of the disease.

(–) John reported an acrimonious relationship with his ex-wife since the divorce and custody dispute. They no longer spoke to each other directly, as is common in many custody cases, and relied on their attorneys to communicate. John reported being so distraught over his divorce that he lived an isolated life filled only by his work as a stockbroker, his attendance at monthly AA meetings, and the visitations with his son.

(–) Sara's longest primary relationship has lasted two years with Maria C. The relationship with the father of her daughter, Mark D., lasted only two months. Sara reported that physical violence was common during the two months she lived with Mark, though she evaded any clarification of whether or not her behavior toward Mark was also violent. Although initially indicating that her current relationship was stable, toward the end of the third interview, Sara reported that, "the end" with Maria C. "was in sight."

Is the Spouse Attending AA or Al-Anon?

A spouse in recovery, whether AA, Al-Anon, counseling, or psychotherapy is a positive asset for the alcoholic and addict. With all the mood swings, vulnerability, and stress in the first year of recovery, having a spouse that supports sobriety is an asset compared with living alone or with a spouse who is actively using, drinking, or coercing the newly sober individual back to using.

In many custody disputes, the spouse of the alcoholic or addict will assume that divorce is a sufficiently corrective measure to a painful situation. Rarely will a spouse identify and seek help for his or her own problems or view the alcoholic and addict's seeking help as a positive move. Unfortunately, protective or vindictive spouses often use a diagnosis of chemical dependence as an opportunity to get a legal upper hand.

(–) Though she reported being concerned about his drinking since the beginning of their marriage five years ago, John's wife never sought treatment herself nor did she think it might be of help to her now. John's wife reported that she had a single DUI near the time of her pregnancy. Like many spouses of alcoholics, John's wife thought that their divorce was a sufficient measure of action, even though through their son, Nathan, she would remain in relationship to John, an alcoholic, for many years.

(–) According to Sara, neither Marietta's father, Mark, nor Maria C., nor any previous significant individuals in relationships with Sara attended any Twelve Step Program, psychotherapy, or related treatment for alcohol or drug dependence.

2) Family

Are There Long-Standing Supportive Relationships with Family Members?

Family support can be emotionally and financially beneficial for the recovering alcoholic and addict. Though the change to sobriety is often positive, it is rarely easy for family members, especially when there is a long history of mistrust and emotional pain associated with the alcohol and drug use. When family members seek help for themselves, either through Al-Anon, other Twelve Step programs, church groups, counseling, psychotherapy, or other forms of treatment, it can provide a measure of relief for the addict as well. When the family is in treatment, it is often less likely that they will add to the addict's difficulties, and they will begin to understand the difference between care and caretaking, between concern and co-dependence.

(+/–) John reported supportive relationships with his mother, his father, and his sister. He reported having little contact, other than yearly visits, since moving to California a decade ago.

(–) Both Sara's parents are deceased, the father of cirrhosis, the mother from a gunshot wound in a bar fight. Sara reported no ties to family members or friends that could provide support during the initial stages of a recovery.

Are Family Members and Friends Alcoholic, Addicted, or in Recovery?

When friends and family members are drinking or using, subtle or even direct pressure can be brought to bear on the newly sober person to give up abstinence and join the party. Conversely, family members who are in recovery are often better equipped to avoid the pitfalls common in alcoholic families, such as feeling overly responsible for the addict and alcoholic's behavior, covering up, giving him money, or using or drinking with him. This type of co-dependent behavior stands in contrast to what has been described as *support*: when a family member is available to baby-sit while the addict or alcoholic goes to a Twelve Step meeting, provides a ride to work because the driver's license has been revoked, or loans the alcoholic or addict money but only for treatment and never for alcohol or drugs.

(+/–) John reported neither alcoholism nor recovery in his family. Since he was ashamed of his alcoholism he had yet to inform his family of the difficulties that resulted from his drinking.

(–) The social worker and police reports indicate that Sara had a history of residing with "criminals."

Are Family Members and Friends Available for Support or Baby Sitting?

Respite care is essential for the single parent in recovery, especially during the first year of sobriety, where the need to participate in counseling and meetings can be demanding. This need for support and stability is so important that the newly sober individual is often recommended not to tackle any significant, life-changing activity, such as new relationships, marriage, divorce, or job change, for at least a year.

(–) Since John's family lived on the East Coast, they were unavailable for practical support or help. He reported few, if any, close personal friends aside from business acquaintances.

(–) Sara indicated no contact with friends or family able to provide respite care aside from her current though shaky relationship to Maria.

3) Recovery/Treatment

Is This the First Recovery?

A first-time recovery with comprehensive treatment and family support is sometimes a positive indicator for long-term sobriety.

(–/+) John continued to drink after his first DUI, abstained for a two months following his second arrest for driving under the influence, and dated his sobriety from the day after his wet reckless driving in December of 1995. If John entered treatment now, this would be his first real recovery.

(–) Sara has a long history of attempted recovery in the last ten years though she has reported no length of sobriety greater than one month, in spite of the severe consequences imposed by the courts resulting in her probation, incarceration, and loss of custody of her daughter.

Does Recovery Include Inpatient, Outpatient, Residential, Aftercare, Twelve Step Attendance, Working the Steps, Working with a Sponsor, Group or Individual Psychotherapy?

A basic rule of thumb I consider clinically, when making recommendations for treatment, is that the more chronic the disease or the greater the history of relapse, the more structured treatment I recommend. Those who have had little disruption in their lives from alcohol and drug problems I have found do well with psychotherapy and participation in AA. On the other hand, when an individual's life and resources revolve around acquiring, using, and selling drugs, it is much harder to develop the emotional, social, and financial network to maintain sobriety. In such cases, inpatient, residential, or day treatment may provide a strong foundation for an individual's sobriety.

(+/–) While not currently involved in any treatment or recovery program, John completed all the required coursework related to his convictions. It is important to distinguish, however, between alcohol and drug education (DUI classes) and treatment (outpatient, inpatient, or aftercare).

(+/–) Both Sara's statements and the social work records indicate an attempt to comply with court-ordered treatment. She attended, though never completed, several court-ordered treatment programs including both group and individual counseling sessions. She completed a court-mandated parenting class and was given a very positive report.

The records also indicate that, in spite of Sara's participation in various programs, her attitude toward her sobriety varied dramatically from acknowledging that she had a problem to denying it, from seeking treatment to noncompliance, from negative testing for short periods of time (a week to one month) to testing positive for various substances including cocaine, PCP, and methamphetamines, with the most consistent being marijuana. Sara also has a history of being terminated from treatment programs, and on one occasion she stated that she completed a program when the program counselor's report indicated her eviction from the program due to continued drug use.

4) *Pattern of Use*

Is There a History of Daily Use and/or Bingeing?

The pattern of use may indicate a progression of the disease, the extent of loss of control, and the ability or inability to abstain. While intermittent use may be acute and problematic, daily use frequently leads to the development of acquired tolerance, the complications of withdrawal or use to avoid withdrawal, and chronic health problems. Binge using, if continued long enough, may lead to tolerance, and may contribute to accidents under the influence, acute health problems, or psychosis. A basic guideline I use for treatment caution is that the greater the progression of the disease the greater the risk of relapse, with the caveat that binge users are often at a greater risk of relapse.

(+) While John reported only one incident of drinking to the point of passing out as a senior in college, only one blackout, and blood alcohol levels of .10, .14, and .20 respectively for his three DUIs, his drinking, though problematic and daily (1–3 drinks three times per week and 3–8 drinks four times per week), was not indicative of bingeing, where drinking continues to the point of passing out, hospitalization, or jail.

(–) Sara reported a history of alcohol and drug use, confirmed by social work and treatment records indicating a history of both daily maintenance use and extended periods of bingeing to the point of neglecting the basic needs of her daughter for food, shelter, and clothing. At one point, denied by Sara though extensively documented by both police and social work reports, Sara lived in an abandoned car during the month of November, 1995. She then admitted the status of her homelessness, stating that it was due to lack of money. The arresting officer indicated that at the time of her arrest she was in possession of a bag of methamphetamine with a street value of $250. The physician who examined her 6-month-old daughter at the time indicated the child was malnourished and likely had not eaten or taken liquids in forty-eight hours.

5) Work

Is There a Long Term Work History? Has Work been Affected by Alcoholism/Drug Use? Is the Work Environment Supportive of Sobriety?

Frequently, positive indicators for an individual's recovery are that work has not been interrupted due to alcohol and drug use, when the individual has never been fired or given a warning due to alcohol/drug use, and the work environment is conducive and supportive to recovery.

(+) John reported a long and prosperous work history following college, with only one job change unrelated to his drinking. He reported never missing work due to hangovers.

(–) Sara reported an employment history that included a six-month period of work as a janitor at the local state hospital. She reported terminating her employment a month after she became aware of being pregnant. Otherwise, Sara collected AFDC funds throughout her daughter's life. She consistently refused both psychiatric treatment and vocational training.

6) Drugs of Choice

Is There a History of Poly-Drug Use?

Poly-drug users often have a more difficult time staying sober than single drug users. The exception is the stimulant class of substances such as amphetamines, methamphetamines, cocaine, and crack, which have one of the highest relapse rates.

(+) Aside from reportedly casual marijuana use in college, disputed by his ex-wife, John reported no other drug use.

(–) While Sara reports a predominant use of marijuana, a long history of blood tests indicate she has a history of using PCP, cocaine, methamphetamine, and alcohol.

7) Dual Diagnosis

Is There a History of Psychiatric Problems?

Within a population of alcoholics and addicts, a varying percentage (see Chapter 2) suffer from a number of psychiatric problems, including schizophrenia, depression, Bipolar disorder, and anxiety disorders, and use a variety of prescription, licit, and illicit drugs to self-medicate their symptoms. In these cases, treating the dually diagnosed patient requires special care and attention. Individuals without psychiatric problems present fewer treatment complications and are likely to have a lower rate of relapse.

(– very minor) Since his divorce and custody dispute, John was prescribed Xanax for anxiety and Zoloft for depression.

(–) Numerous references in the documents provided by the social worker indicate a long history of Sara's psychological problems. They include "depression," "suicide attempts," and "a nervous breakdown." These reports must be weighed carefully, due to the lack of a current, thorough psychiatric evaluation. (Medical records from her hospitalizations were unavailable at the time of this report.) They do, however, raise a serious concern regarding her historical and current psychological status. A thorough psychological evaluation would determine the presence of Axis I (Clinical Disorders) and Axis II (Personality Disorders/Mental Retardation) diagnoses. The diagnosis of highest concern indicated symptoms consistent with a Bipolar (manic-depressive) Disorder, although a psychiatric evaluation may reveal other diagnoses.

8) Relapse Plan

Is There a Realistic Relapse-Prevention Plan?

Regardless of an individual's drinking or recovery history, having a realistic relapse plan that includes the need for more meetings, increasing the number of therapy sessions per week, re-working the steps, and calling Twelve Step contacts can be described as "sobriety insurance," especially in the first year recovery.

(+/–) John admitted he was an alcoholic, and on three separate occasions stated clearly that his drinking had made his life miserable. He reported a willingness to comply with any recommendations, but aside from his occasional (1/month) attendance at a local AA meeting, he had no consistent participation in the program, no sponsor, no working of the steps, and therefore had no relapse plan to help him create a foundation for his sobriety.

(–) Sara denied she had a current problem with alcohol or drugs and, therefore, did not have a relapse plan. In regard to her "medicinal" use, Sara was unable to articulate the disorder she was self-medicating. It is possible, given her most recent hospitalization, when she demonstrated psychotic symptoms including paranoia, hallucinations, delusions, and avoidance of medical and psychiatric treatment, that Sara is using marijuana as a sedative.

9) Lifestyle

Does the Individual Continue to Associate With People or Locations Identified With Using and Drinking?

Associating with drinking and using buddies in old haunts such as clubs, bars, or liquor stores presents problems for individuals at risk for relapse due to coercion or the psychological triggers that may initiate craving.

(+) In John's case, given his isolation, focus on work, and the central importance of his relationship to his son, he avoided all the bars and people with whom he drank.

(−/+) Sara reported a tendency to isolate, aside from her relationship to her friend Maria. Maria is not reported to be involved in nor does she have a documented history of alcohol or drug abuse.

(+/−/+) Though John admits he is an alcoholic and goes to at least one meeting a month, he has yet to really "work the program." He reported no thoughts or fantasies about drinking. His stress level and depression, however, have increased as a result of his temperance. He appeared genuinely concerned about the downward progression of his drinking and his current legal problems.

John was unsure of whether he would remain abstinent the rest of his life, a common thought with early-stage alcoholics who get sober and have fewer significant problems and no chronic physical disabilities.

John emphatically stressed his willingness to comply with any and all of my recommendations, not only for himself but for the wellbeing of his son.

(−) Sara's inability to understand the historical problems associated with her use of alcohol and drugs, her hostile attitude toward psychiatric and drug treatment, and barely compliant responses to mandated counseling indicate an individual uninterested in seeking help, either for herself or her daughter. Sara's inability to comprehend her legal, psychiatric, and drug problems have been consistently interpreted as either "resistance" or "denial" by a long history of social workers and drug counselors. Given the most recent psychologist's report, the possibility of a dual diagnosis and a below-average IQ (86) may be of greater significance in explaining her response.

10) Attitude

What is the Attitude Toward Recovery and Sobriety?

The more subtle signs reflected in the alcoholic and addict's attitude often herald Coyote's presence in a profound way. The patient toying with relapse often displays a regression to previous levels of self-centeredness, self-aggrandizement, or a sudden burst of enthusiasm and creativity. Often related to an over-confidence in sobriety, this inflation places the recovering individual at increased risk for relapse. Likewise, if a recovering alcoholic or addict is deflated by the loss of a loved one or a job, physical injury, or financial difficulties, he may withdraw from therapy, skip meetings, or isolate from close relationships in a sulk, get depressed, or act out the wish to drown in a pool of pain and self-pity. This withdrawal from the resources that support an alcoholic and addict's sobriety contribute to a risk of relapse.

When the addict or alcoholic is using or on a dry drunk, you can almost hear Coyote howl at the moon, and declare either "Oh, how wonderful I am!" or "Oh, the pain of it all!" We might see Coyote whisper advice to end therapy and save money, because either the therapy has worked and "Thank you very much," or it hasn't and Coyote suggests looking for a different (meaning "better") therapist. In the former case you might initially feel flattered, and in the latter saddened at the declaration of another failure. If we neglect to look more closely at the alcoholic and addict's sudden mood change and interest in changing therapists, Coyote has won. He has distracted us from the truth beneath the hype. Coyote may state that he was thinking about it for weeks anyway, whether or not we inquire about the suddenness of his decision. It is still important at least to ask what might be going on beneath the surface.

Without careful consideration and discussion, the recovering addict and alcoholic, whether inflated or deflated, may rationalize the need or greed to buy a fast car, take a vacation with friends who drink, start a new and exciting relationship, go on a shopping spree, or become increasingly promiscuous. Flattering a therapist's vulnerable self-image, the alcoholic or addict might toss in a compliment, "I'm trying to take care of myself as a reward for all the good work we've done." Smiling, binding us to a kind of slippery logic, the alcoholic and addict might add, "After all, that's what you've been trying to teach me isn't it, to have fun without alcohol or drugs?"

In a dry drunk, a single thought starts out with a good objective. The objective may be a treat with a good meal, but in a restaurant known for fine wines. It may be the thought of taking a vacation with friends, but to a place known for wild parties. Unaware of the slight change in attitude from humility and self-care to arrogance and greed, the alcoholic and addict will reach a bit too high and bring others down with him toward another hard bottom. And the sight is often painful to see.

Many newcomers to Alcoholics Anonymous find a high degree of pathos and humor in virtually every meeting. Even when the pain of a life awash in alcohol and drugs is laid bare for all to hear, it is unlikely an hour will go by without some humorous relief. And while humor can be an excellent defense against the pain that lies beneath the pain and loss of a life saturated with alcohol and drugs, it has a profound ability to heal as well. Though quite provocative, the next story reveals Coyote's greed, his sense of irony, and his good will and curious humor toward his brethren. Ironically, while his greed leads to a high degree of cooperation, it ultimately has harmful effects. On the other hand, by laughing at the misfortune and death of his brothers, Coyote, of course, is also laughing at himself.

THE COYOTE CHAIN

One day when Coyote was hungry and looking for food, he came to the edge of a wide flat mesa. Squatting down to rest he saw a crow fly up to the edge of a cliff below. He leaned over the edge and saw a nest of young crows.

"Caw, caw, caw," they cried.

"What a noise," Coyote said. "Such fine young crows will make a tasty meal," he said, licking his lips. "But how will I reach them?"

Coyote paced back and forth along the edge of the mesa and tried to find a way down to the little crows. But the cliff was steep and there was no way down. He looked around and saw a bush near the edge of the cliff. He grabbed the bush with his hind legs and leaned out over the cliff. But he could only see the young birds calling from below. He stretched and reached and reached but he could not get close to the nest.

Tired, frustrated, and hungry, Coyote gave up but that didn't stop him from thinking about the crows as he started back toward his home.

After he had been walking for quite some time, a jack rabbit leaped out from his burrow just in front of Coyote, and though he was startled he quickly caught up to the rabbit and killed it. Coyote skinned and roasted the rabbit right on the spot. But he just couldn't stop thinking about the crows.

"Wuuuwuuuu," he cried. "Wuuwuuuuuuu."

Now, four of his brothers had been nearby, and when they heard him call they came running.

"Brother, what is the problem that you call us so sadly?"

"Well," replied the first Coyote, "this morning I was hunting over by the mesa and I spotted a nest of tasty young crows. But the nest was too far down the cliff for me to reach by myself and so I gave up. On the way here I killed this rabbit. But wouldn't it be nice if we all went together and caught the crows? Then we could share the crows and the rabbit and have a feast."

The eyes of the four coyotes lit up when they thought about the tasty young crows, and smelling the freshly roasted rabbit made their mouths water. And so they all trotted off toward the mesa where the first coyote spotted the nest.

When they arrived, the largest Coyote took charge.

"Now, this is what we will do," he said with authority. "You," he said, pointing to the littlest Coyote, "because you are the smallest, you will go first. We will lean you over the edge of the cliff, and your brother here will hold your hind legs and he will lean over the cliff too. Then his brother will grab his legs and lean over the cliff and so on. Then you," he said, pointing to the first Coyote, who had found the crows, "you will hold my hind legs, grab the bush with yours and we will all have crows for dinner."

By this time they had forgotten about the roasted rabbit.

Whimpering, and not all that sure this was a good idea, the littlest Coyote crawled toward the edge of the cliff.

"Oh," the largest Coyote commanded. "We should all close our eyes so we don't get dizzy and let go."

So they all crawled toward the cliff, grabbed hold of each other's hind legs and slowly lowered themselves down over the edge of the cliff.

"Caw, caw, caw," the young crows cried.

I must be close, the littlest Coyote thought, and he reached out with his front paws and tried to touch the nest. He strained and strained to reach.

I am so close, he thought, but because he was concentrating so much he failed to notice that he had defecated on himself.

Now the Coyote behind him became impatient.

What is taking my brother so long? he thought. *Maybe I will just peek. I won't get dizzy.* And he looked. Now, when he saw that his brother had soiled himself he burst out laughing. He laughed so hard that his body jerked with spasms and he let go. The littlest Coyote yelped as he fell all the way to the canyon floor and hit with a puff of dust.

Now the next Coyote wondered what all the laughing was about, and, like his brother before him, he thought he could look and not let go. When he opened his eyes he saw that his brother below him had also soiled himself. The next Coyote burst out laughing, let go of his brother, and the same thing happened to the next Coyote and the next until the first Coyote opened his eyes.

When the first Coyote saw his brother in front of him, soiled from his own laughter, and the pile of Coyotes at the bottom of the canyon he tried to hold back. Then his chest heaved. He held it back. His head jerked. He held tight. Finally, he couldn't restrain himself and, bursting into laughter at the misfortune of his brothers, he jerked so hard that he too let go and fell to his doom.

And of course none of the Coyotes tasted either the young crows or the roasted rabbit.

RECOMMENDATIONS

When asked to give expert testimony, through either a written report or cross-examination, it is important to pay attention to when one has crossed the threshold of clinical objectivity. This tendency toward inflation can be tempered by the willingness to ask more questions and admit to the simple phrase "insufficient information to determine." Providing treatment recommendations allows some leeway to err on the side of caution.

In John's case the task was relatively simple. Given his high motivation, John needed to increase his attendance at AA, and might benefit from psychotherapy to treat his anxiety and depression. He also needed some way to provide the court with a relatively secure means to justify unsupervised visitation. Any concerns regarding his risk of relapse, following a period of supervised visitation and random drug testing, might be addressed by a one year follow-up evaluation.

In Sara's case, the situation was significantly more dire, though easier to provide recommendations. Even without knowledge of the psychologist's report and her daughter's condition, through her own statements it was clear that Sara's dependence on alcohol, crack cocaine, and methamphetamine severely limited her ability to parent. Given her extensive history of relapse, lack of economic stability, and the high likelihood of more than one psychiatric diagnosis, I suggested the highest level of structure, treatment, and support available. In the event that my suggestions were countered with a second professional's differing opinion, an additional cautionary note was included to provide an absolutely clear impression of my concerns.

Recommendations for John H.

1. A minimum of 1 year (50 sessions) outpatient group or individual psychotherapy with a specialist in the field of alcohol and drug dependence. Mr. H. is highly motivated and reports feeling out of place in the AA meetings and classes he attended due to his relatively moderate drinking. This is common for early stage chemical dependents where use is primarily characterized by psychological reliance, and loss of control is episodic. The anxiety and depression associated with his legal difficulties will be more effectively addressed in individual psychotherapy. Because of his motivation, Mr. H. is likely to utilize

either group or individual psychotherapy well, though I imagine group therapy will be more challenging for him due to the shame associated with his alcoholism. In place of the outpatient psychotherapy, he may consider six to ten weeks of outpatient treatment in an alcohol and drug treatment program followed by aftercare.

2. More experience with AA. A single meeting a month, while helpful, may be compared to building a house on a foundation of wood. It's better than nothing. But concrete would be better still. I would recommend Mr. H. attend two or three beginner's meetings a week for a year. A therapist will be able to help guide him in this regard.

3. Unsupervised visitation, if all recommendations are complied with.

4. If the court is sufficiently concerned regarding Mr. H.'s ongoing sobriety, the court may consider furnishing Mr. H. with a pager and the mandate to report to an agreed-upon laboratory to furnish urine within an hour of any random page. Noncompliance would be logged as negative results affecting the status of his visitation. Recommendations for the timing of random tests should be made in consultation with either another alcohol and drug professional or this evaluator.

Recommendations for Sara M.

1. Complete psychiatric evaluation to determine *DSM-IV* Axis II diagnosis and possible developmental disability.

2. One year residential treatment followed by 1 year sober group home living.

3. Weekly psychotherapy with a specialist in the field of chemical dependence and the additional psychiatric disorders.

4. Working the steps, and working with a sponsor.

5. Random drug testing with consistently negative results for one year prior to any unsupervised visitation of the minor child.

6. Monitoring of any prescription medication from a physician knowledgeable about drug dependence, with full knowledge of Ms. M.'s history of addiction.

Whether a therapist is working with alcoholics and addicts at the beginning of sobriety or years down the line, the difficult (if not impossible) task of identifying and intervening prior to a relapse is a daunting challenge. And while a statistically significant tool has yet to be developed, an evaluation of these ten criteria (Relationships, Family History/Treatment, Recovery/Treatment, Drug(s) of Choice, Patterns of Use, Work History, Dual Diagnosis, Relapse Plan, Lifestyle, and Attitude Toward Sobriety) can provide a measure far better than a casual guess. Whether in the context of a consultation, evaluation, or ongoing therapy, the risks associated with an individual's loss of sobriety make the inconvenience of this type of assessment seem small when compared to the consequences, the shame, and the deflation following a relapse.

❖ CHAPTER 8 ❖

Drinking and Using Contracts: A Couple's Tale

BOB AND DOROTHY

On the day Dorothy and her husband walked into my office, it was obvious, given the lumbering way Bob dragged himself through the door, that this was going to be another case of shotgun therapy. Few couples enter therapy to deepen the positive bonds they share. The majority seek out help either when it is too late to repair the consciously or unconsciously inflicted wounds, or following a final ultimatum delivered by the less dependent partner.

As they settled into the couch across from my chair, Bob took a defensive position near the door and Dorothy sat as far to the right as she could sit and still stay in my office. The look on Bob's face expressed a mix of suppressed rage and muted fear. The look also let me know that if I was lucky, I had one session to make an empathic connection with him. Otherwise, I believed, he was history.

"Can you give me an idea about what brought you here today?" I asked, inviting someone to begin.

"She did," Bob said, pointing to Dorothy. Then, turning his head toward the door, he threw his keys on the small table next to the couch.

"Do you have any idea why Dorothy wanted the two of you to come in?" I said, since Bob spoke first.

"Ask her," he answered harshly. Bob had been forced into a role as a recalcitrant husband, discussing his private business in front of a stranger, and he didn't like it.

"Well, I think that we've been having problems for a while," Dorothy began. And without the slightest glance in her husband's direction or pause, she went on to describe a six-year marriage rapidly heading for the skids.

As in most cases when couples begin therapy, Bob and Dorothy started the session by describing their situation in the vaguest possible terms to determine whether it was safe for them to talk in the presence of a stranger. At these moments a therapist is in the awkward position of being invited into the most personal aspects of a couple's life while simultaneously being expected to prove his or her worthiness to receive such an intimate introduction. It is a moment when all antennae are on alert and the ambivalent wish that a therapist will guess what the problem is so it can remain unsaid is shared by all parties. The ambivalence was played out in this first session through Dorothy's unconscious wish that I would focus on her husband and, for Bob, that I would say everything was fine so they could stop all the talking and just go home.

As I glanced at Bob briefly, I sensed a familiar fear that most men bring to couples therapy. His fear held the familiar fantasy that his wife would symbolically, emotionally, or (if paranoia crept in) physically have an affair with me. He looked terrified underneath a controlled exterior. If my intuition was accurate, he was afraid of being humiliated in the presence of another man. Having grown up in a family where problems were rarely talked about, I felt the need to reach out to Bob but tried to be careful not to lose the more empathic connection I already felt with Dorothy. On the other hand, sensing a mixture of exhaustion and smoldering rage in Dorothy, I hoped she would spill the beans sooner rather than later. The tension was palpable.

"You might try being a little bit more affectionate," Bob criticized, hinting at what might have been missing from their relationship for a long time.

"Was there a particular incident that brought you here today?" I inquired, trying to encourage Dorothy to talk and not let the first session deteriorate into an argument they undoubtedly knew well.

"Well," she said, looking down, and obviously wounded by Bob's implication. "Last week there was, well, an incident," Dorothy answered, and then went on to describe the latest in a series of arguments about money and Bob's version of the bohemian writer's lifestyle that meant his ongoing unemployment. On the previous weekend, in a fit of rage, having verbally attacked his wife Bob stormed out of the house to his favorite bar, returned home drunk in the early hours of the morning, and made unwanted sexual advances to his repulsed and frightened wife.

Ahhh! I thought, *now we're on familiar ground.* And while considering the obvious possibility that Bob had a drinking problem, I found myself thinking of a whole list of questions: How bad was it? Was there a history of physical violence? Was there a familial history of addiction? What other drugs might be involved? Was there a history of incest in Dorothy's family?

But luckily, rather than racing headlong into an interrogation, I let Bob and Dorothy speak for themselves.

And they did.

"I didn't touch you," Bob said, distancing himself from the impression that he was physically abusive.

"He doesn't hit me," she countered, "but last week . . ."

"I told you I was sorry for the stuff I said."

"He said some . . . really ugly stuff. He ended up . . . throwing . . ."

"You know I don't mean what I say when I've been drinking," Bob interrupted, cutting short his wife's elaboration and description of the episode.

I wondered if Bob threw something out of rage or at his wife. I wondered to what extent Dorothy was physically or emotionally afraid for her life.

"We just happen to be a fairly passionate couple—in some areas," Bob added.

WEIGHING THE RISKS

Once the presenting problem of alcohol and drug use has been identified, whether in the context of couples or individual therapy, the utility of drinking and using contracts, while not the most direct avenue toward sobriety, offers the alcoholic and addict an opportunity to wrestle with his distorted view of his loss of control while under the observance and guidance of a therapist. Drinking and using contracts offer alcoholics and addicts one more chance *to prove to themselves*, not to the therapist, spouse, or family, that they can control their drinking or using. They challenge the alcoholic and addict internally, because making an agreement (through the contract) with someone else externalizes the locus of commitment, and risks injecting an emotional virus into the task at hand. Alcoholics and addicts, challenged to control their substance use, will look for any opportunity to blame others for their loss of sobriety. If the agreement is made with another person, it gives the power to the other and provides an easy out when alcoholics or addicts are looking for someone else to blame. If the locus of control is contained by making the agreement with and to themselves, any loss of control is set apart from the conflicted relationships with spouse or therapist.

DRINKING/USING CONTRACTS

In general, the drinking and using contract involves a three-month period of abstinence followed by a three-month period of limited use. The challenge to the psychotherapist considering the use of a drinking contract is threefold. The first task necessitates evaluating the risk of withdrawal in the first phase of the contract and the likelihood of a patient's losing control during the second phase of the contract. The risks are less likely in the early stages of the disease and more so in the late stage when addicts and alcoholics present a greater danger to themselves and others on a daily basis. I never agree to a drinking and using contract with alcoholics or addicts in the late stage of the disease. The risk of damage to themselves or others is uniformly too great.

The second task requires that a therapist locate the alcoholic or addict's motivation to take the challenge and endure the absence and loss of alcohol or drugs. Occasionally, this may be accomplished in an individual session, if couples therapy is the mode of treatment. Other times, locating the alcoholic or addict's motivation to challenge his ability to abstain and control drinking or using can take several sessions to discover just who and what the patient holds dear enough in order to consider abstinence a positive experience.

The third task is more taxing, and requires that a therapist wait for the appropriate moment when the patient, rather than the therapist, presents the therapeutic challenge of "I can control it!" This may happen implicitly and necessitate a little coaching from the therapist when the patient spontaneously realizes the risk to what is valued most in life, or explicitly as in the case with Bob. The risks associated with abstinence relate primarily to the symptoms of withdrawal and should be monitored carefully. If any of the major symptoms of withdrawal appear the contract should be interrupted and the patient immediately referred for medical treatment. The risks associated with a period of controlled use may be medically associated with withdrawal, or related to driving while intoxicated, acting out violently, or making decisions while under the influence. The risks can be minimized, though not eliminated, by an agreement not to drive, argue, or have custody of minor children when drinking or using.

Over the course of the first session Bob reluctantly discussed his current drinking (4–6 drinks, 4x/week with weekend binges), occasional marijuana use (3x per week), and a history that included: LSD (100 trips over ten years), cocaine (episodic bingeing, though he never bought any himself), speed (10–20x over five years), and experimentation with mushrooms, hashish, and peyote. Given his current drinking and marijuana use I estimated that he had a moderate chance of experiencing minor withdrawal symptoms and only a very slight chance of expressing more extreme symptoms if he had minimized his current use. Though I was unaware of whether or not he was willing to explore a controlled drinking contract, Bob had already met the first criterion, minimal risk.

"Has this happened before, after you've come back from the bar?" I asked, wondering about the frequency of his drinking.

"The bar doesn't have . . ."

"Yes," Dorothy said, interrupting.

". . . anything to do with it."

"It's happened before."

"What can I say? I'm a writer!" Bob defended, clarifying that from his point of view the two went hand in hand.

I nodded as if to say "Of course!," not wanting to alienate the angry man in front of me.

"You knew that when you married me," Bob reminded his wife, then crossing his legs and leaning further away, he exhaled a sarcastic "hmmmmf!"

"Maybe I'm just sensitive to this because in my family," Dorothy said, offering an olive branch to Bob's challenge, "my dad drank and . . ."

"Uh, yeah, I think that has a lot to do with it. And, by the way, I'm not your father!"

Startled at Bob's raising his voice, Dorothy leaned back against the couch.

"She's one of those, like, you know, ACAs, or whatever."

"So when Bob comes home drunk," I said to Dorothy, "he reminds you of your father?" And as I spoke, a whole host of scenes played out before my eyes, not scenes of my own family but those of the family violence I had become familiar with over the years, scenes of day-long tirades, incest, and neglect. I blinked hard trying to remember that I was talking to Dorothy. The task at hand, however, defined in the session, was Bob's drinking.

"Yeah," she said, looking down at the floor. "And I worry."

"Has Bob ever had an accident before?" I asked, curious about his history with accidents and DUIs.

"Nothing significant, man, you know, little fender benders . . . shit like that." And Bob put his thumb and index fingers close together to emphasize his impression of just how small the accidents were.

"And that scares me. Then, if he comes home and he's still drunk, he goes into a rage. And he's never hit me, but . . ."

"I'm a pretty mellow guy."

I wasn't convinced.

"Not when he's drinking," Dorothy countered.

"So you agree that he's generally laid back," I said, trying to find a way to agree with both Bob and Dorothy simultaneously.

"Um-hm . . . yeah." Dorothy agreed.

"I'm an old hippie, man, you know."

And I nodded, remembering the early seventies and my own extended adolescence. I could hear Janis Joplin crying out in the distance, her voice hoarse and raw. I remembered bell-bottoms, psychedelic posters, peace rallies, and love-ins. I felt a sudden bond and nostalgia reminiscing with Bob, closer than I'd felt at any time in the interview. For a moment, my building irritation with his lack of empathy slackened.

"But when he's drinking . . ." Dorothy continued, grounding us in the present moment and disturbing our shared reverie of the past.

"No hope without dope," Bob said.

I was pissed. I felt betrayed. I was trying my best to be understanding, compassionate, and tolerant. I was waiting for the opportunity to find a connection to the pain beneath Bob's pale bravado, his bohemian lifestyle, and his laid-back attitude. I felt stepped on and, before I could hold my tongue, I retaliated with my own countertransference and anger at his narcissism.

"Yeah," I said trying to put him in his place, "I've heard that one before."

"Shit, I lived it," he said, one-upping me back.

"Well, " Dorothy said, trying to bring us back from our testosterone-filled duel. "When he's drinking it's different, and that scares me."

"Why are you worried about his being in an accident?" I asked.

"Yeah!" Bob added. "Why are you worried? You ride with me all the time!! I'm a good driver!"

"Because he has had a couple of accidents and I . . ."

"A couple of tiny accidents," Bob corrected. Then, in his determination to put an end to the discussion, Bob gave me what I needed to realize the name of the game.

"I have it under control!" He said defiantly.

And I thought, "Bingo! Criterion number two: the challenge."

THE STRUCTURE OF A CONTRACT

An effective drinking and using contract utilizes the following format (or variations thereof) to test the recalcitrant patient's ability to abstain and control drinking or using. The contract format I have used in the last decade includes:

1. A three-month period of abstinence from all substances that contain narcotics, depressants, stimulants, or hallucinogens, including over-the-counter diet and sleep aids, cold remedies, and allergy formulas. It also includes any prescription medications that may, under the advice of a physician, be withdrawn or exchanged for nonaddictive substitutes, including pain pills, diet pills, antianxiety agents, and the milder cold remedies and

analgesics that contain either alcohol, Hydrocodone (synthetic morphine), or codeine.

2. Weekly sessions to monitor compliance and the patient's experience, whether abstinence is easily achieved or the patient struggles, thinks about, dreams about, craves, near misses, or relapses.

3. A three-month period of controlled use that includes one or two drinks once or twice a week or a relative equivalent of the drug of choice. This, however, does not mean two drinks (joints, hits, lines of coke) at 11:59 P.M. and two at 12:01 A.M.. It also does not mean bingeing or two ten-ounce drinks.

4. Weekly therapy sessions to monitor compliance and experience.

Failure to maintain either abstinence or control is therefore considered symptomatic of *at least* problematic use. This necessitates explaining, at the time of engaging the contract, that when the patient says he or she can control their alcohol and drug use *we're talking about total control and total abstinence.* *Occasional* loss of an ability to abstain or control use is as much as *total* loss of control, because, in the context of comparing non-problematic users to alcoholics and addicts, one of the primary criteria is the ability to say no either before the first drink or after the second.

Why three months? In this regard I can rely only on clinical experience. Three months of abstinence provides a significant amount of time that is likely to expose the alcoholic or addict to a majority of life situations and the problems likely to instigate a relapse to previous levels of use or produce withdrawal. Though a large portion of even middle-stage chemical dependents are capable of abstaining without relapse for a period of three months, in ten years of making drinking and using contracts with patients, not one alcoholic or addict out of several hundred has been able to achieve both three months of abstaining and three months of controlling use without relapsing.

A three-month period of time also helps gauge a patient's resistance during the initial discussion of the alcohol and drug use and provides a period of sobriety to stand in contrast to the period of controlled use. If both three-month time periods are met successfully, a patient can look back on the last six months and decide whether or not to enter recovery, return to abstinence, remain controlled and risk a relapse to previous levels of use, or resume unrestricted drinking and using.

BARGAINING

Few patients enter into a drinking or using contract without a fuss. For some alcoholics and addicts, the challenge to prove a therapist or others wrong may be enough to leave behind a daily or episodic routine of alcohol and drug use. For most however, the six month period of abstinence and controlled use will loom far ahead and invite Coyote into the room to make his mischief. The recalcitrant patient is then likely to revert to denying the problem or bargaining with the therapist to minimize the challenge. Bob gave me the hardest time of any patient in my entire clinical career.

"Uh, Bob, " I said, taking advantage of the opening he gave me. "Have you ever tried to prove to Dorothy that alcohol and the dope wasn't a problem?"

"Dope?"

"Marijuana," I quickly corrected, having failed to use the same term he did. I hoped my error wouldn't increase the cognitive distance between us.

"Well," Bob said, "I don't see why I have to *prove* it. You know, it's not a problem."

"Yes, I understand that," I said, joining his declaration, "but given Dorothy's sensitivity, you know, to her father and all, have you ever, like, tried an experiment to see if things improved?" I knew I was on shaky ground using Dorothy's sensitivity as a tool and hoped he wouldn't take advantage of it. It was a calculated risk.

"You mean, like, what improves?" Bob asked implying he needed to know what was in it for him.

"The r-r-relationship." I stuttered, not wanting to be the first to imply that they hadn't had sex in a painfully long time. "The way the two of you get along."

"You mean sex?" Bob sneered, saying it outright.

"I can't believe we're talking about this!" Dorothy chuckled nervously.

"So I'm, I'm wondering if you've ever thought of an experiment?" And I looked Bob right in the eyes.

"Yeah," he said leaning forward. And with the most direct eye contact he'd made so far he said, "Yeah, I've thought of some experiments." Then leaning back and crossing his legs suggestively he asked, "What did you have in mind?"

Bingo! I thought, there's his motivation. *He wants sex.*

> When you've got them by the balls
> Their hearts and minds will follow.
> —Charles Colson

"Well," I said, grabbing at the straw Bob dropped. "I'm wondering if you've ever thought of not drinking and not smoking to see if it helped the situation?"

"Well, I don't think the pot has shit to do with it. I know her dad was a horrible drunk. He was a really bad dude. And he was hurtful to her. I guess there are probably times when I shouldn't drink whiskey. Like, what are you suggesting?"

In couples or family therapy, once the alcoholic or addict is invested in a drinking contract, the subtle homeostatic sabotage of other family members may surface in an attempt to derail the proceedings and maintain the chaos and previous distribution of power in the relationship. Initially, it appeared that Dorothy held the power in the relationship due to her income. She made the phone call for the first appointment. Her husband was both defensive and hostile about being dragged into my office. But when the power shifted in Bob's direction through his willingness to engage in the drinking contract, an equal counter-measure surfaced in order to maintain the status quo where Dorothy was the responsible victim in the relationship, and Bob was the laid-back, hedonistic, abusive father figure of a man.

"I don't think he'll stop," Dorothy challenged.

"I can stop. I don't have to drink. You know . . . I don't have to drink."

"Well," I added, trying to jump in and not let the struggle for power take precedence over the positive changes at hand, "I know an experiment that would test what effect not drinking might have on the relationship, given her sensitivity, given Dorothy's experience with her father and how terrifying it was for her."

"What are we talking here?" Bob demanded in a tone that established both his interest and need to define to what extent his life might be affected. "What are we talking like, no booze?"

He's hooked, I thought.

"He'll never do it!" Dorothy challenged.

Ahhh, Coyote, I thought again, *I see you.*

"You say you can control your drinking, so no booze for . . ." and before I could begin to clarify the normal three-month abstinence and three-month controlled drinking contract, Coyote leaped through the window and landed next to Bob.

"What's in it for me?" he said, picking up Coyote's cue.

"Well, you've talked about wanting to have more of an active sex life. You've talked about wanting more affection. You . . ."

"Yeah. And I'd like to get this woman off my back."

"And you've talked about wanting to get her off your back. So you have a lot to gain."

"That would be a new experience," Bob laughed.

Immediately, I glanced at Dorothy to see her reaction to Bob's comment. If Bob had spoken to me in such a condescending tone I would've blown my stack. But to my surprise, Dorothy just sat there taking it all in. Maybe the reality of his actually engaging in therapy had thrown her off balance. Maybe later on, when her self-esteem improved and her intolerance of his behavior and verbal sarcasm increased, a comment like that might set her off. But for the moment I was glad she hadn't reacted as I might have because it would have derailed the process up to that point.

"So you have a lot to gain," I said, catching my breath.

"If you were to stop drinking . . . I wouldn't nag him for however long he doesn't drink," Dorothy added, refraining from defining the timetable.

"Say, for example, would you be willing to go for a month?" I offered, already having reduced the time period from my usual three.

"A month?" Bob said incredulously.

"Well, you said you could control your drinking," I replied, feeling Coyote tugging at the cuff of my pants, pulling me closer to Bob's side of the couch. I wondered how we were going to agree. I felt a tense silence building. Then Dorothy broke in.

"I don't know if I can stop nagging him for a month."

And we all broke up laughing.

"No whiskey for a month?" Bob asked. "I can do that!"

And I could have sworn I saw Coyote lean over the back of the couch and whisper some advice into Bob's ear.

"But if you're really going to make a go of this, to really test whether she's reacting to you or the memory of her father, you would have to give up everything."

"No beer?" Bob asked.

Needless to say, I'd met my match. Bob bargained me down farther than any patient in a decade of drinking contracts. Unwilling to try total abstinence for a period of three months he finally agreed only to *not getting drunk for just one month*. Bob maintained the right to have a joint now and then, a beer at the ballpark or with burritos. But, as he stated, "I won't get drunk for a month because I know when I'm going to get drunk." Bob agreed, we agreed, and as they left my office smiling, I could've sworn I saw Coyote trotting between them as they walked down the stairs to the street. And I felt like I'd been taken.

THE HONEYMOON

"Well! I gotta say, we've had a great time," Dorothy boasted the following week, even before she and Bob sat down holding hands. "We went on a picnic."

"It was fun," Bob joined in with an unusually supportive manner. "We had a really good time."

"It was great," Bob said, and smiled in a way that made me wonder whether it was the picnic or what happened afterward that curled the ends of his mouth upward.

"He didn't drink at all," Dorothy added, even before my curiosity found a voice.

"Nothing?"

"Well, I didn't get drunk," Bob said clarifying his part of the agreement.

"He went out drinking during the week. But he didn't come home drunk," Dorothy added proudly.

I nodded, genuinely pleased.

"Yeah, well, I stopped at the bar," Bob went on. "I had a beer. I watched the ballgame. I talked to some friends."

"Things are just a lot calmer."

"And you've been great!" Bob said, praising his wife for keeping her part of the bargain.

"It hasn't been easy not to nag," Dorothy admitted.

"You've been fantastic!"

"Wonderful!" I joined in, cautious and curious.

Relaxed and shyly affectionate, Bob and Dorothy spent the remainder of the session reminiscing about the beginning of their relationship and the history of their previous divorces. They spoke lovingly about each other. They celebrated what they remembered and cherished about the beginning of their courtship. When Dorothy mentioned how encouraged she was by their quick progress, Bob suggested they "had it in them all along" and maybe they didn't need to come to therapy anymore. Though I was genuinely pleased with their progress, I was alarmed when Bob suggested terminating therapy. I was as convinced of the sustainability of their newfound intimacy as I was of my miraculous abilities as a therapist. Perhaps it was the gleam in his eye, the way in which Bob looked almost puffed up and confident. Or maybe it was how he quickly forgot the past that reminded me of Coyote's strength and cunning, and ultimately his downfall.

COYOTE LOSES EVERYTHING

One night when Coyote was on his way to Zuni to get married, he came across a group of animals gathered together in a circle. Coyote knew he shouldn't be late for his own wedding but he couldn't resist his own curiosity. He stopped to take a look.

"What are you doing?" he asked, but before one of the animals could answer, he knew. They were gambling.

"Can I join in?" Coyote asked, and of course they said yes. Coyote was a notorious gambler. Coyote was sure he would win something. *I always win*, he thought to himself, though this was not true. *I will take my winnings to my wedding to impress my new wife.*

Unfortunately, Coyote lost everything he brought with him. He lost the gifts for his wife, his wife's family, and her clan. Even after he lost everything he couldn't stop gambling.

Maybe this time I will win, he thought. And he lost even his fur.

Now until that moment Coyote had the prettiest, softest, shiniest fur of all the four-legged animals. His was more handsome than Bear, Beaver, and even Rabbit. But Coyote lost it all in one moment.

Whimpering, he stepped out of his skin and handed it over. Since it was night, it was cold and Coyote started to shiver. In his shame he walked away from the group, sat on a rock, and started crying.

Hearing his sad whimper, some mice wandered over to him. They felt sorry for him.

"Poor Coyote," they said. "Tomorrow he will get married and look at him now."

So they hunted around and gathered some old scraps of fur and glued them to Coyote with pinion pitch. And ever since, Coyote has had the saddest fur of all the animals, but that hasn't stopped him from gambling.

"Just for the sake of curiosity," and perhaps slyly taking advantage of their good mood I said, "why don't you both take in a Twelve Step meeting," and clarified that I meant Dorothy might go to Al-Anon and Bob to Alcoholics Anonymous, "just to gather information while things are going so well." Obviously puzzled at the suggestion I tried to sneak in as they stood up, they merely shrugged and acknowledged my comment. They smiled and walked hand in hand down the stairs to the street.

DOWN FROM THE HIGH

Ten minutes late to the next session, Dorothy walked into my office a few yards ahead of Bob. They sat down and stared at the floor. As in the first session, Bob took a seat at one end of the couch and Dorothy sat as far away from him as she could. I waited for them to start. I felt instinctively that I knew what happened. I could practically see the power of Dorothy's rage flow out in waves and I saw an image of Bob's emasculated emptiness as a large black hole in the middle of his chest.

"Maybe you should tell him about what happened," Dorothy said, urging her husband to explain why the honeymoon was over.

"Why don't you talk about it?" Bob replied turning away and looking out the window.

And she did. After receiving news that a screenplay he'd been working on for years was being considered for a pilot TV show, Bob celebrated at his local bar and set up a round for his friends. Forgetting and not forgetting about the agreement, Bob got drunk.

I looked at Bob and saw a man defeated, a man wasted. I felt genuinely sad and depressed even though I knew that ultimately this was the best thing that could have happened. And at the same time it pained me to see the sad look in his eyes, let alone the agony in Dorothy's voice.

"I've picked him up from bars so many times I can't even remember." Dorothy cried and reached for a tissue. "It makes me think how sick I must be that I'd do that. And I just realized, I just can't take this any more. I can't. I mean I feel like I'm going crazy. I can't do this anymore. I think we need to separate. Something has got to change 'cause I can't do this anymore, I don't want to."

And she burst into tears.

"I think you're just gettin' carried away," Bob discounted Dorothy's pain.

"Maybe I am! All I know is I can't take this any more."

Bob was genuinely shocked. He obviously didn't realize the depth of Dorothy's pain and her growing intolerance of his drunkenness. When I asked him what happened, after an initial defensive response that "nothing is any different than before," Bob described how "one drink led to another" and that he couldn't say no when his drinking buddies at the bar set up drink after drink until he could barely stand. He couldn't remember who called Dorothy to pick him up and his blackout protected him from remembering that he vomited in the car on the way home.

Bob looked lost and afraid. I wanted to encourage him. I wanted to tell him it would be all right. I wanted to ask Dorothy to give him another chance. I wanted to shake him and say, "Don't you see what you're doing? You need help." I wanted to, but I knew I had to let him sit in his fear of losing Dorothy, his anxiety about being alone, and the loss of his meal ticket. I knew that if I stepped in I would diffuse the drama unfolding in front of me. I knew that if I interrupted the painful silence, Bob might lose sight of the bottom rushing up toward him. It was incredibly difficult to hold my tongue. I wanted to save him from the pain and at the same time I wanted him to feel it.

"Y'know, I didn't have it in mind to get wasted."

"I know you didn't." Dorothy conceded softly.

"Honestly, I didn't . . ."

"But you did." And she wept silently.

"You know, I mean, this is not something that hasn't happened before."

"And that's the thing. It *has* happened before. A lot of times. When do I start taking care of myself instead of always taking care of you? When do I stop picking up the pieces? I can't, I can't do this anymore. I can't. I just can't. . . ."

Sensing the inevitable, Bob leapt in and brought out his final attempt to manipulate his wife. Coyote was getting desperate and I could hear him whimpering off in the corner.

"I don't think you wanna leave," Bob said. "You know what that would do to me. You know, it would be like pulling the rug right out from under me!"

WHEN ENOUGH IS ENOUGH

Dorothy's eyes flared and she gasped at her husband's blatant attempt to control her with guilt. She took in an audible gasp and became silent and still. I tracked the second hand of the clock beside the couch and pinched myself. I bit my tongue and tried to hold back from relieving the pressure that took six years to build. At a minute-five, Bob conceded.

"Well," he said, "I guess I could have celebrated just fine with the two of us. We coulda gone out to dinner. I see your point. I didn't know you were hurting that much about it. I guess I need to start bein' home more, huh?" he said, offering a crumb to a starving woman.

"Would that be enough for you?" I asked Dorothy. "For Bob to spend more time at home? Would that make the difference?" And I prayed Dorothy wouldn't cave in to such a small gesture. I hoped she would stick to her implied threat. I could see she was thinking about it.

"That would be a start. But I don't know if that would be enough."

Yes! I thought, and in my mind I leapt in the air.

"Bob," I asked, "have you ever been to AA?"

"Yeah, I went once. I was researchin' a story four or five years ago."

"You went to AA?" Dorothy said, obviously surprised.

"I was researching a story and I went to a couple of meetings."

"I didn't know that."

"I was, like . . . you know. It wasn't that big of a deal. The story really didn't get very far."

Of course, I thought. And neither did his interest in sobriety. While not entirely the norm, it *is* common for many alcoholics and addicts to find their way to a meeting under the guise of helping a friend, gathering information for a family member, or, in Bob's case, researching a story.

"It was about four or five years ago around the time that everyone started to get sober all at once, you know."

"Uh-huh."

"I was kind of interested in the phenomenon."

"What were the meetings like?"

"Uhh, they were pretty boring. You know, the level of discourse wasn't all that stimulating. 'Hi, I'm Bob, I'm an alcoholic. I drank myself through fourteen marriages and beat up eighteen kids.'"

I nodded.

"Everybody's got a story, you know?"

I nodded again.

Noticing how close to the end of the hour we were, I spoke directly to Dorothy. "If Bob went to thirty meetings in the next month would you consider hanging around to see if he could stay sober with help?"

Dorothy was silent. In the midst of her silence I hoped she wouldn't back down and let Bob off the hook. I was looking out for Coyote because I was afraid he would take advantage of the situation and talk Dorothy into letting Bob off the hook for so many meetings. And I hoped Bob wouldn't jump in and start negotiating from thirty down to some lower number.

"I would consider it," Dorothy said.
And Bob let out a sigh of relief.

The following month presented a number of scheduling difficulties. The first two weeks I was out of town and the week after that Dorothy was away on business. Unfortunately, we couldn't meet for an entire month and I feared that without the structure of therapy, Bob might slip back into his old routine. Over the weeks we kept contact by phone, traded messages back and forth, and finally spoke for a few minutes the day after Dorothy returned from her business trip. She called just as I was about to leave the office for the night. She got home earlier than she expected and was fearful Bob might have fallen off the wagon. She was more than a bit anxious. She wondered whether she should call around to the hospitals to see if Bob had been in an accident. But just as we were about to hang up Bob returned from his second AA meeting that day.

In the beginning of the session that week Bob talked about how he took to AA after recognizing a close friend at the meeting.

"This is weird," he said, leaning forward on the couch next to his wife. "I went to a meeting the day after we met last month and there was this guy. They call them the speaker at these meetings."

I nodded and let Bob teach me about Alcoholics Anonymous.

"This guy, the speaker, was somebody that I knew really well, like fifteen years ago. And, uh, we used to hang out." Bob laughed in a way that brought images of drunken parties filled with smoke to mind. "We used to party a lot. We even lived together at one time. Anyway, somehow he disappeared. I never knew what happened to him. As it turns out he stopped using. He stopped getting high. And when he talked about it, I felt like he was talking right to me."

I nodded again, smiling, and as I listened a cautious feeling of relief rose up from my gut and allowed me to share in Bob's newfound sobriety.

"It was like old home week. So I went up to him afterwards and we started talking. It was so weird. After he listened to what I had to say, he just told me point-blank that I had to stop drinking."

"Really?"

"And I had to stop getting high."

"What did you tell him?"

"This is the weird part. I told him that it sounded like he was right. So I've been absolutely clean since then."

"He came back from that meeting," Dorothy chimed in, "and, I don't know, but there was some kind of change. He came home and we just talked for hours. And we haven't done that in ages. I mean it was like we were trying to understand rather than blame each other."

"What did you talk about?" I asked.

"Well," Dorothy said, "just kind of everything, I mean, his part in things, my part in things. I've been going to those Al-Anon meetings."

I nodded, trying to contain a grin that unchecked might have been received as a bit goofy.

"It just makes me really aware of my behavior."

"It seemed like I was finally ready for someone to say, 'Bob, stop this shit!'"

"Well, I've been saying that," Dorothy chided, and I wondered if Bob would bite back as he had in the previous sessions.

"Well, I guess I just couldn't hear you say it," he replied almost tenderly.

I was impressed. Bob took the fact that Dorothy had said the same thing his friend and savior had said to him without biting back. And he admitted he couldn't hear it. For a somewhat narcissistic man like Bob, this was a big concession.

For the next half-hour Bob and Dorothy talked about how much better their relationship had been since he stopped drinking. When Dorothy chimed in, Bob paused rather than correct or criticize her. When Bob owned his sobriety in a self-congratulating and narcissistic way, Dorothy held her tongue. She spoke about how hard it was to stay out of Bob's life and let him struggle with his own problems. She admitted it was just as hard for her to stop criticizing or rescuing Bob as much as he was struggling to stay sober.

Without making any agreements, both Bob and Dorothy acknowledged the necessity to continue to work on themselves and, as many couples who enter therapy with the hope that one or both will get into recovery, they recognized that sobriety brought with it a new set of difficulties. Previously, their relationship had been characterized by short periods of enmeshment through sex, passionate arguments, power struggles, and longer periods of distance defined by Bob's binges and Dorothy's wounded aloofness. Now that a new stability was forming between them based on mutual respect, autonomy, and intimacy, Dorothy was concerned that they might grow apart.

"Well," she said hesitantly, "it's not like it was a couple of weeks ago when things were so great. It's weird. Cause we're both different and we don't know quite how to, you know, relate to each other. I'm just afraid we're going to drift apart."

I nodded.

"I'm not so sure what's going on between us but it's not like I want to go back to the way things were."

Sensing their confusion I jumped in to help clarify the awkwardness of early recovery and gave Bob and Dorothy a template to understand the ground that lay ahead.

"It can be awkward in the beginning," I said. "In one way your recovery is the same, and in another it's very different. The things that each of you will explore over the next few months, as you continue in the program, are very different from each other. For example, Bob, you might find yourself feeling understood in the presence of other alcoholics and addicts. And Dorothy, there's a good chance that you will feel understood in the presence of other co-dependents. There might be times when you can talk to each other about it and it will make sense. And there might be times when you'll talk about what is going for you and it won't make sense. There won't be an understanding."

"Yeah," Bob said, defining his territory, "I don't want to hurt your feelings by saying this but I don't think you really understand me right now. I mean it's weird."

"I guess I get a little scared when you say that. Are we just gonna drift apart now that we're making these changes?"

Just as I was about to answer and be the know-it-all therapist, Bob stepped in and saved *me*.

"I dunno. I don't think so." And he gazed gently at his wife. "But I just know that what's goin' on for me doesn't have, I don't want to hurt your feelings, but it doesn't seem to have very much to do with you right now."

And he was partly right and partly not. For Bob, the focus of his recovery rapidly revolved around his attendance at meetings and his doing the steps. I guessed, based on his previous self-centered attitude, that in a short period of time, Bob would rise through the ranks of the Program to build his self esteem, literally, step by step. Hopefully, if his sponsor recognized it, he might also be gently prodded to acknowledge how he might be replacing a Twelve Step related self-centeredness for his previous arrogance. With the help of a sponsor or an individual therapist, he might begin to embrace a path of humility at the center of a recovery from alcohol and drugs.

"It just seems ironic," Dorothy added. "You know, last month I was talking about wanting to separate . . ."

"I don't want to split up," Bob said tenderly. "Uh, that's not what I'm talking about."

"I don't want to split up, either. I mean, as long as we both are moving forward. I just wonder is there any way we can move forward together, too?"

My experience in private practice has led me to conclude that after entering recovery couples often terminate therapy or put aside their relationship struggles in order to concentrate on their individual growth and development. While some survive this separation, others split apart under the strain of past wounds and the difficulty of balancing their relationship needs with their individual healing. At the end of the session, sensing that we were at a decisive point, I asked Bob and Dorothy where they thought they might be heading at this point in therapy. Characteristically, Bob opted for terminating, but after giving a second thought to how important the sessions had been, he suggested that they come back once a month for a while to see how things progressed in his recovery. Relieved, Dorothy agreed and we all shook hands.

Not all drinking contracts end with such harmony and insight. If the alcoholic chooses to keep drinking it may result in the loss of a job, estrangement from family members, or divorce if an employer or spouse has had enough. Whether in the context of individual, couples, or family therapy, a drinking/using contract offers the alcoholic and addict a chance to decide whether or not to enter treatment after facing an undeniable inability to abstain or control using. It offers an opportunity to remain abstinent because things have improved following the cessation of drinking or using. Or if the alcoholic and addict decides to continue in controlled drinking or return to previous levels of using, the abstinent and controlled period of time can act as a reference point when later drinking and using produces negative consequences. Either way, it's a win–win scenario.

Countertransference and Compassion

COYOTE'S LAIR

Working with recovering alcoholics and addicts in psychotherapy, I often see myself talking with Coyote in front of his lair. What may initially appear to be a straightforward task, when the initial diagnosis is made, often seems daunting once a threshold of sobriety is crossed where problems lurk deep inside the chambers of the alcoholic's and addict's past. A majority of the problems associated with the dually diagnosed patient have defined clinical characteristics and fit neatly into the *DSM-IV* framework, but what the disorders fail to describe are the human dramas, the pain, and the fears that keeps a whole host of feelings and memories at bay.

For every diagnosis of alcohol and drug dependence, once a threshold into sobriety is reached, slowly, over time, a therapist is likely to hear a voice in the darkness, a voice of pain waiting to speak out. The voice may be heard when the alcohol and drugs are withdrawn allowing previously suppressed feelings, memories, or nightmares to surface. It may be heard in the midst of the Fourth Step, when a fearless moral inventory encourages a sober individual to look back on the past. Or it may be heard when the safety of the therapeutic container is established and the alcoholic and addict in recovery begins recalling a lifetime of sadness. The sadness may take the form of guilt and shame arising amidst the memories of a drunken past from a new, sober perspective. It may surface in the wake of acknowledging the tremendous loss in a lifetime of drinking or using drugs that left behind friends, marriages, children, jobs, fortune, self-respect, dignity, and the shattered pieces of one's soul. Or it may be connected to having committed or witnessed emotional or physical violence, incest, a variety of destructive compulsions, prostitution, or even homicide.

Just when you believe you've heard it all, when you find yourself deep inside Coyote's den, your fingers may find a narrow passage to yet another chamber. Carefully exploring the opening, you wait for your eyes and ears to adjust to the stillness, the silence, and the blackness. And if you listen closely, you may hear a voice speaking for the alcoholic and addict's unhealthy relationships. Because within every alcoholic or addict a co-dependent (and frequently an adult child of an alcoholic) is alive and not quite well.

CO-DEPENDENCY AND ADULTS
TRAUMATIZED AS CHILDREN

At one point or another all alcoholics and addicts associate with others who drink and use, especially during the latter stages of the disease, when their behavior becomes intolerable to the uninebriated. At some time during sobriety, when recovering alcoholics pull away from their drinking and using buddies and away from enmeshed, chaotic relationships, they may find themselves exhibiting many of the co-dependent characteristics hidden beneath the more obvious face of the alcoholic and addict. These characteristics, described by Cermak (1986), may include:

A. A continued investment of self-esteem in the ability to control both oneself and others in the face of serious consequences.
B. An assumption of responsibility for meeting other's needs to the exclusion of acknowledging one's own.
C. Anxiety and boundary distortions around intimacy and separation.
D. Enmeshment in relationships with personality disordered, chemically dependent, other co-dependent, and/or impulse disordered individuals.
E. Three or more of the following:
  1. Excessive reliance on denial
  2. Constriction of emotions

3. Depression
4. Hypervigilance
5. Compulsions
6. Anxiety
7. Substance abuse
8. Has been or is the victim of recurrent physical abuse or sexual abuse
9. Stress-related ailments
10. Has remained in a primary relationship with an active substance abuser for at least two years without seeking help.

[Cermak 1986, p. 11]

Later, after several years of therapy and a naturally evolving reflection about the alcoholic and addict's relationships, after stories of drunkenness, hangovers, painful breakups, loss, and anguish, you may find yourself hearing the muffled sound of a young child deep within your patient's story inside the darkness of the past. Touching the damp earth of Coyote's den with your fingers, if you reach out carefully you may discover an opening to yet another chamber revealing the pain from the recovering alcoholic and addict's childhood experiences.

Due to the genetic predisposition of chemical dependence, a high percentage of alcoholics and addicts grow up in drug-dependent families. Whether as a result of the stage of the disease at the time of the child's early physical and emotional development, the lack of resources available, the family's lack of cohesion, or a parent's psychiatric disorder, many children either witness or are subjected to intense experiences that may involve being:

Rejected: when the adult refuses to acknowledge the child's worth and the legitimacy of the child's needs.
Isolated: when the adult cuts the child off from normal social experiences and relationships, or makes the child believe he or she is alone in the world.
Terrorized: when the adult verbally assaults the child, creates a climate of fear, bullies and frightens the child, or makes the child believe the world is capricious.
Ignored: when the adult deprives the child of essential stimulation and emotional responsiveness.

Corrupted: when the adult mis-socializes the child to destructive, antisocial behavior and reenforces deviance.

[Garbarino 1986, p. 8]

Although a great deal has been written over the last decade on the impact these experiences have on the child and the adult patient (Jaroff 1993, Loftus 1993, Reviere 1996, Wright 1993), the impact of *exploring* a lifetime of pain in the context of psychotherapy or *witnessing* the emergence of traumatic memories is rarely discussed. Work in the field of long-term depth psychotherapy long enough, as opposed to the kind of short-term treatment promulgated by managed health care, and you'll see your patient tremble, become nauseous, and arrive for an appointment sleep-deprived, fearing the return of a repetitive nightmare. You will feel your gut tighten when your patient recalls a parent's drunken rage that led to repeated beatings. And you will recoil when your patient reveals, after years of confessed promiscuity, a stepparent's face when he first entered a darkened bedroom. You will shudder when you hear how she prayed that the darkness would disappear and when it didn't, a large part of her did. And it will change you, forever.

HADDIE

A 39-year-old woman in her third year of sobriety, Haddie entered therapy because she had nightmares, unexplainable anxiety, and difficulty concentrating at work. Slightly over five feet tall, she wore her straight black hair slightly above her shoulders and dressed in a conservative fashion that covered virtually every square inch of her skin aside from her hands, neck, and face. Four months into therapy, virtually at the end of the session, Haddie told me a dream.

"I'm alone in the darkness. I can't see anything but it feels wrong. Something isn't right. It feels like spiders are crawling all over me. I can't stand spiders. At the office yesterday I saw a small spider. It was so tiny but I freaked. I couldn't handle it. I was trembling and wanted to scream. Anyway, in the dream, I try to look at my hands but I don't have a body. I woke up screaming. Oh," she said nonchalantly, realizing that the hour was nearly over, "I'll see you next week." And without the slightest acknowledgment or hesitation, Haddie stood up. She shuffled toward the door, opened it slowly, and disappeared.

In the past decade, several high-profile lawsuits and investigations have raised questions regarding the validity of adult memory recall in cases involving early childhood trauma, incest, and satanic abuse. Though not all children who grow up in alcoholic families are subject to such trauma, a number of studies indicate a high correlation between child neglect and child abuse and parental alcohol or drug problems (Hindman 1977, Orme and Kenner 1981). A psychotherapist treating the recovering alcoholic or addict who begins to remember past trauma is faced with a number of difficult tasks: to believe or not believe the patient who states categorically, "I was molested because I have all the symptoms" but no specific memories; whether to use active measures such as directed visualization, hypnosis, or even more controversial techniques that risk tainting the integrity of the therapeutic process; or try to maintain an open perspective and let the material unfold in its own time.

In the last decade, numerous articles and books have drawn attention to the ways in which investigators and therapists may have unconsciously introduced suggestive material into the experience of a patient. A collective tendency among therapists might be to interpret this criticism as unjustified or characteristic of the backlash against the growing number of child abuse allegations in this country. From a personal and professional perspective, I feel an obligation to examine my work in light of these important questions. As a result, two types of countertransference dilemmas discussed below may shed light on the difficult task we face as psychotherapists.

THE NIGHTMARE

As I waited for Haddie just prior to her next session, I wondered if she would bring up the dream she briefly mentioned at the end of the last session or whether she'd ignore it, forget it, or move on to some other topic. Sensing the hesitation in her voice when she said "Hello" as I invited her in to my office, I sat back in my chair and waited for her to begin. Carefully and meticulously, as she did at the beginning of every session, Haddie arranged the coat she never removed. It was a ritual worthy of my attention and restraint.

"It was horrible," she said.

"Another nightmare?"

She nodded and stared at the floor for a few moments. Her head rose slowly and she paused. Her face went blank, her body went limp, and Haddie sat virtually motionless. Her breathing appeared shallow, almost nonexistent. Slowly, her eyes closed as if she were asleep. A few moments later, her head jerked back slightly and her eyes opened wide.

"What just happened?" I asked as gently as I could.

She shook her head and took a minute to look around the room as if she were reorienting herself.

"I guess I nodded off," she said, and was silent. "I'm in a room in the house I grew up in. It's nighttime, it's dark. I see a figure standing in the doorway. I can't quite see who it is because the light from the hallway is too bright. The figure is moving toward me. Closer, closer."

I quickly became aware of how the dream was happening to Haddie in the present moment and not in the past. She looked alone.

"I'm afraid. I can't move," she said, frightened. "The figure is coming closer." And as her eyes opened wide she sucked in and held her breath. "I can't move. There's a huge, figure towering over me. I'm trying to scream but no sound comes out."

In the silence that followed her terrified disclosure I noticed that Haddie had stopped breathing. She sat motionless. Her chest no longer moved in and out. I counted off the length of her immobility to the pulse of my increasingly loud heartbeats.

Five, six, seven, eight, nine.

She gasped and her breathing told me she had returned to the room.

Reading the story of Haddie's dream you may have noticed a number of subjective responses, as I did listening to her. I noticed a shallowness in my breathing as I watched her breathing virtually disappear. My concentration focused sharply on each word she spoke. I was transfixed as she hesitated before speaking and then held on to the last consonant of the last word in each sentence. I heard the tension beneath the monotone in her voice. I had a deep sense of fore-boding tightening around my stomach. And I felt uncomfortable not knowing what happened at the conclusion of the story.

In the extended moments of her breathlessness I considered a variety of questions that might shed light on the dream, its possible meaning, and the fears that welled up in my chest. I thought about the anxiety we all have of the unknown, of the shadow, and of the darkness. I thought about how small and vulnerable a child can feel. Then, in the midst of several possible interpretations, it occurred to me that the dream might represent an incest memory.

As therapists, we walk a fine line between denial and hysteria. If we ignore the signs and symptoms a patient presents we may miss a trail of psychic bread crumbs left by a child in need. We may miss a precious opportunity in the natural movement toward healing. Or we may leap too soon and force a patient to acknowledge something on our schedule and not hers. If we fail to discriminate, however, among what is recalled by a patient as a memory, a feeling, a dream, or an image, we may take the material concretely as fact and end up constructing a past on shifting sands.

If we leap too quickly out of our own excitement, out of our need to confirm our hypotheses of abuse, neglect, incest, or trauma, we may stop the patient's recollection from evolving or revealing itself. One week's memory ("It was standing over me") may change over time and become an image with psychological, not physical, meaning. A patient may come to realize that the image represented emotional and not physical trauma. "You know . . . it doesn't feel right. I don't think he came into my bedroom, but he was intrusive and humiliated me frequently." Then, when the patient is able to tolerate the memory and affect associated with it, the image, memory, or dream may evolve and the figure may take on more recognizable features, the darkness may be replaced by a dim light or bulb, and the room may change entirely to a different location.

When we finally think we know what actually happened we must also remain open and hold in abeyance even our relief at a psychological interpretation because there is no certainty that *this* is the final form of the realization. A patient's declaration that "I wasn't really abused. The dream just represents his badgering me" may be true or it may be a retreat from the former physical manifestation to a benign, safe, symbolic interpretation. The problem is, that if we put *our need* to know the significance, *our need* to know the source of the dream, the nightmare, and the intrusive image, *our need* to release the palpable tension held aloft in the space between our chest and the patient's, we may offer a comment or question prematurely and risk *concretizing* or *embellishing* the patient's recollections.

CONCRETIZING THE PROCESS

Concretizing the patient's story may occur when a therapist attempts to clarify a partial offering by placing the material in a context inconsistent with the patient's current experience or timing of the recall. This might have occurred if I inadvertently asked, "Who came into your bedroom at night when you were a child?" introducing the idea that someone actually intruded into *her* bedroom, though Haddie had yet to mention whose bedroom it was. Or it may have occurred if I had suggested that "Your dream is consistent with dreams reported by other adults who were molested as children," validating her dream and my interpretation by backing it up with a partial truth. Or it may have occurred in the extreme if I had *insisted* that "The dream is proof that you were molested," in an attempt to bolster my need to know, to contain my countertransference, or to appear omniscient.

Comments such as these, while for the most part understandable with the last considered extreme, may also risk overwhelming the patient. Patients who recall terrifying nightmares are, in general, extremely vulnerable. By introducing an interpretation or, worse, the insistence that an image means something even more frightening, a therapist may exacerbate the patient's anxiety, raise dormant defenses, and run the risk of short-circuiting an emerging revelation. Or the interpretation, commentary, or insistence, may offer the patient a convenient excuse to compartmentalize, dissociate, and contain the experience *and be done with it.*

"Once I remembered what happened, it becomes solid. I could hold it, and put it away. Then it doesn't affect me any longer."

Very few patients are intrinsically motivated, when they reach this point in treatment, except to relieve themselves of a variety of problematic symptoms that may include: insomnia, anxiety, agitation, paranoia, disorientation, blackouts, fainting, a kind of pseudonarco-lepsy, intrusive recollections or images, phobias, somatic complaints, difficulty with intimacy or sexual relations, depression, an overwhelm-ing sense of dread or powerlessness, dystonic obsessions, a sudden focus on physical safety and strength, nightmares, and daymares. At times Haddie would even become disoriented, dizzy, and see images superimposed on what she knew was concrete and real. Patients in such a high degree of psychic stress often require multiple sessions per week and medical consultation when the anxiety, stress, and sleep deprivation risk decompensation or suicidal thinking. If a therapist unwittingly suggests wrapping it up in a single concept, a patient is just as likely to grab at the chance to embrace an oversimplified, cause-and-effect explanation to avoid any further emerging images, dreams, or affect.

A therapist's comment may result in the patient initially calming down but it may also extinguish the potential relief intrinsic to a ter-rifying and eventually healing discovery. Calmed by an assertive an-swer provided by an intervening therapist, a patient may awake as if from a dream, blink, embrace the therapist's comment, and move on. Though still numb and slightly deadened, she may initially appear calm but will leave your office with the image, the feeling, and the dream alive and waiting just beneath the surface.

EMBELLISHING THE MATERIAL

When a therapist "leads the witness" by adding information to the patient's story in the midst of asking a question or making a specific statement, a therapist is at risk of *embellishing* the patient's material. In Haddie's session, this might have happened if I had asked pointed questions in order to gather more information. It might have occurred if I had asked, "What do you think the figure was going to do to you?" when there was no indication that the figure was necessarily going to *do* anything. Or it might have occurred if I had said, "The figure seemed menacing, as if he was going to hurt you," when all we knew at this point was that, in the dream, Haddie was terrified by the pres-ence of the dark figure.

An interpretation about incest may seem obvious and even have been accurate. *But if the patient is vulnerable to suggestion, the voiced interpretation or comment may also become part of the patient's stated story and confuse further revelation.* This contamination is unlikely when a patient's ego is strong enough to evaluate the therapist's comment objectively, and when internal and external stressors are minimal. Unfortunately, when a patient is recovering from some form of early childhood trauma, this is rarely the case. On one occasion, when Haddie drifted off as she spoke about her anxiety and fear that she was being followed by menacing forces of darkness, a feeling that lasted several days after a nightmare, an intrusive question on my part actually blocked her recall by throwing her off her own path of associations. Moments after she mentioned feeling afraid of a man she saw in a shopping mall, a man that looked familiar and frightening, she appeared to fall asleep as she often did in the session. After several minutes, I interrupted her dazed state too quickly by asking, "Are you back in *the room* again?" implying the room she regularly recalled when she had a nightmare. She hadn't been, as I later learned. But my question sidetracked her. For two or three sessions she readily associated the man on the street with the room in her dreams. Several days later we retraced the incidents of her associations with the man on the street, my interruption, and picked up where we left off, mending the distraction and my blunder. I was lucky I caught it.

THE HERO UNMASKED

The question is: Why would I act so quickly? What contributes to my tendency to name, interpret, and contain the material rather than wait for a patient's own timing to reveal the whole story? I believe the tendency comes from two basic human responses. First, what we do as therapists is often inordinately difficult. We sit and listen to other people's pain hour after hour, week after week, year after year. At times when the patient's story is particularly painful or horrific, as it frequently is when alcohol, drugs, disease, and death are involved, we may react in ways consistent with the patient's own response: we wince, we feel pain, we shut down, we try to do something to make it better, we try to clarify what we're up against, and then try to make it go away.

In response to the pain, and I believe it is normal although not necessarily helpful, *I may try to name the horror as soon as possible.* I may call out the beast and define it outside the realm of the patient's experience. I may try, in effect, to contain the revelation. Or I may try to gain control over the pace of the revelation itself by stepping in and interrupting the patient's story. I may feel the urge to do this with the intention of validating the patient's experience, but I may also be attempting to reassure myself and gain some measure of control over the sympathetic pain I feel witnessing a traumatic revelation.

I am not implying that it is appropriate for a therapist to be entirely passive. The therapist's presence, goodwill, and inquiring attitude all help make sense of, tolerate, and contain an often overwhelming experience of horror. A more thoughtful and less intrusive alternative to making an immediate interpretation might be to:

> invite the patient to comment on the dream and wait for a response, regardless of the silence we are required to tolerate;
> work with the dream by asking nonleading questions, such as "What do you see?" "What do you feel?" "Where are you now?";
> invite the patient to consider the meaning of the dream.

This approach is based in the assumption that a patient's defenses must be respected and (at times) utilized rather than discarded, dismantled, or penetrated. It is an approach that respects the *patient's* timing and not the therapist's need to act heroically as a burrowing instrument of memory recall. I find myself deeply concerned when I see a patient whose attempt to know the truth of what happened led them to seek out recovered memory workshops where hundreds of people were simultaneously hypnotized and led through visualizations, where the intent and promised relief focused on revealing the past without support for the panic, chaos, and self-loathing that often follows for days or even months after such discoveries.

Secondly, *I believe I may act out of my fear of the unknown.* I may try to name the event, name the wound or the perpetrator prematurely because not knowing what happened is nearly as uncomfortable for me as it is for the patient. Not knowing may be unnerving, agitating, and at times intolerable. As a therapist I am often hungry to know what is inside. Because if I can get inside, I believe I may find something of value. In my desire to get in there and help, my heroic inflation may lead to opening a deliberately closed container releasing unforeseen, humbling, and painful consequences.

HOW THE STARS GOT IN THE NIGHT SKY

In the beginning of the world, when the animals came up from the darkness to live above the ground, before the two-leggeds came up from below, Coyote was sent by Thought Woman on a special journey to the South.

"Carry this buckskin pouch," she told Coyote, "but do not open it or I will punish you."

For many days and nights Coyote journeyed to the South with the pouch on his back. But because the world was new there wasn't much for him to eat, just a bit of grass here and there and he got hungry. But he kept walking, and as he kept walking his stomach grumbled.

I wonder if there is some food in this pouch, Coyote thought. But he remembered Thought Woman's command and feared her punishment. So he kept walking. Finally, one night, his hunger was more than he could bear and it spoke to him.

"Open the pouch," his hunger said. "Maybe there is something to heal your pain."

And so he took the pouch from his back and opened it. As soon as he unloosed the leather thong wrapped around the pouch, thousands of stars poured out. Coyote was startled and jerked back and the stars flew up into the night sky all this way and that, which is where they are to this day.

At that very moment, Thought Woman appeared and said, "Look what you have done, Coyote. Now the stars have no order. You disobeyed me and from now on you will always get into trouble wherever you go."

And suddenly, Coyote had a toothache. At night, when the other animals were asleep or resting, he could only sit and howl at the stars and has been crying so every since the beginning of the world.

When holes in the patient's memory threaten to remain hidden I often feel an impulse to step in to fill in the blanks and find closure in the patient's story where only emptiness and fear exist. The question is, am I acting in the patient's best interest or am I acting out of my own discomfort and impatience? Am I acting out of my own countertransference to have everything in nice neat packages that fit into fifty-minute hours and easily contained concepts? Or am I trying to heal the pain related to my own past, my own fears, and my intolerance of the unknown?

The current professional climate regarding memory recall ranges dramatically, from the denial that recovered memories exist to assurances on the part of a therapist (following the briefest of recollections) that the patient must have been molested. Incomplete memories or lack of recall are often taken *a priori* as evidence of abuse by a therapist quick to define the problem and possibly reduce the therapist's as much as the patient's anxiety and fear (Bass 1988). As a psychotherapist in private practice, I feel a need to exercise great care when working with all patients including addicts, alcoholics, and adults recovering from early childhood trauma. Taking a therapeutic stance that the patient's recall is precious, I struggle to resist the heroic urge to call out and name the beast, contain it, and lock it away. I struggle to resist neatly contained answers to unmentionable questions. And I resist the urge to sound omniscient.

Struggling to embrace the partial offering in Haddie's dream, in the image, and in the crumb of a recollection, I wait, I listen, and I struggle to stay present. Then, when the pain washes over me, the fear through me, and the terror dissolves in the midst of a shared horror, I struggle to respect the unknown. When I can no longer bear it, I try to remember that I am human and that I have limits. I call up a senior colleague to schedule an hour to talk, to feel the sadness and the horror linking her pain to my own compassion and suffering. I remind myself of the healing amidst the pain and I remember and feel grateful that I am alive inside.

❖ ❖ ❖ ❖

References

Abrams, D. B., Rohsenow, D. J., et al. (1992). Smoking and treatment outcome for alcoholics: effects on coping skills, urge to drink, and drinking rates. *Behavior Therapy* 23 (2):283–297.

Alcoholics Anonymous (1984). *Alcoholics Anonymous Comes of Age.* New York: AA World Services.

Alterman, A., ed. (1985). *Substance Abuse and Psychopathology.* New York: Plenum.

American Psychiatric Association (1980). *Diagnostic and Statistical Manual of Mental Disorders DSM-III-R,* 3rd ed., pp. 163–180.

Bass, E. (1988). *The Courage to Heal: A Guide for Women Survivors of Child Sexual Abuse.* San Francisco and New York: Harper & Row.

Blane, J., and Leonard, K. E., eds. (1987). *Psychological Theories of Drinking and Alcoholism.* New York: Guilford.

Blum, K., Noble, E., Sheridan, P., et al. (1990). Allelic association of human dopamine D2 receptor gene in alcoholism. *Journal of the American Medical Association* 263:2055–2060.

Blum, K., Noble, E. P., Sheridan, P. J., et al. (1991). Association of the A1 allele of the D2 dopamine receptor gene with severe alcoholism. *Alcohol* 8:409–416.

Blume, S. (1989). Dual diagnosis: psychoactive substance dependence and the personality disorders. *Journal of Psychoactive Drugs* 21 (2):139–144.

Brown, S. (1985). *Treating the Alcoholic.* New York: Wiley.

Cermak, T. (1986). *Diagnosing Co-dependence*. Minneapolis, MN: Johnson Institute.

Cooper, S. E., and Robinson, D. A. (1987). Use of the Substance Abuse Subtle Screening Inventory with a college population. *Journal of the American College Health Association* 36:180–184.

Daley, D. C. (1989). *Relapse Prevention: Treatment Alternatives and Counseling Aids*. Blue Ridge Summit, PA: TAB Books.

Diagnostic and Statistical Manual of Mental Disorders (1987). 3rd ed., rev. Washington, DC: American Psychiatric Association.

——— (1994). 4th ed. Washington, DC: American Psychiatric Association.

Eliot, T. S. (1937). The Hollow Men. In *The Oxford Book of Modern Verse*: *Chosen by W. B. Yeats*. New York: Oxford University Press.

Ewing, J. A. (1984). Detecting alcoholism: the CAGE questionnaire. *Journal of the American Medical Association* 252(14):1905–1907.

Freud, S. (1884). Uber coca. In *Cocaine Papers*, ed. Robert Byck, pp. 48–73. New York: Stone Hill Publishing.

——— (1905/1955). Three essays on the theory of sexuality. *Standard Edition* 7.

Garbarino, J. (1986). *The Psychologically Battered Child*. San Francisco: Jossey-Bass.

Goodwin, D. W. (1984). Studies of familial alcoholism: a review. *Journal of Clinical Psychiatry* 45 (12, sec. 2):14–17.

——— (1988). *Is Alcoholism Hereditary?* New York: Bantam.

Goodwin, D. W., and Erickson, C. K., eds. (1979). *Alcoholism and Affective Disorders*. New York: SP Medical & Scientific Books.

Heather, N., and Robertson, I. (1981). *Controlled Drinking*. New York: Methuen.

Henderson, J. (1956). A psychological commentary. In *The Pollen Path*, ed. Margaret Schevill-Link, p. 2. Stanford, CA: Stanford University Press.

——— (1959). *The Masks of God: Primitive Mythology*. New York: Viking.

Hestler, R. K., and Miller, W. R. (1995). *Handbook of Alcoholism Treatment Approaches and Effective Alternatives*, 2nd ed. Boston: Allyn & Bacon.

Hindman, M. (1997). Child abuse and neglect: the alcoholic connection. *Alcohol, Health and Research World* 1:2–7.

Hofmann, F. G. (1983). *A Handbook on Drug and Alcohol Abuse: Biomedical Aspects*, 2nd ed. New York: Oxford University Press.

Indian Health Service (1988). Indian Health Service Chart Series Book. Washington, DC: U.S. Government Printing Office. DHHS Pub. No. 1988 0–218–547:QL3.

Jacobs, J. B. (1989). *Drunk Driving*. Chicago: University of Chicago Press.

Jainchill, N., DeLeon, G., and Pinkham, L. (1986). Psychiatric diagnoses among substance abusers in therapeutic community treatment. *Journal of Psychoactive Drugs* 18(3):209–213.

Jaroff, L. (1993). Lies of the mind. *Time Magazine*. Nov 29, pp. 52–59.

Jung, C. (1959). *The Archetypes and the Collective Unconscious*. New York: Pantheon.

Kanas, N. (1988). Psychoactive substance use disorders. In *Review of General Psychiatry*, 2nd ed., ed. H. H. Goldman, pp. 286–298. San Mateo, CA: Appleton & Lange.

Khantzian, E. J. (1990). The self-medication hypothesis of addictive disorders: focus on heroin and cocaine dependence. *American Journal of Psychiatry* 142:11.

Laign, J. (1990). Field groups redefine alcoholism. *U.S. Journal of Drugs and Alcohol Dependence* June, pp. 1–16.

Lawson, A. W. (1989). Substance abuse problems of the elderly: considerations for treatment and prevention. In *Alcoholism & Substance Abuse in Special Populations*, ed. G. W. Lawson, and A. W. Lawson, pp. 95–113.

Loftus, E. (1993). The reality of repressed memories. *American Psychologist* 48(5):518–537.

Luckert, K. W. (1979). *The Coyoteway: A Navajo Holyway Healing Ceremony*, Johnny C. Cooke, Interpreter. Tuscon, AZ: University of Arizona Press and the Musuem of Northern Arizona Press, Flagstaff.

Metzger, L. (1989). *From Denial to Recovery; Counseling Problem Drinkers, Alcoholics, and Their Families*. San Francisco: Jossey-Bass.

Morgenstern, J., and Leeds, J. (1993). Contemporary psychoanalytic theories of substance abuse: a disorder in search of a paradigm. *Psychotherapy* 30(2):194–206.

Naifeh, S. (1995). Archetypal foundations of addiction and recovery. *Journal of Analytical Psychology* (40):133–159.

National Council on Alcohol and Drug Dependence (1972). Criteria for the diagnosis of alcoholism. *American Journal of Psychiatry* 129(12):127–135.

O'Connor, L. E., and Weiss, J. (1993). Individual psychotherapy for addicted clients: an application of control mastery theory. *Journal of Psychoactive Drugs* 25(4):283–291.

Orme, T., and Kenner, J. (1981). Alcoholism and child abuse. *Journal of Studies on Alcohol* 42(3):273–287.

Paredes, A., Gregory, D., Rundell, O. H., and Williams, H. L. (1979). Drinking behavior. *Clinical and Experimental Research* 3(1):3–10.

Porter, C. (1959). I Get a Kick out of You. In *The Cole Porter Song Book*. New York: Simon and Schuster.

Reed, E. D. (1988). *Coyote Tales*. Santa Fe: Sunstone Press.

Regier, D. A., Farmer, M. E., Rae, D. S., et al. (1990). Comorbidity of mental disorders with alcohol and other drug abuse: results from the Epidemiologic Catchment Area (ECA) study. *Journal of the American Medical Association* 264(19):2511–2518.

Reichard, G. A. (1977). *Navaho Religion: A Study of Symbolism*. Bollingen Series XVIII. Princeton, NJ: Princeton University Press.

Reviere, S. L. (1996). *Memory of Childhood Trauma: A Clinician's Guide to the Literature*. New York: Guilford.

Ries, R., Consensus panel chair. (1994). *Assessment and Treatment of Patients with Coexisting Mental Illness and Alcohol and Other Drug Abuse*. U.S. Department of Health and Human Services (DHHS). Rockville, MD: Substance Abuse and Mental Health Services Administration (SAMHSA) and Center for Substance Abuse Treatment. DHHS publication #SMA 94-2078.

Rombauer, I. S., and Beker, M. R. (1964). *Joy of Cooking*. New York: Bobbs-Merril.

Sandner, D. (1979). *Navaho Symbols of Healing*. Rochester, VT: Healing Arts.

Sandor, R. S. (1991). Relapse to drinking: does cigarette smoking contribute? *CSAM News* 18(2).

Schuckit, M. A. (1985a). Genetics and the risk for alcoholism. *Journal of the American Medical Association* 254(18):2614.

―――― (1985b). Genetics of alcoholism. *Alcoholism: Clinical and Experimental Research* 9(6):475–491.

―――― (1986). Genetic and clinical implications of alcoholism and Affective disorder. *American Journal of Psychiatry* 143(2):140–147.

―――― (1994). Low level of response to alcohol as a predictor of future alcoholism. *American Journal of Psychiatry* 151:184–189.

Secretary of Health and Human Services (1990). *Seventh Special Report to the U.S. Congress on Alcohol and Health*. Rockville, MD: U.S. Dept. of Health and Human Services, Public Health Service (DHHS).

―――― (1995). *Eighth Special Report to the U.S. Congress on Alcohol and Health*. U.S. Dept. of Health and Human Services. Alcohol, Drug Abuse, and Mental Health Administration. Rockville, MD: National Institute on Alcohol Abuse and Alcoholism.

Selzer, M. S. (1971). The Michigan Alcoholism Screening Test: the quest for a new diagnostic instrument. *American Journal of Psychiatry* 127(12): 1653–1658.

Seymour, M.A., and Smith, D. E. (1987). *Guide to Psychoactive Drugs: An Up-to-the-Minute Reference to Mind-Altering Substances*. New York: Harrington Park.

Seymour, R., Smith, D., Inaba, D., and Landry, M. (1989). *The New Drugs*. Center City, MN: Hazelden Foundation.

Smith, D. E., and Gay, G. R. (1972). *It's So Good, Don't Even Try It Once: Heroin in Perspective*. Englewood Cliffs, NJ: Prentice-Hall.

Sobell, M. B., and Sobell, L. C. (1978). *Behavioral Treatment of Alcohol Problems: Individualized Therapy and Controlled Drinking*. New York: Plenum.

World Health Organization (1978). *Mental disorders: glossary and guide to classification in accordance with the Ninth Revision of the International Classification of Diseases*. Geneva: World Health Organization.

Wright, L. (1993). Remembering Satan. *New Yorker*, May 17, pp. 60–81; May 24, pp. 54–76.

Youcha, G. (1986). *Women and Alcohol*. New York: Crown.

Zweben, J. E. (1986). Recovery oriented psychotherapy. *Journal of Substance Abuse Treatment* 3:255–262.

Index